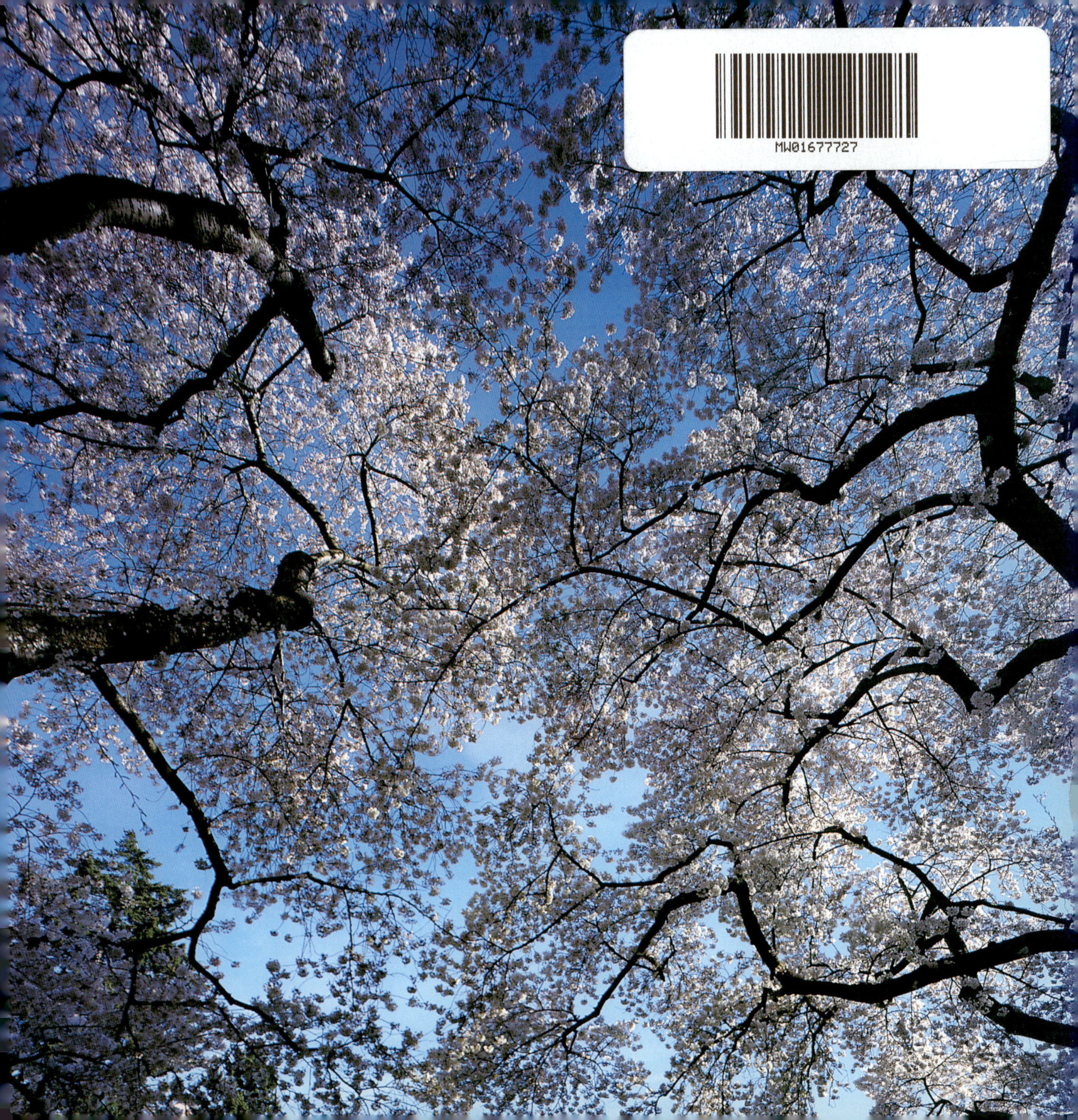

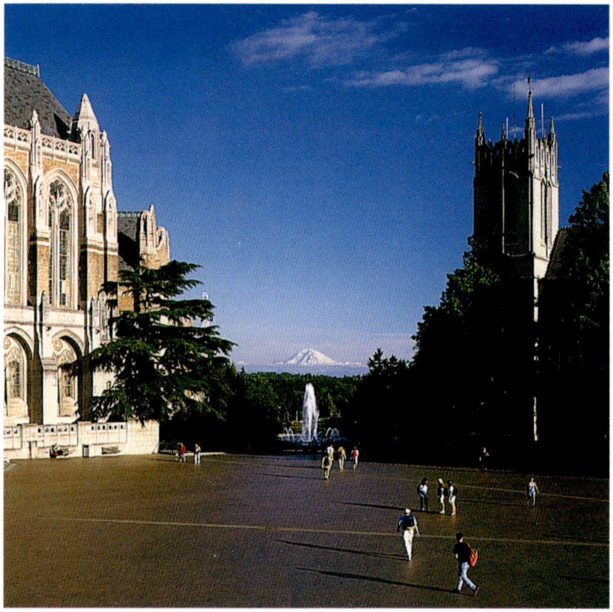

The University of Washington Experience

Text
Thomas Griffin

Photography
Stewart Hopkins

Contributing Photographer
Jaimie Trueblood

Documentary Media LLC
Seattle, Washington

The University of Washington Experience

Published by Documentary Media LLC
3250 41st Ave SW
Seattle, Washington 98116
(206) 935-9292
books@docmedia.org
www.documentarymedia.com

Author: Thomas Griffin
Photographers: Stewart Hopkins, Jaimie Trueblood, Paul Souders and Jeff Zaruba
Editorial Director: Petyr Beck
Book Store Editorial Committee: Bryan Pearce, Mark Mouser and Jasmin Weaver
Editor: Judy Gouldthorpe
Book Design: Paul Langland Design
Printed in China

Library of Congress Catalog-in-Publication Data
Griffin, Thomas, 1951-
The University of Washington experience / text, Thomas Griffin ;
photography, Stewart Hopkins, Jaimie Trueblood ; additional photography,
Paul Souders, Jeff Zaruba.
p. cm.
ISBN 0-9719084-3-5 (alk. paper)
1. University of Washington—Students—Pictorial works. I. Hopkins, Stewart.
II. Trueblood, Jaimie. III. Title.

LD5756.G75 2003
378.797'77—dc21

2003009090

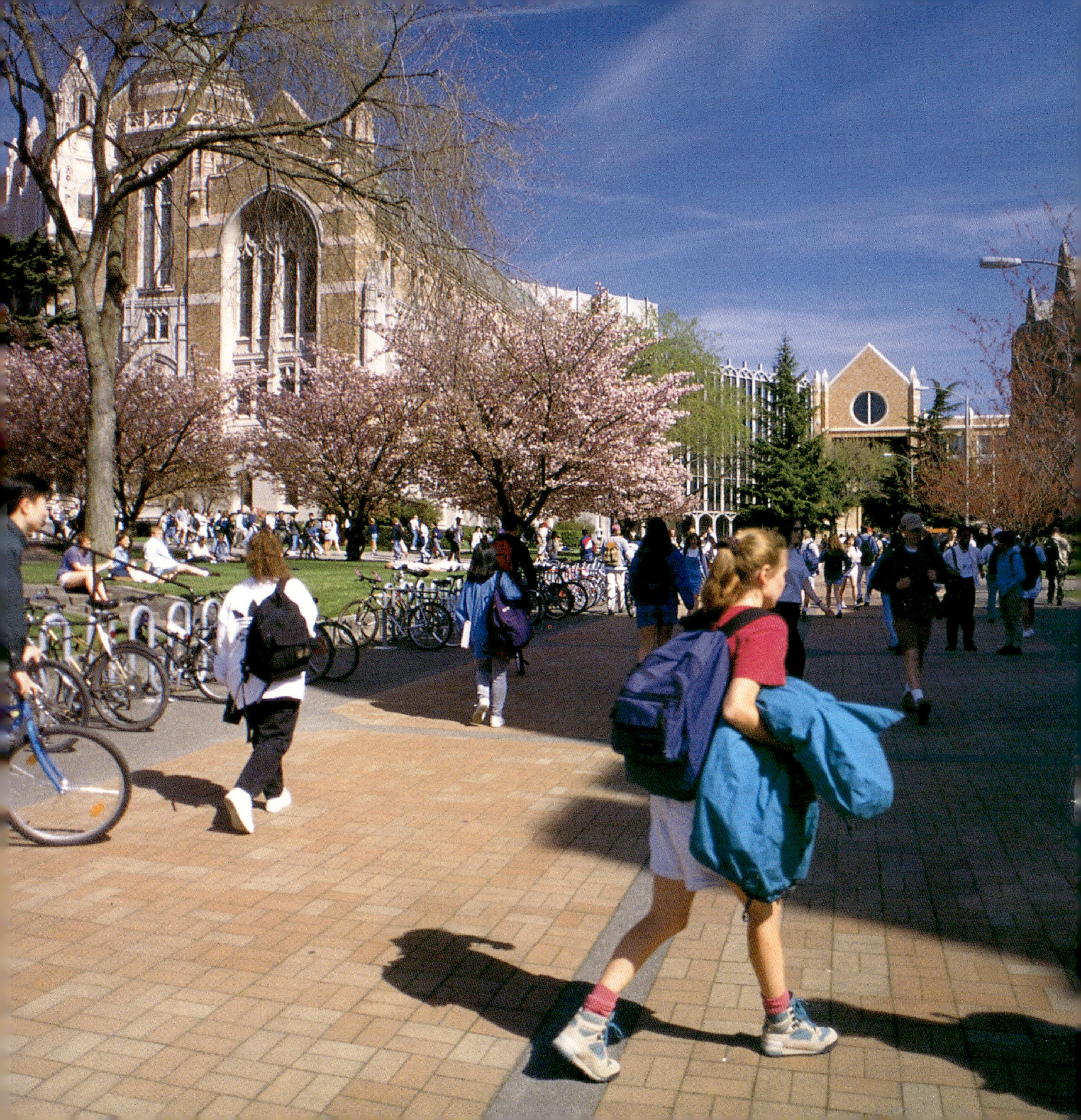

Every September I watch 5,000 people fall in love. No, this isn't a rock concert featuring this year's superstar or a mass wedding ceremony—although there is a ritual to it. It is the arrival of new freshmen at the University of Washington.

You can spot the newcomers easily, and not just because of their age. Like a teenager on a first date, they have a vulnerable air about them. "Are they really going to like me here—and am I really going to like this place?" they ask themselves.

When it comes to first dates, the ritual is to pretend you have lots of experience. Our brand-new freshmen practice the same ruse. They wear whatever they *think* college kids are wearing this year (sometimes they are hopelessly wrong). Campus maps are cleverly tucked in between the pages of newly purchased textbooks. I often watch them take furtive looks at the hidden guide like a preteen peeking at a racy magazine on a newsstand.

As they walk around the University of Washington campus, anxiety gives way to awe. They've never seen 39,000 people of roughly the same age packed into the same space before. They've never encountered so much brainpower in their lives—Nobel Prize winners, National Book Award authors and members of the National Academy of Sciences all teach in the buildings that surround them.

In the midst of this uncertainty, these freshmen soon discover the beauty of the University of Washington. Nowhere else will you find a monumental vista with a 14,000-foot volcano as its focal point. Nearby is Suzzallo Library, a masterpiece of Collegiate Gothic architecture that holds the most spacious library reading room in the nation. The grounds—once a clear-cut forest—now feature lush gardens of roses, herbs and rhododendrons, plus an enclosed quadrangle with 65-year-old cherry trees that take your breath away every spring.

Students at the new UW campuses in Bothell and Tacoma invest plenty of emotion in their surroundings as well. Bothell's students learn in modern structures that pay tribute to classic mountain lodges scattered across the Pacific Northwest. Students in Tacoma walk through 19th-century warehouses that have been transformed for 21st-century education.

So the romance begins. It might not be love at first sight for everyone, but few can resist the passion in this place. That moment might come when you stroll past the scented beds of roses surrounding Drumheller Fountain. Or it might come when you sit in an empty chair that just happens to be next to an attractive classmate eating in the HUB. The bond might begin as you watch a football clear the goalposts in a come-from-behind victory in Husky Stadium or crawl through a conceptual art installation in the Henry Art Gallery.

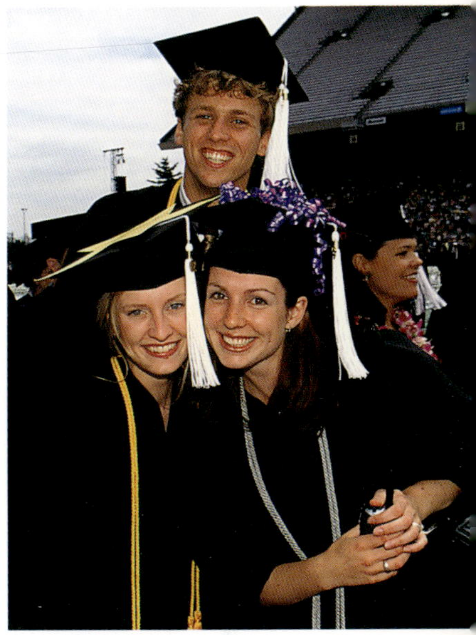

As with any relationship, there are bound to be bumpy spots. Maybe you didn't get into the modern dance class you wanted, your first roommate was an insomniac who liked to do chemistry experiments at 2 a.m., you couldn't find any parking in the Montlake lot just before a crucial final exam, your computer crashed as you were putting the finishing touches on your English lit paper. Maybe all these things happened on the same day.

But somehow you survived the mishaps, and the bonds grew stronger. At times you may have thought, "I can't wait to get out of this place," but when commencement day comes and you walk down the aisle at Husky Stadium, you are amazed at how fast it all went—and how much you are going to miss being a student.

This book is an attempt to capture that romance. Photographers have spent more than a year taking thousands of images at all three campuses. As well as preserving the physical space, they have also recorded the people of the UW. The sum of their 185 images is a visual love letter to the University of Washington experience.

Thomas Griffin
Editor, *Columns Magazine*
University of Washington

Golden leaves fall from the 58 trees lining Memorial Way, the impressive entrance to the northern part of Seattle's campus.

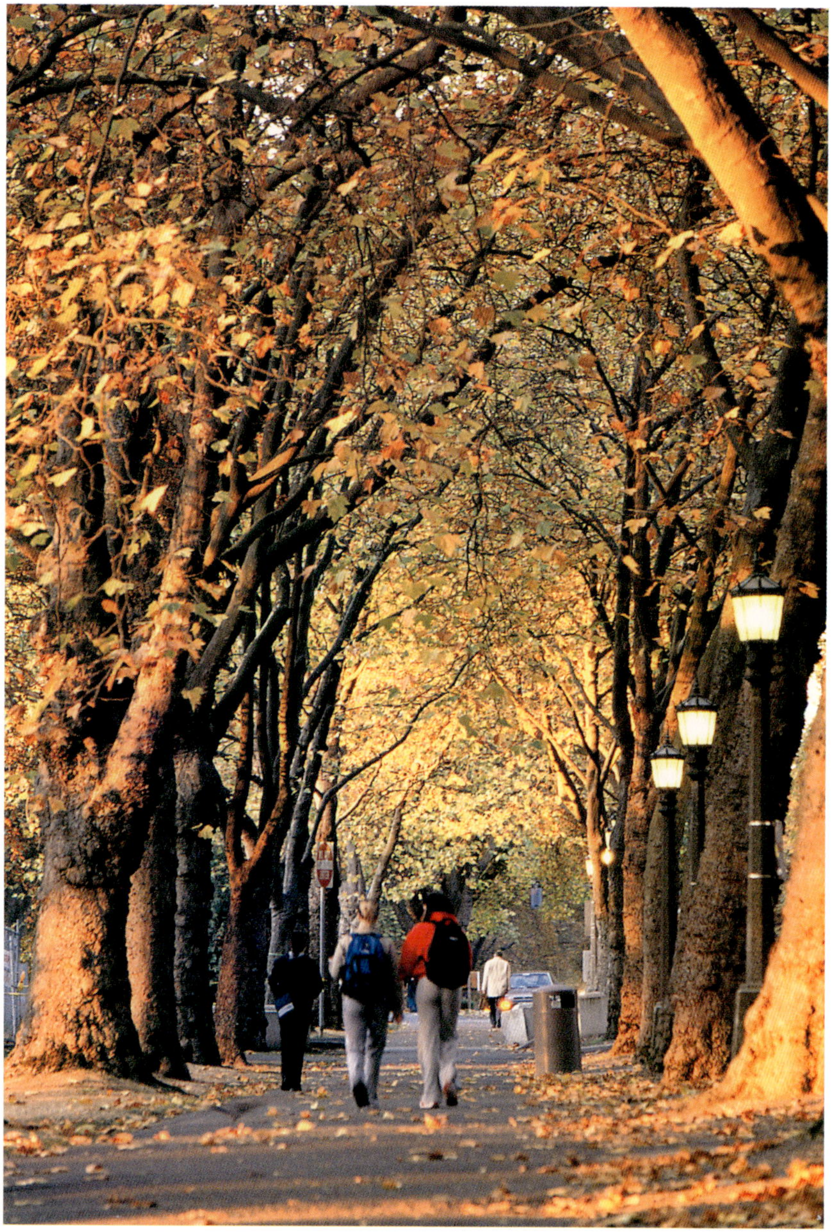

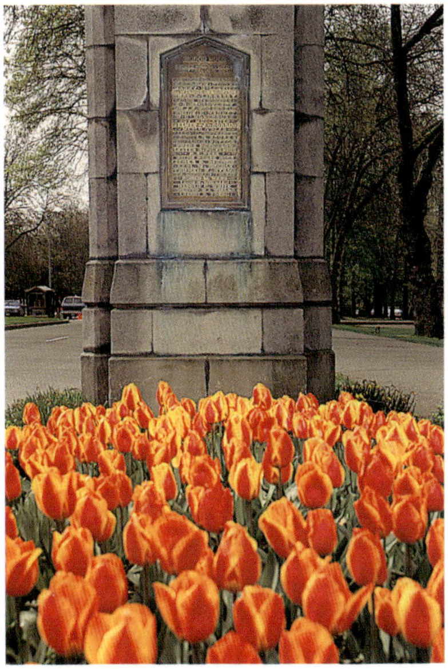

Tulips cover the ground next to the Memorial Gateway, where bronze plaques list students who died in the First World War.

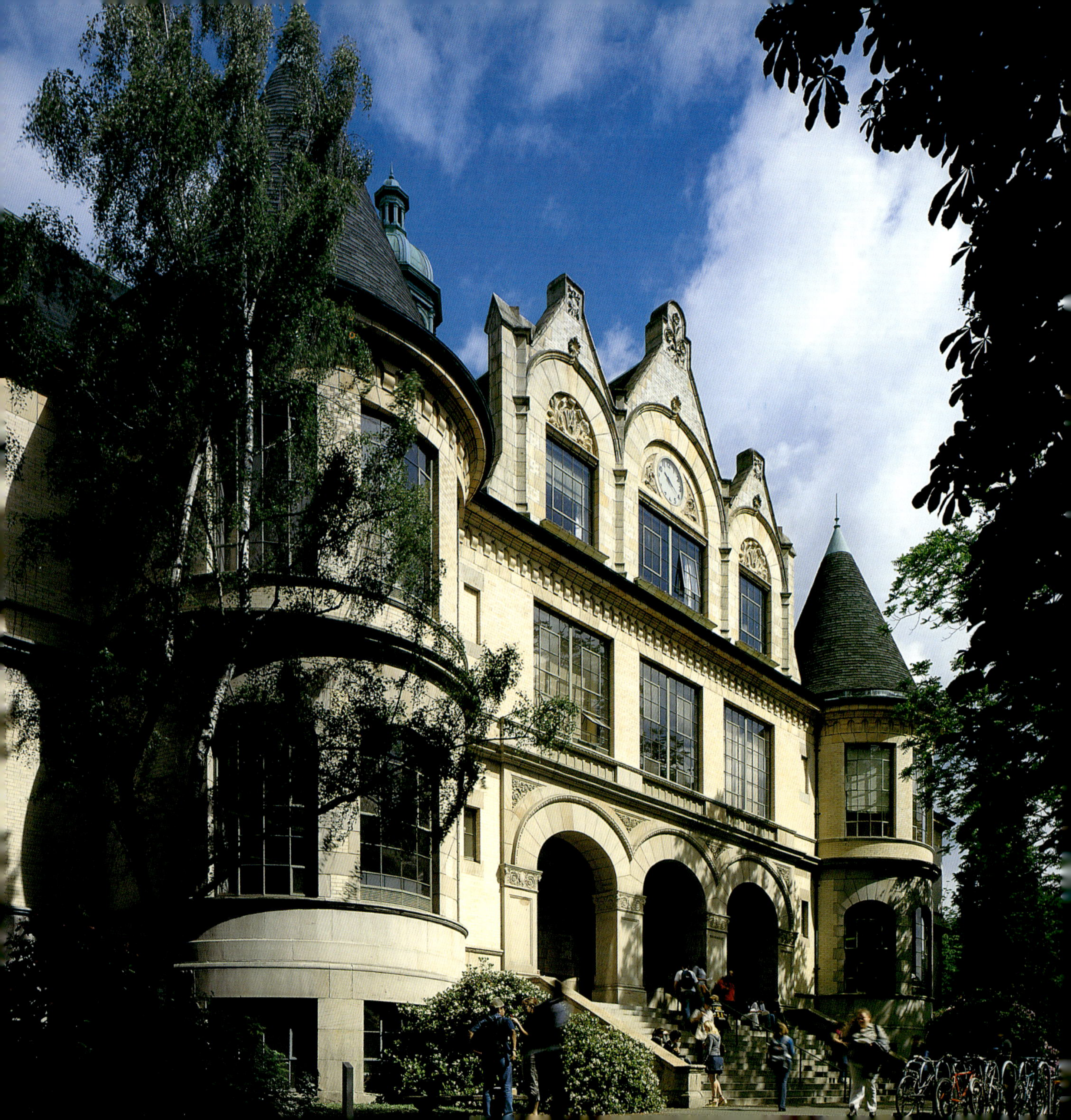

Since 1895, students have been studying in Denny Hall's tower rooms.

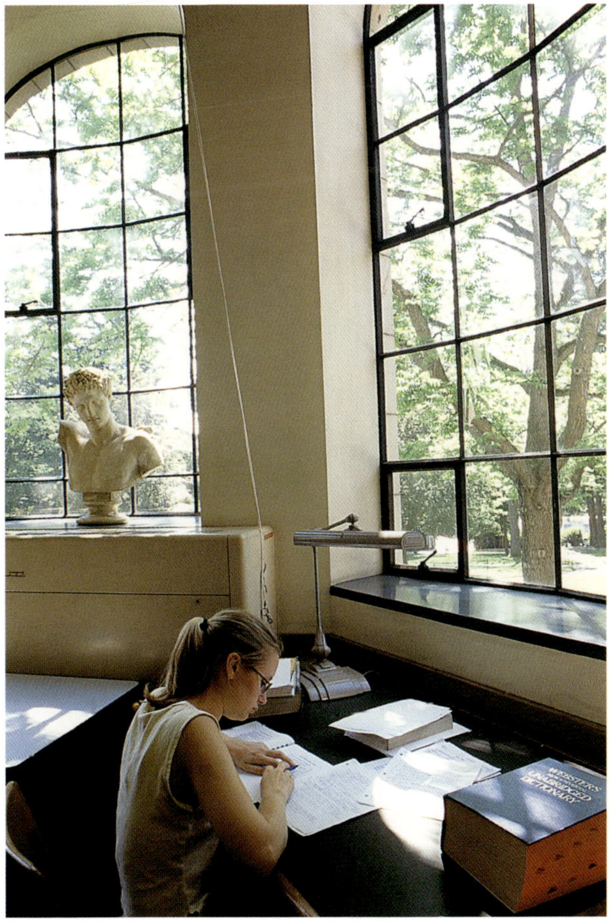

Opposite page: Students park their bikes in front of Denny Hall, the oldest building on campus.

Left: A professor casually greets his students during office hours. *Right:* A student takes a study break in the Evans School office in Parrington Hall.

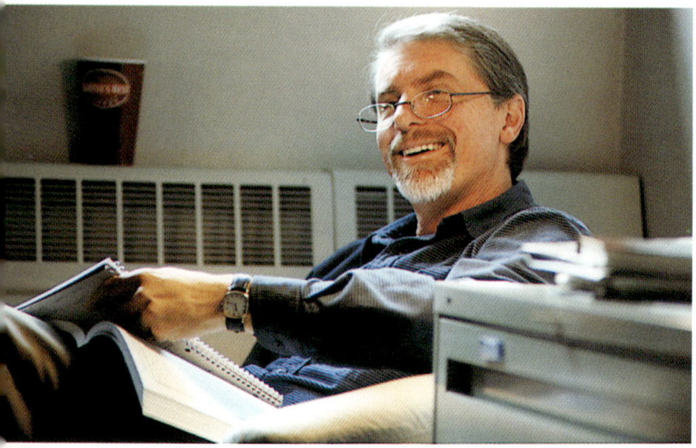

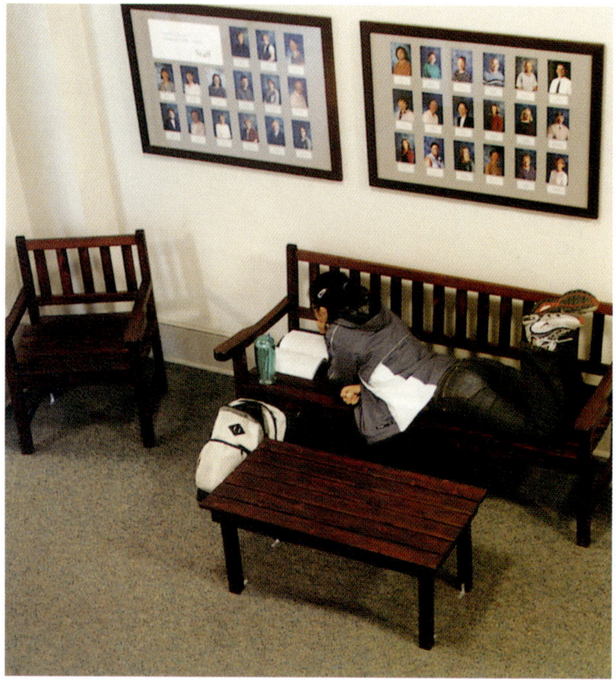

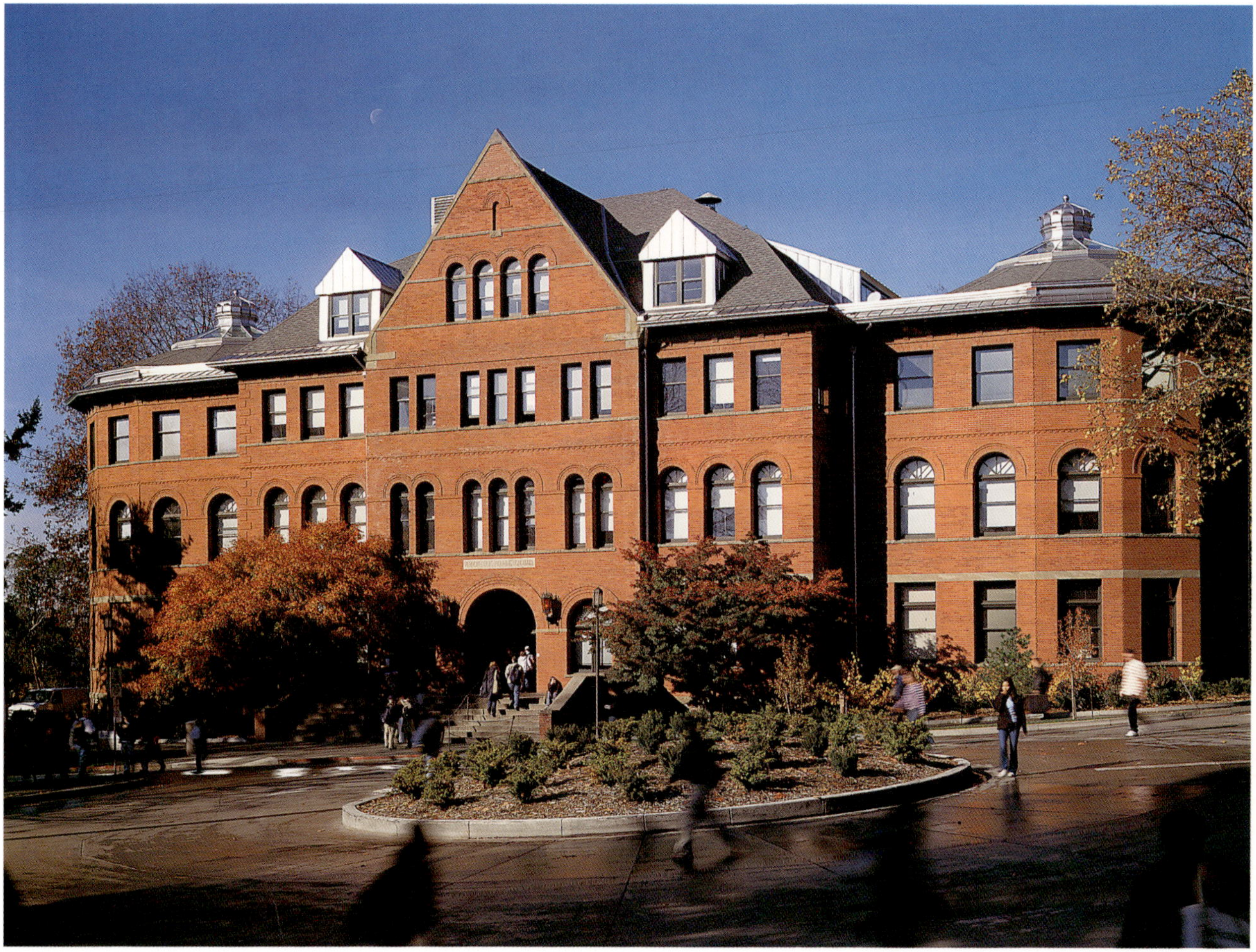

Home of the Daniel J. Evans School of Public Affairs, Parrington Hall shows off its bright red bricks.

For more than eight decades, its outer walls were painted pink. A 1996 seismic upgrade restored its original look.

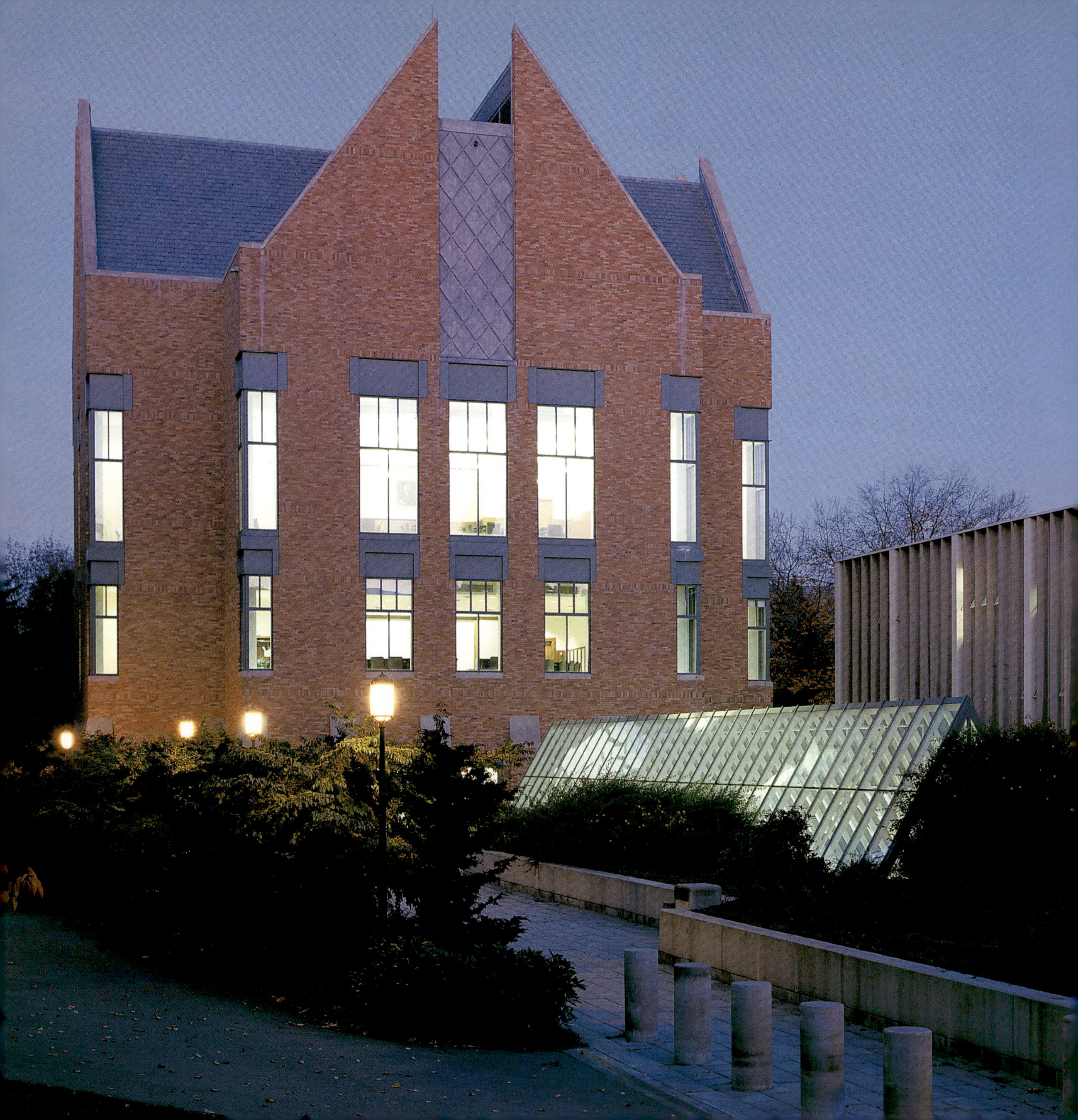

Left: Natural light illuminates study areas in the Foster Library, where many business students hook up their laptops.

Right: The Business School's Boeing Auditorium is the central lecture hall for the top-ranked business school in the Pacific Northwest.

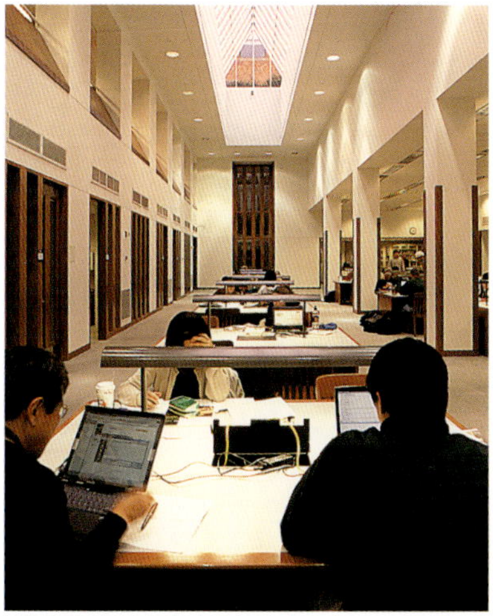

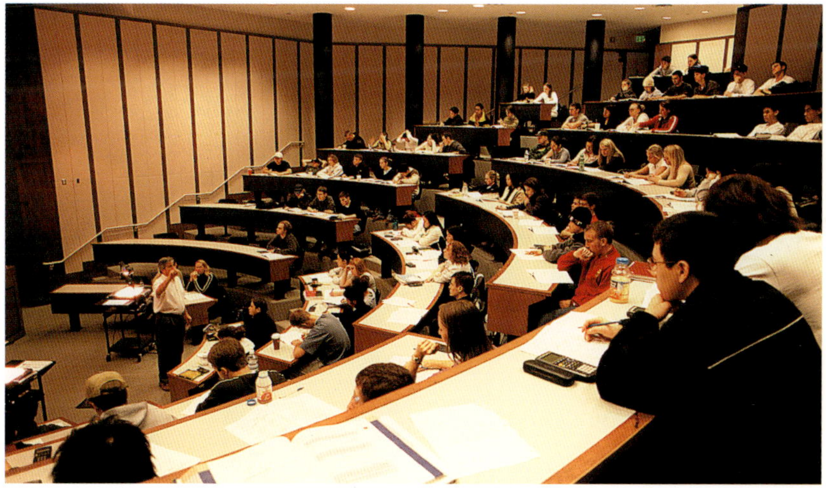

Opposite page: Light pours out of the offices of the Bank of America Executive Education Center at dusk. In the foreground, the skylight of the Business School's Foster Library glows.

Left: A student seamstress concentrates as she alters a skirt in the UW's Costume Shop.

Right: Students rehearse for a performance in the Penthouse Theater, the first building in the world constructed for theater-in-the-round.

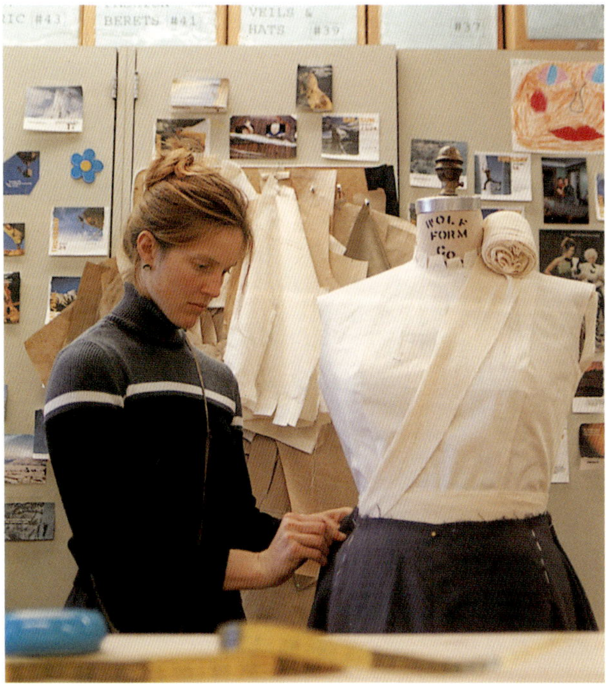

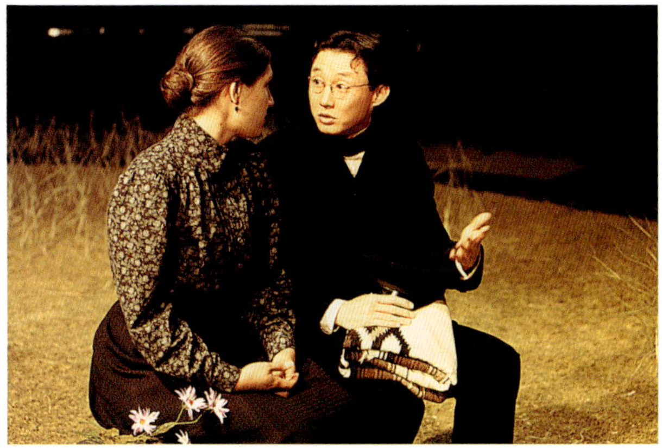

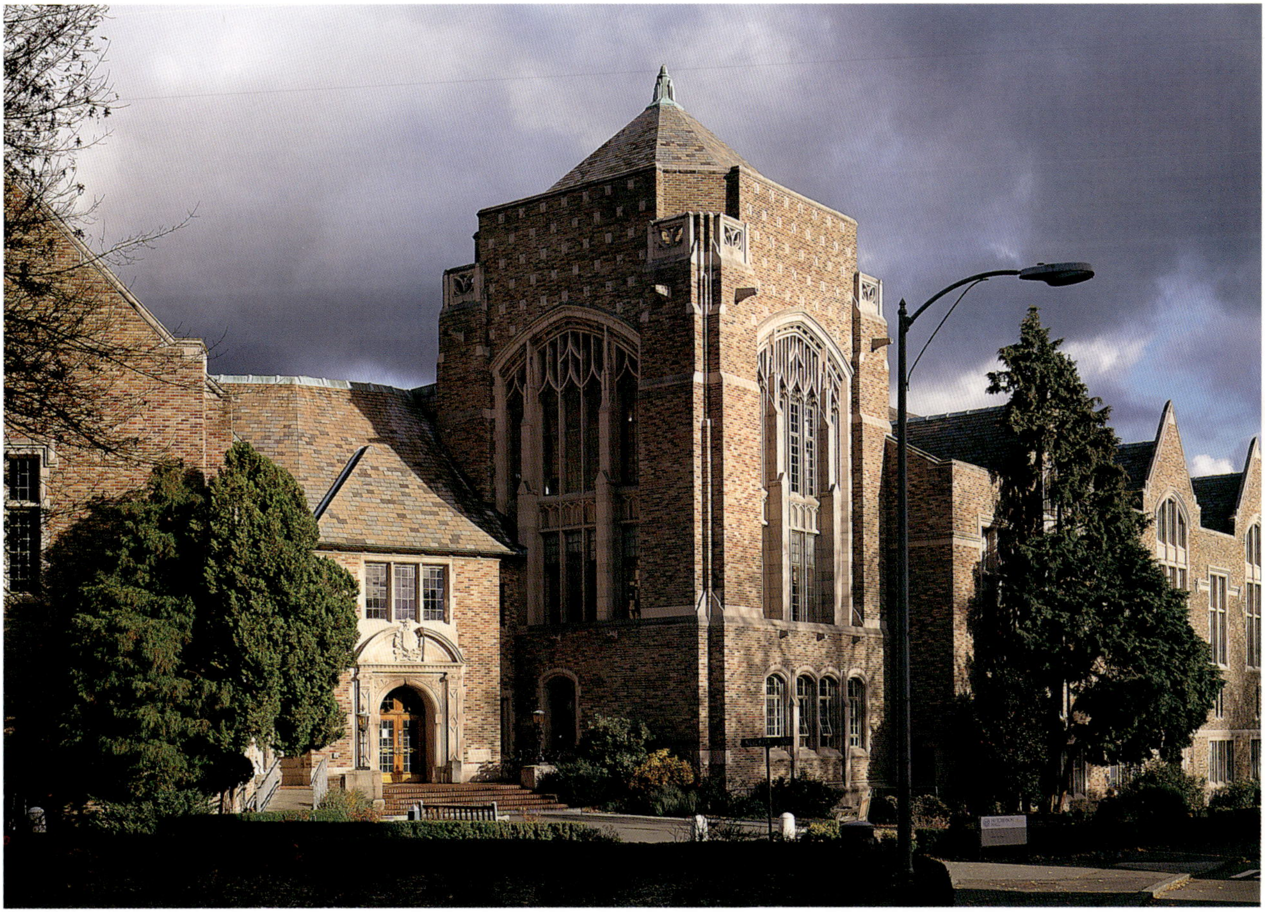

Hutchinson Hall's Collegiate Gothic lines seem more appropriate for its current use—home of the UW School of Drama—than for its original function: a gymnasium for women.

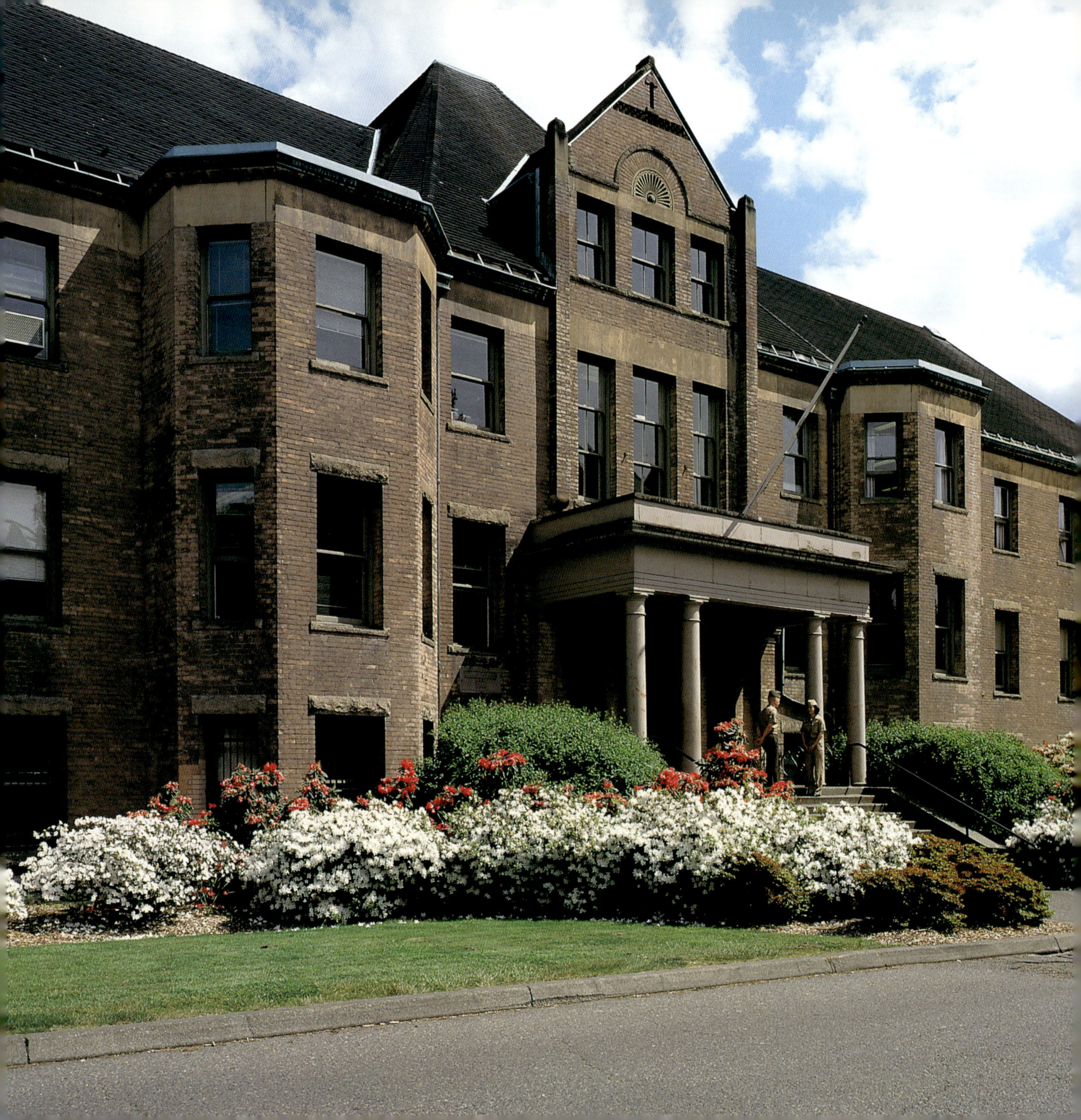

Opposite page:
The Spartan exterior of Clark Hall fits its function as the home of the UW's three R.O.T.C. programs. Named for William Clark of the Lewis and Clark expedition, it was built in 1896 as a student dormitory.

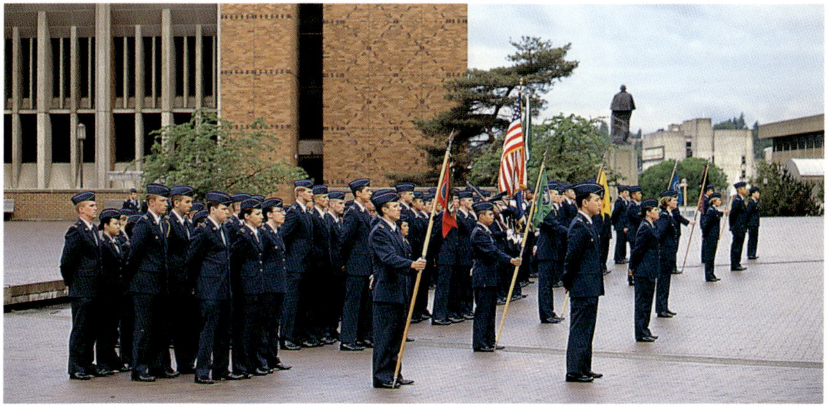

R.O.T.C. units drill on Red Square.

The campus Observatory, built with bricks left over from the construction of Denny Hall, may be too much of an antique for 21st-century astronomy, but it still hosts public viewings of the planets and the stars.

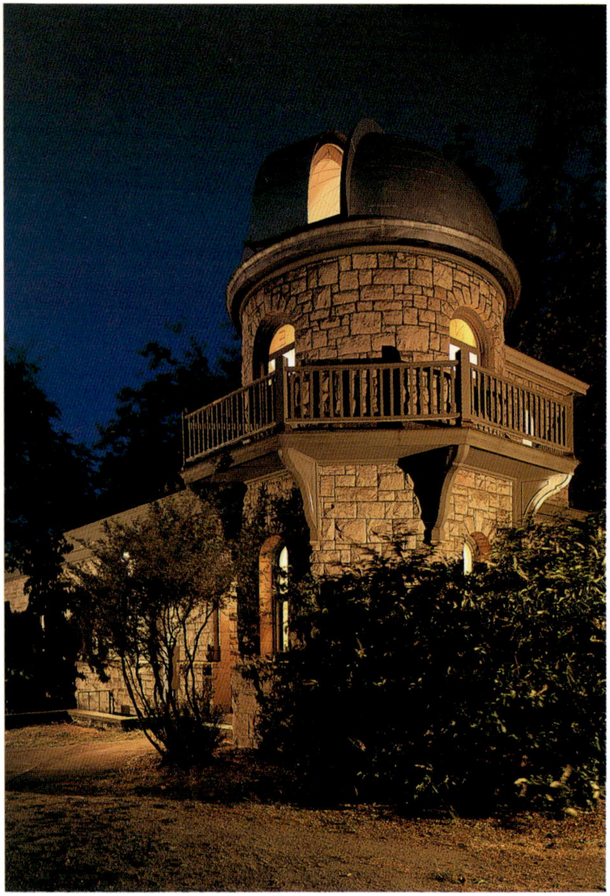

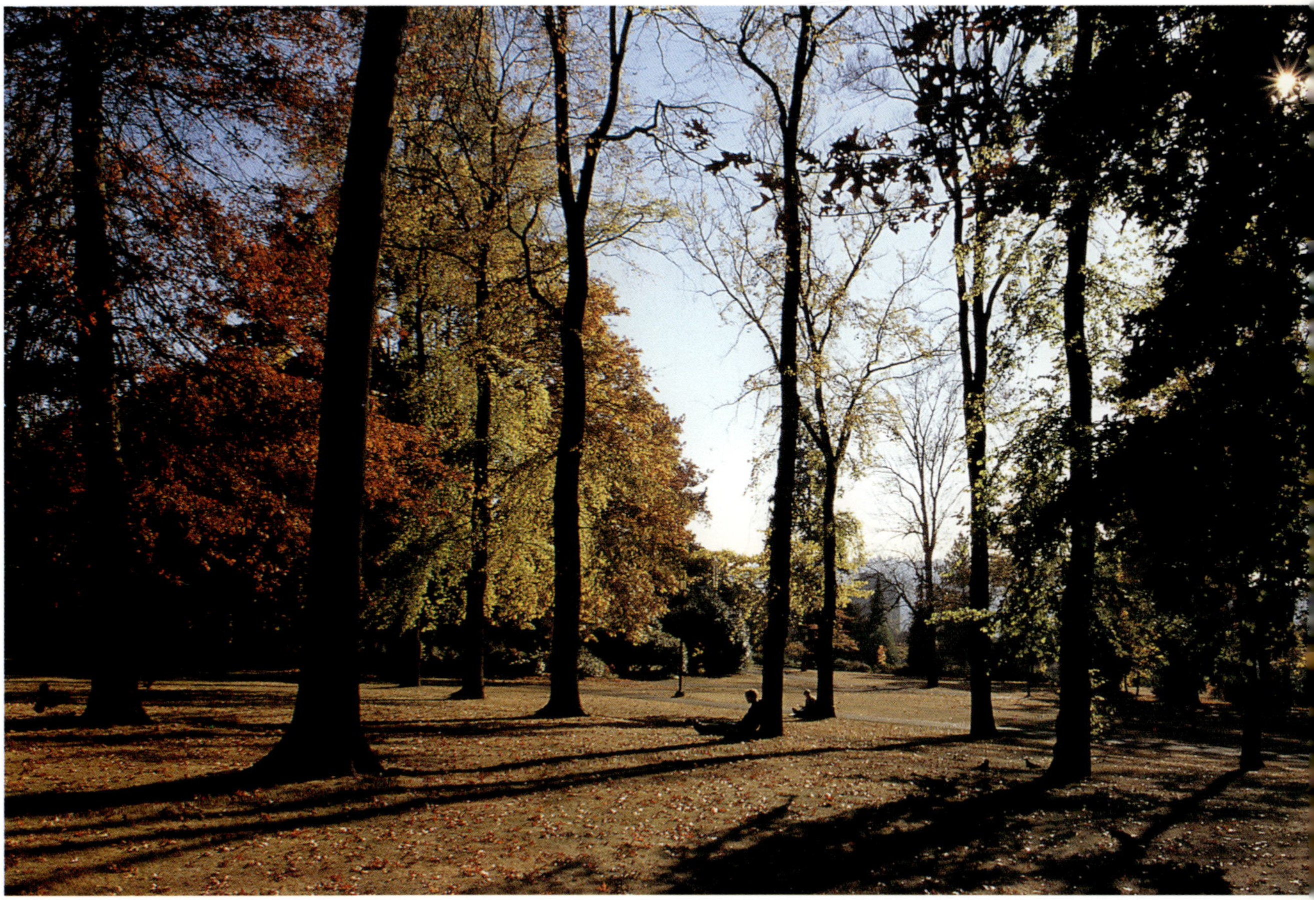

Fall colors and afternoon sunshine create a space for contemplation.

Known in the 1960s as Hippie Hill, this now has the more formal title Campus Green.

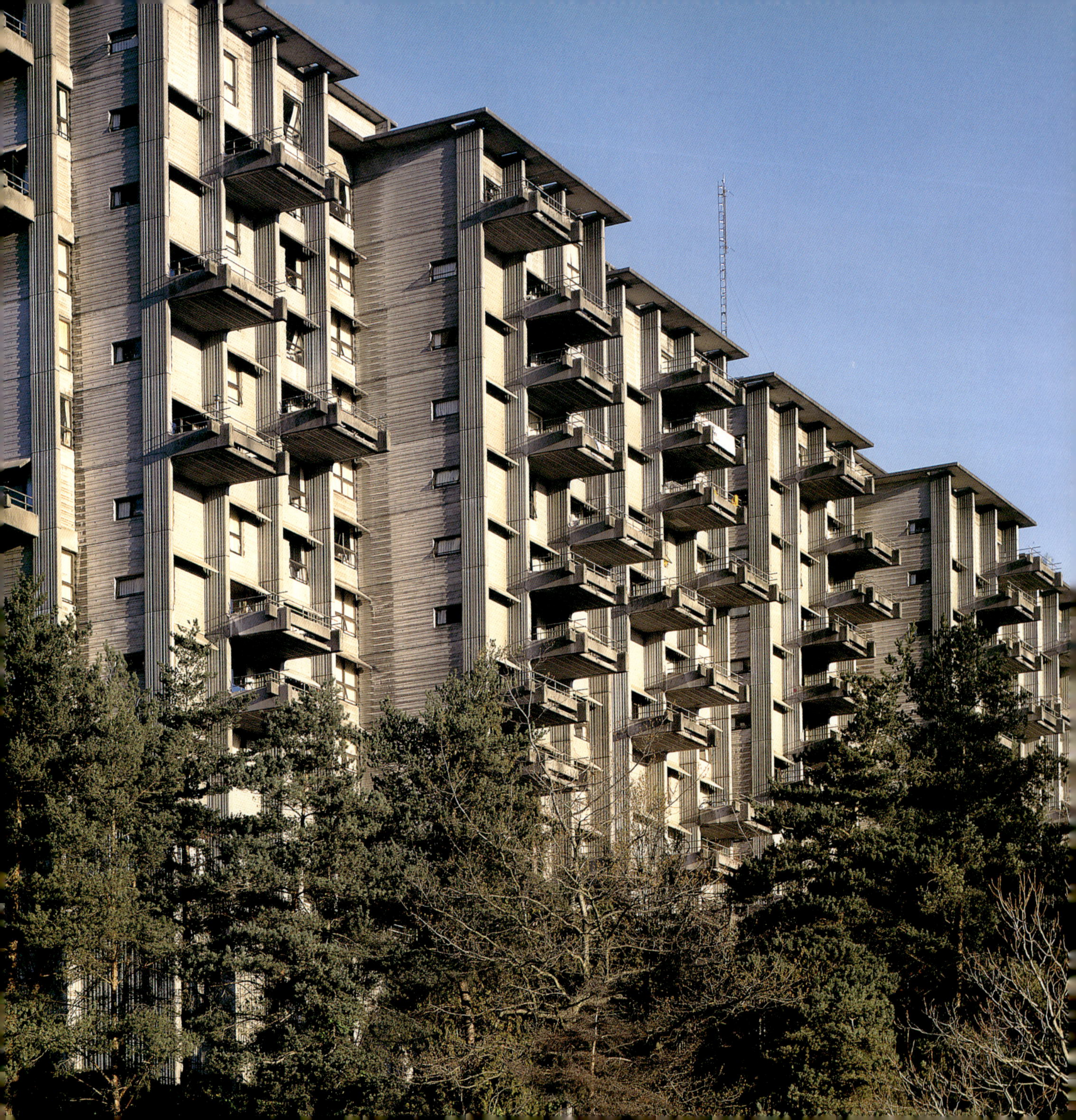

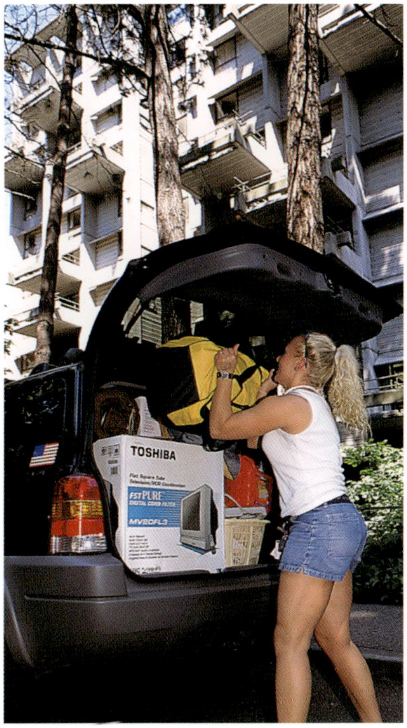

A student juggles bags and boxes on moving-in day.

Opposite page:
These McMahon Hall balconies have territorial views of Mount Rainier and Lake Washington.

Opposite page:
Hansee Hall was originally built as a women's dormitory. Now it's a favorite of juniors, seniors and graduate students.

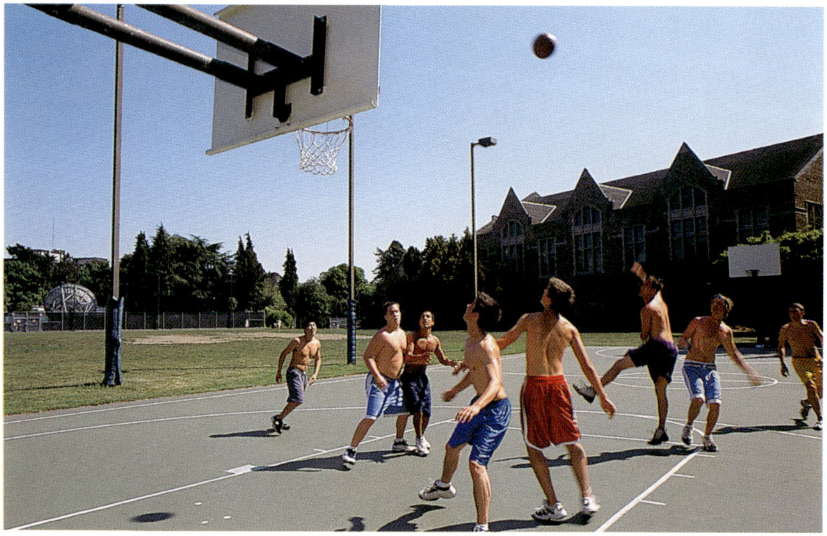

If it's a sunny day, chances are there will be a pickup game of basketball behind Hansee Hall.

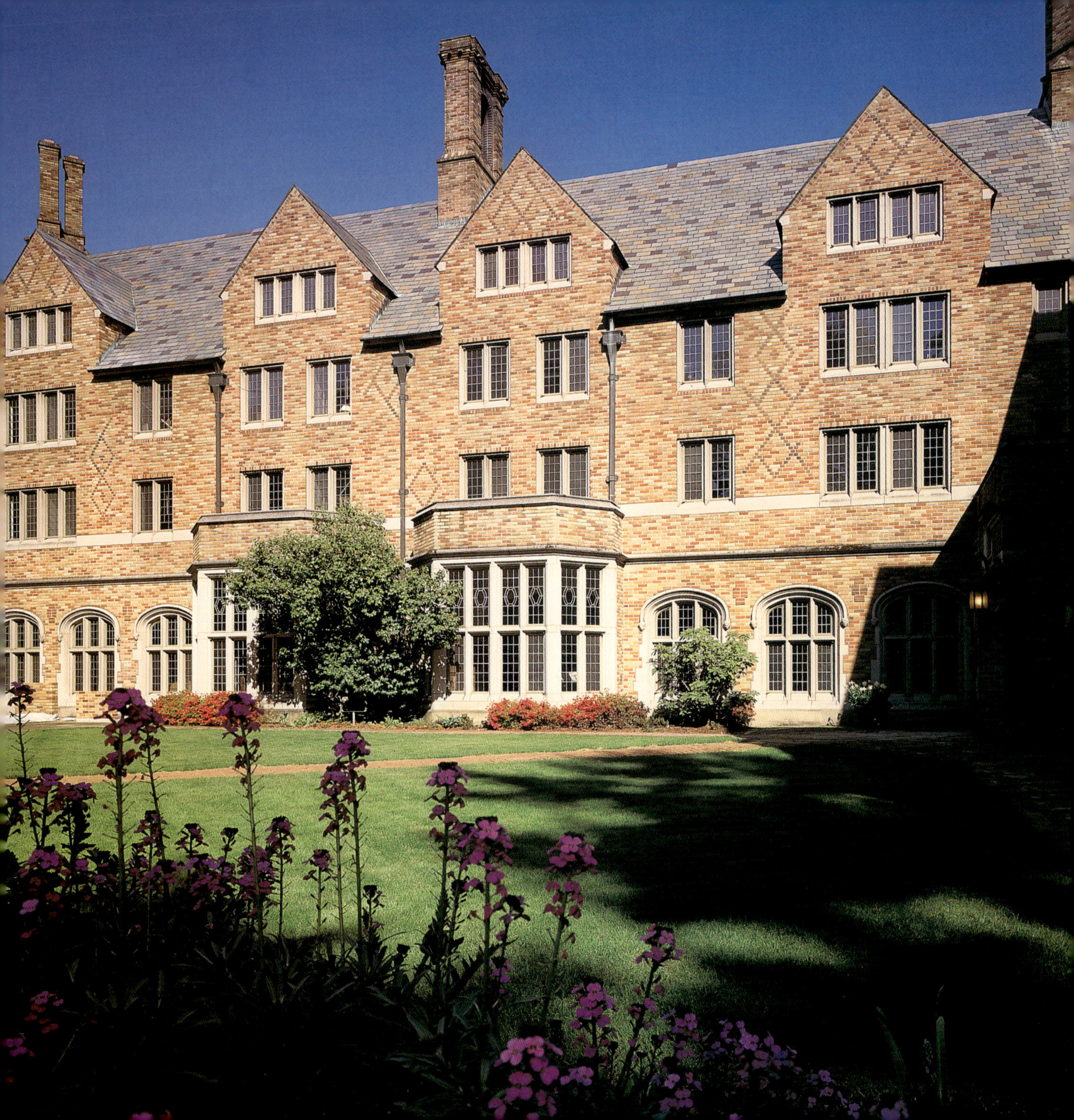

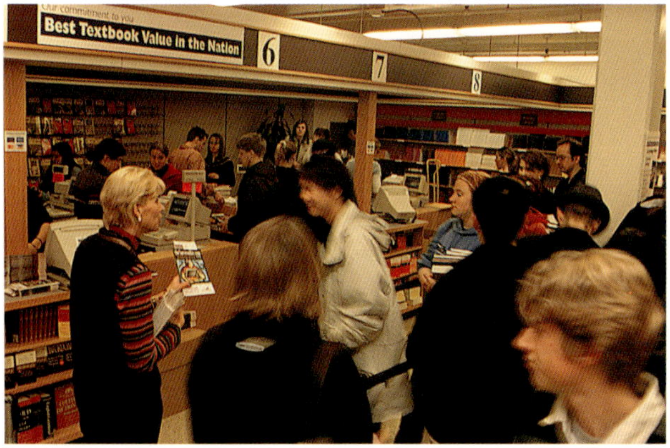

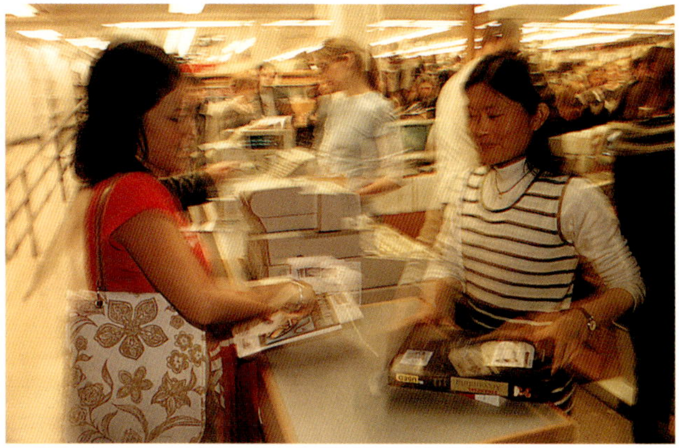

Every UW student since 1900 has had at least one common experience—textbook rush in the University Book Store at the beginning of each quarter.

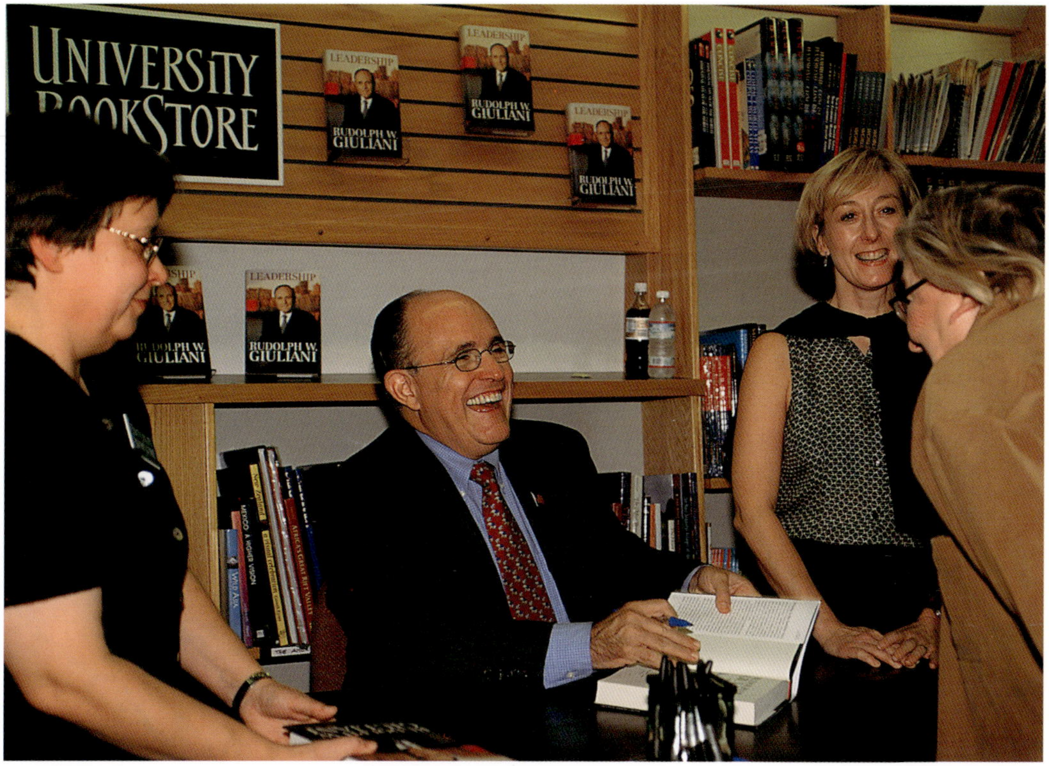

The University Book Store's readings, lectures and book signings add to the culture of campus life. Here former New York Mayor Rudolph Giuliani signs copies of his book.

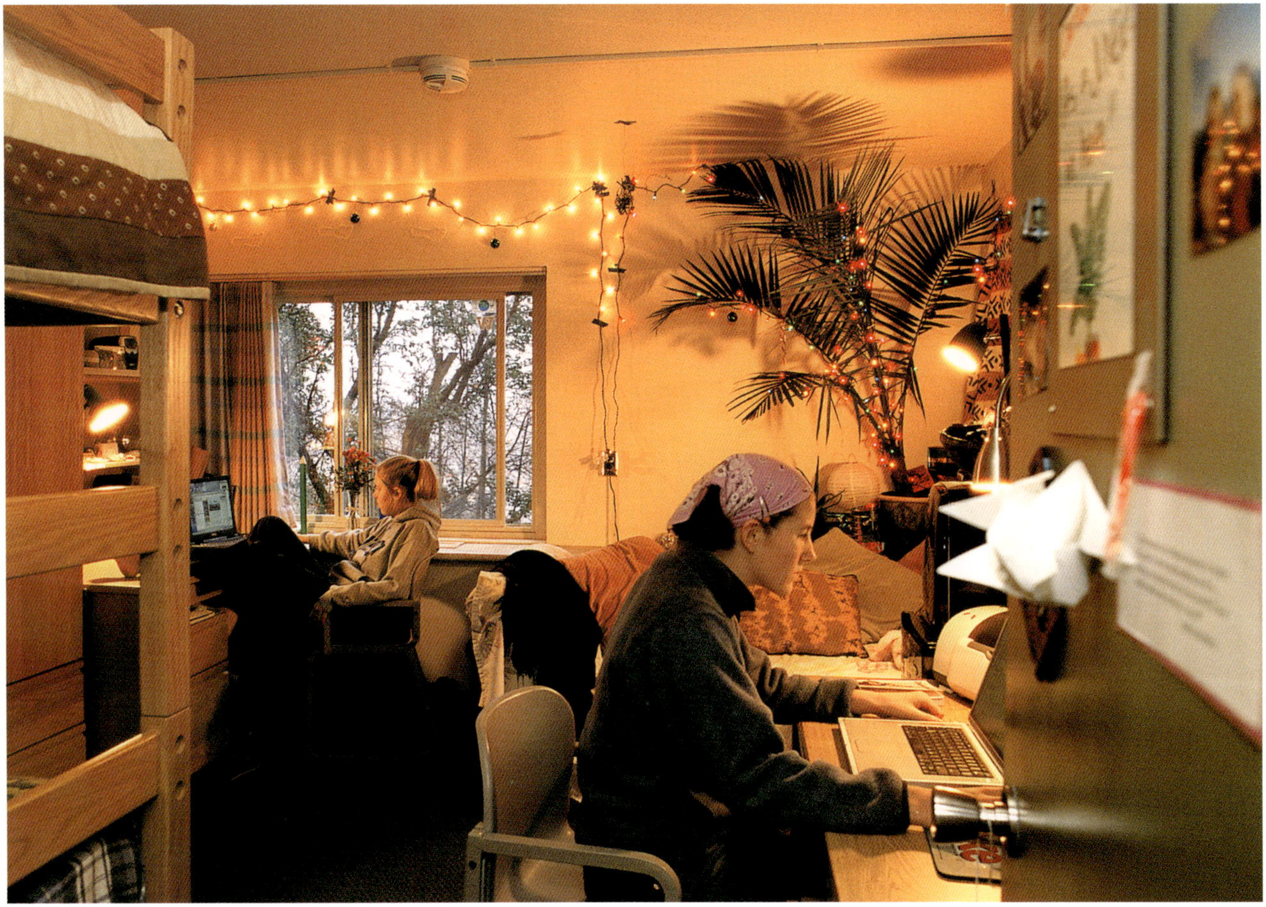

These McCarty Hall roommates use decorative lights to add sparkle to a typical dorm room.

Left: Students line up for pizza, tacos, potstickers and, yes, even hamburgers in the Husky Den. *Right:* Outdoor study time includes reading a book on globalism.

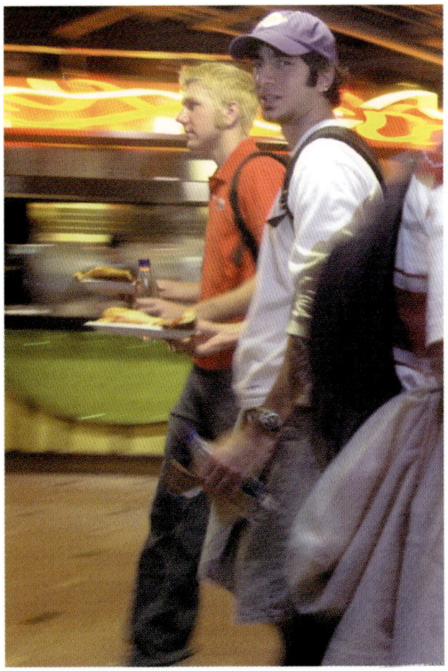

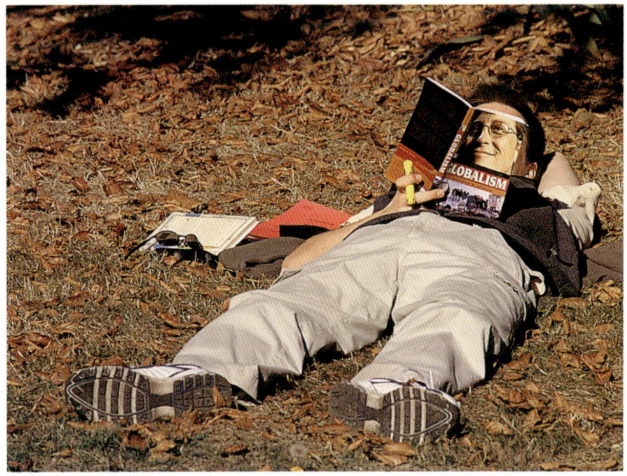

Next page: Sunrise turns the Cascade Mountains—and light reflected from Lake Washington—purple. Students living in some campus residence halls and faculty in Padelford Hall enjoy this spectacular view.

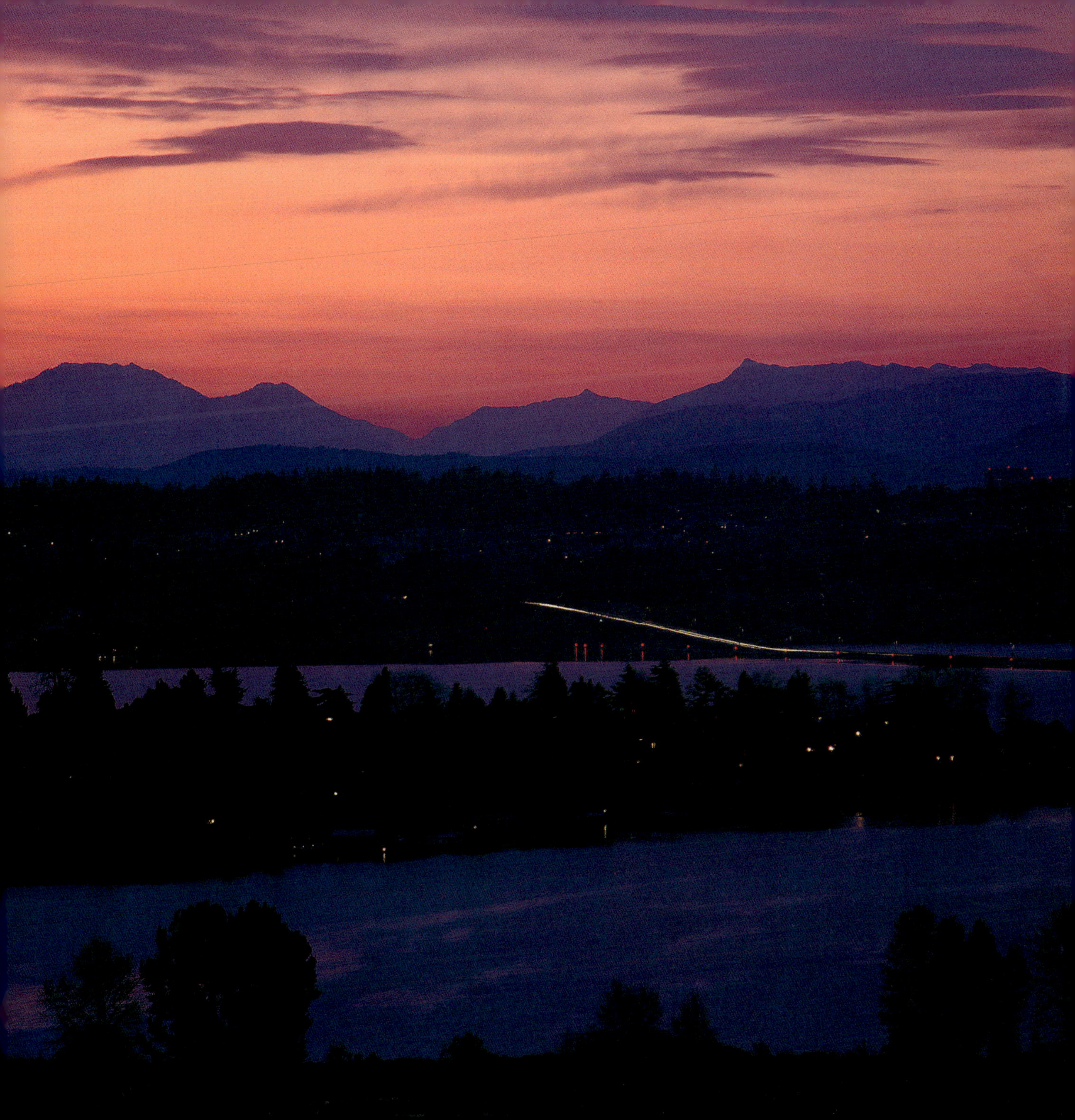

Jogging around Green Lake is one of Seattle's most popular pastimes.

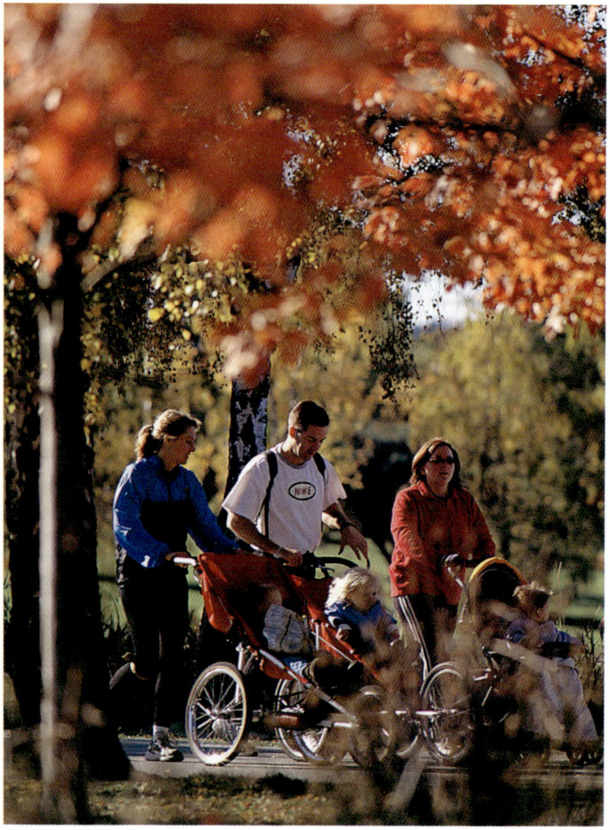

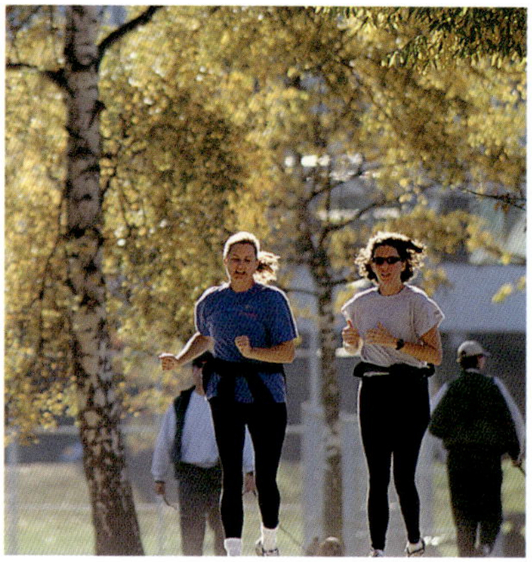

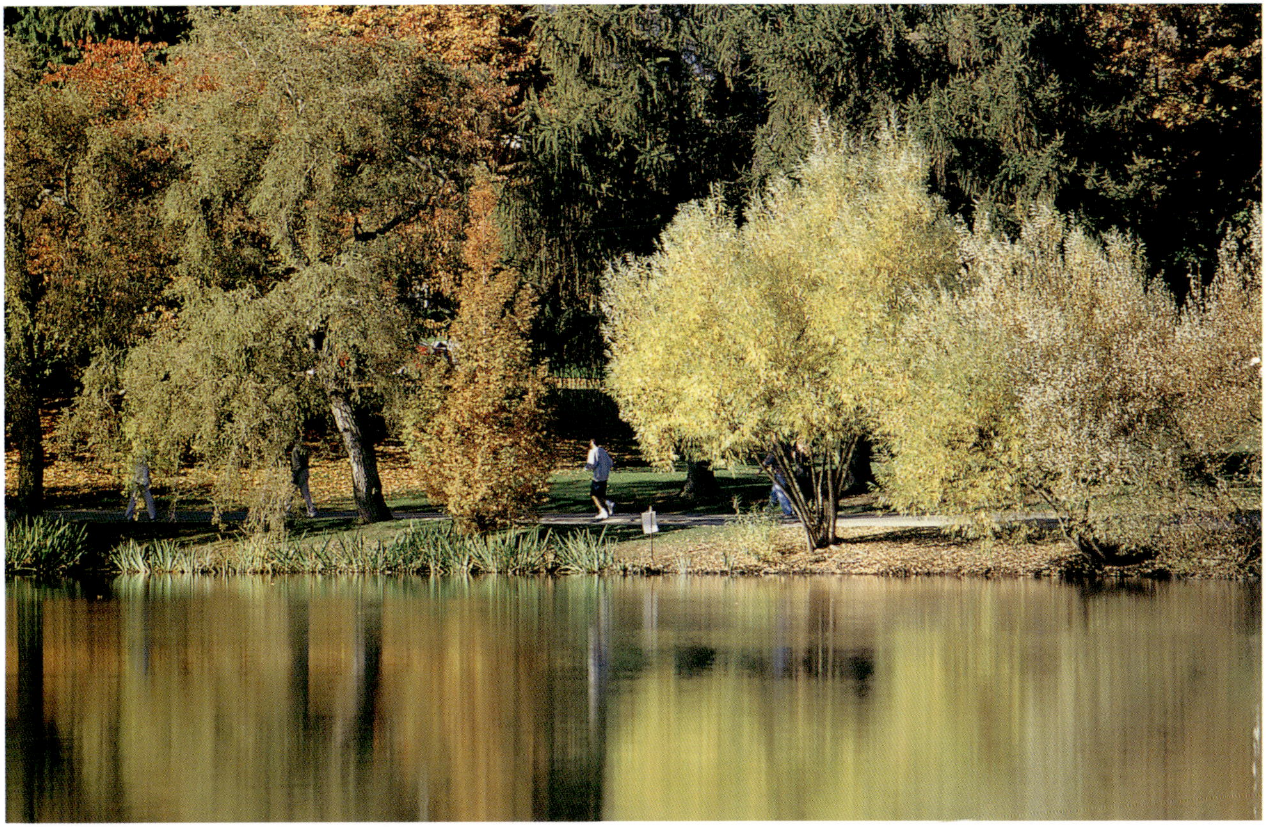

A lone runner travels
the shoreline path
in Green Lake Park.

Members of the Theta Chi fraternity pose in front of their chapter house, decorated for Homecoming. About 12 percent of UW undergraduates are members of fraternities or sororities.

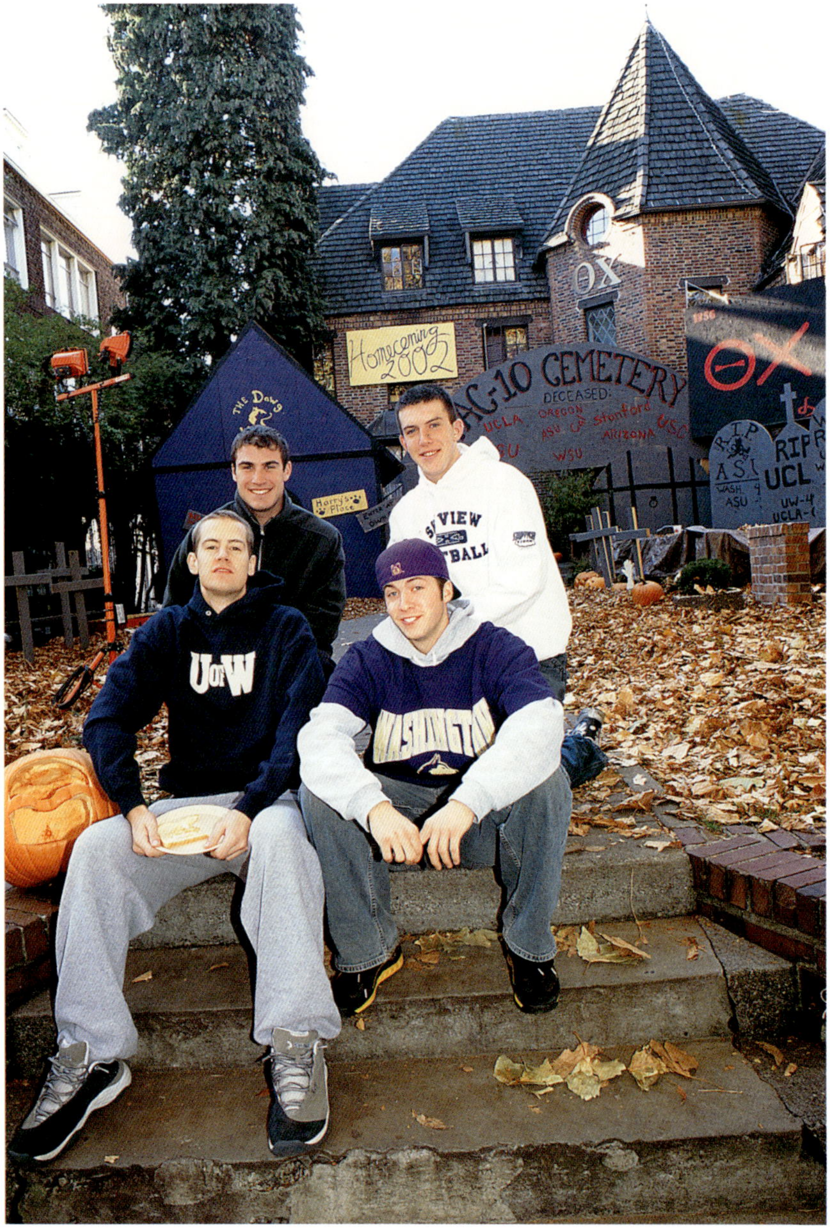

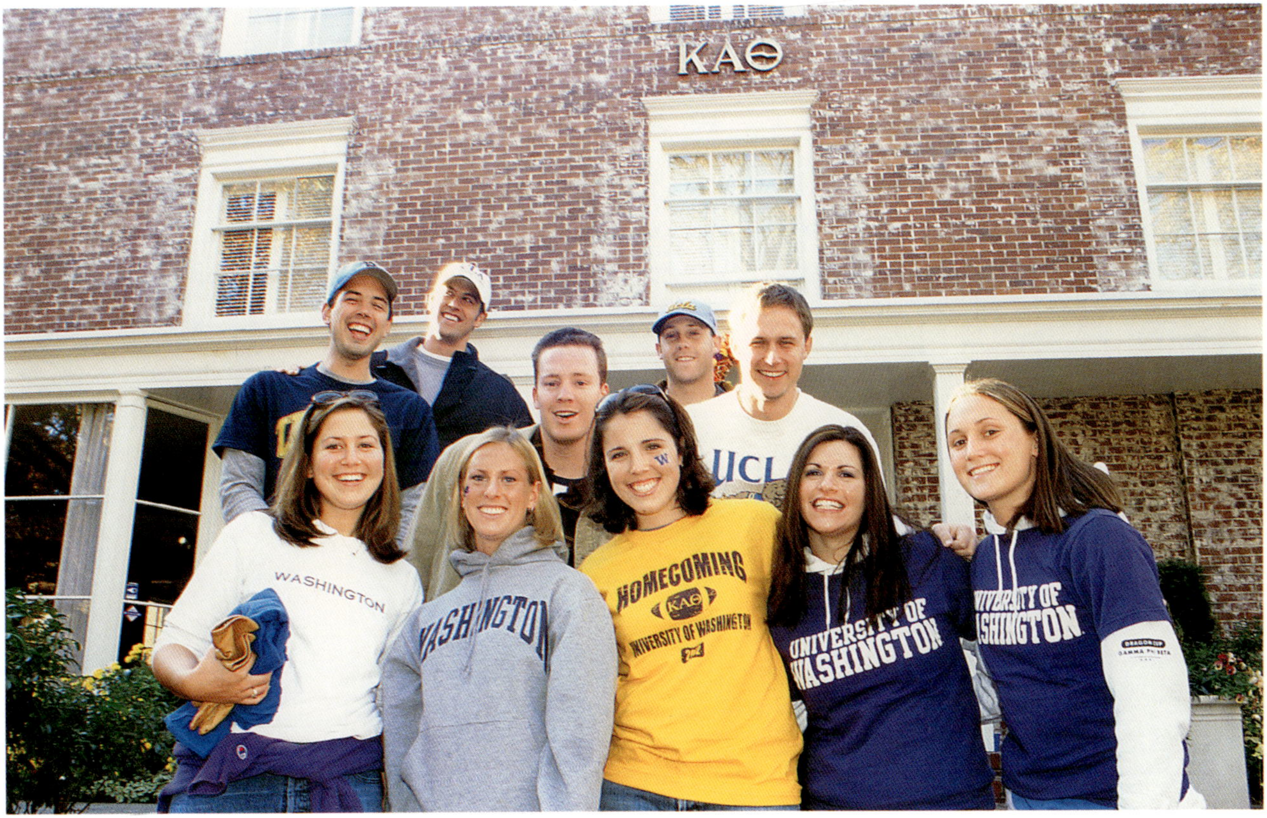

Men and women in the Greek system pose in front of the Kappa Alpha Theta sorority on 17th Avenue N.E., Greek Row.

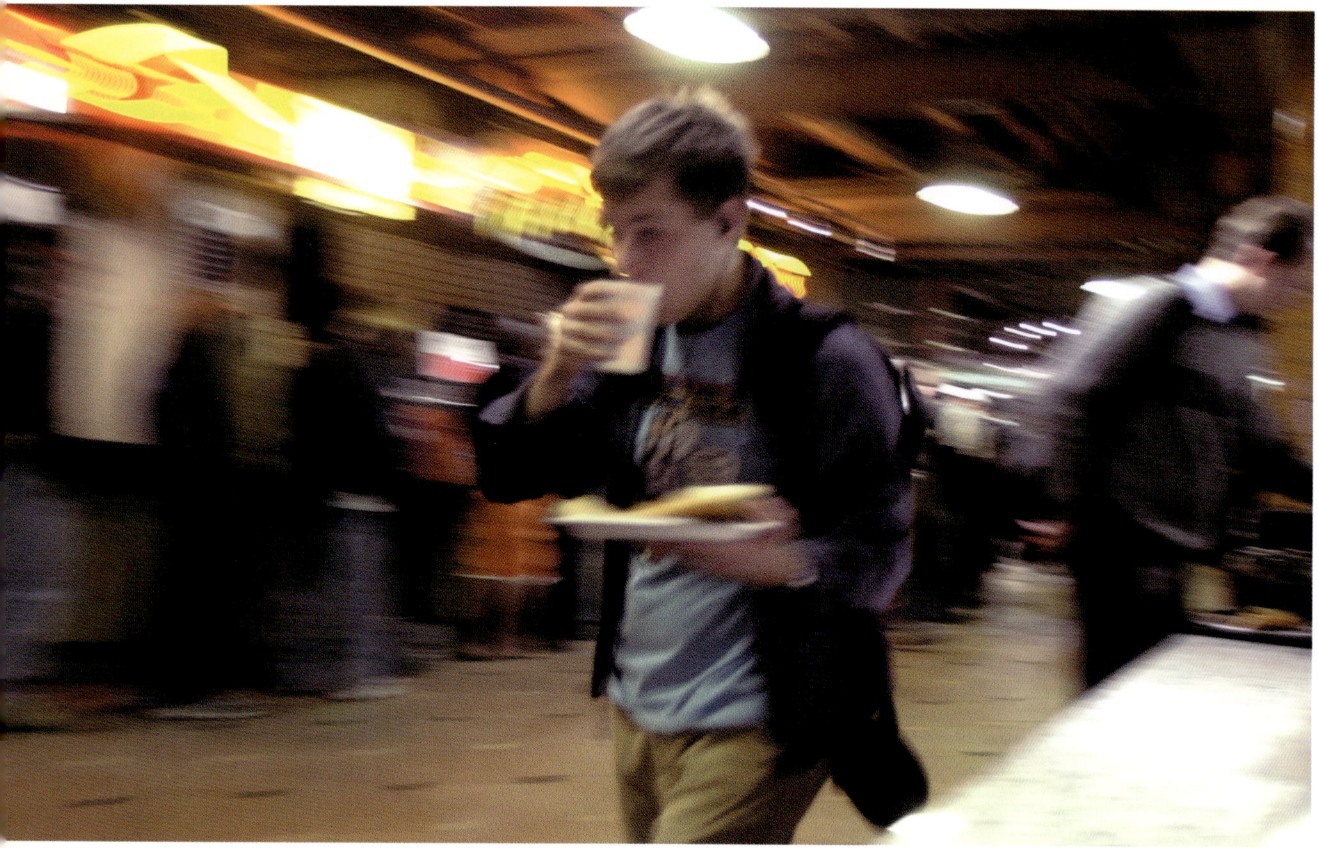

The Husky Den has eight quick-service restaurants to feed students on the run.

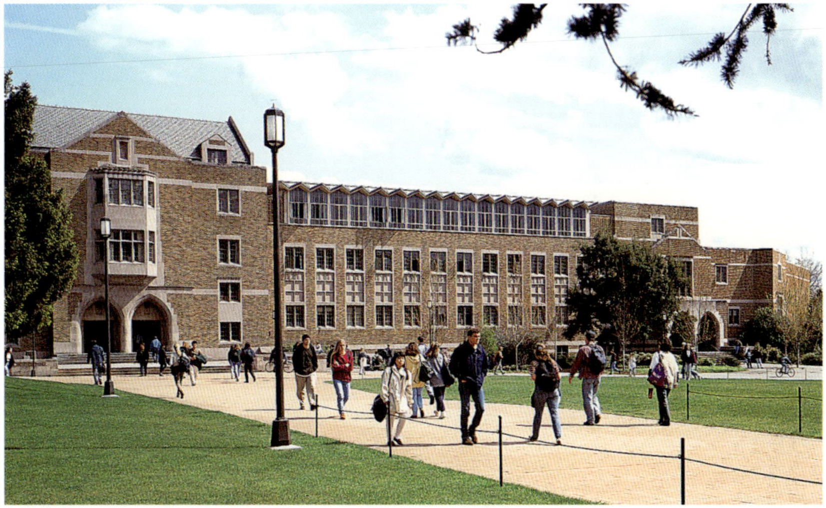

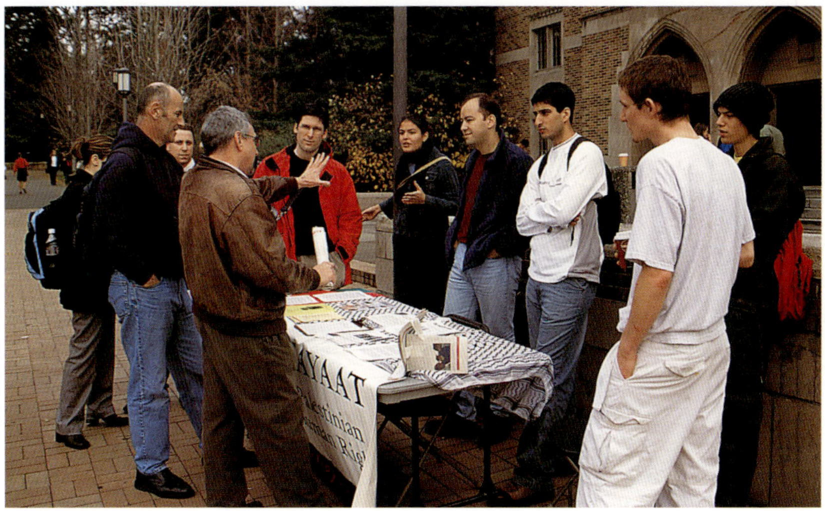

Top: The HUB (officially Husky Union Building) is the center of student social life on campus. *Bottom:* The steps in front of the HUB are traditionally a place for political debate.

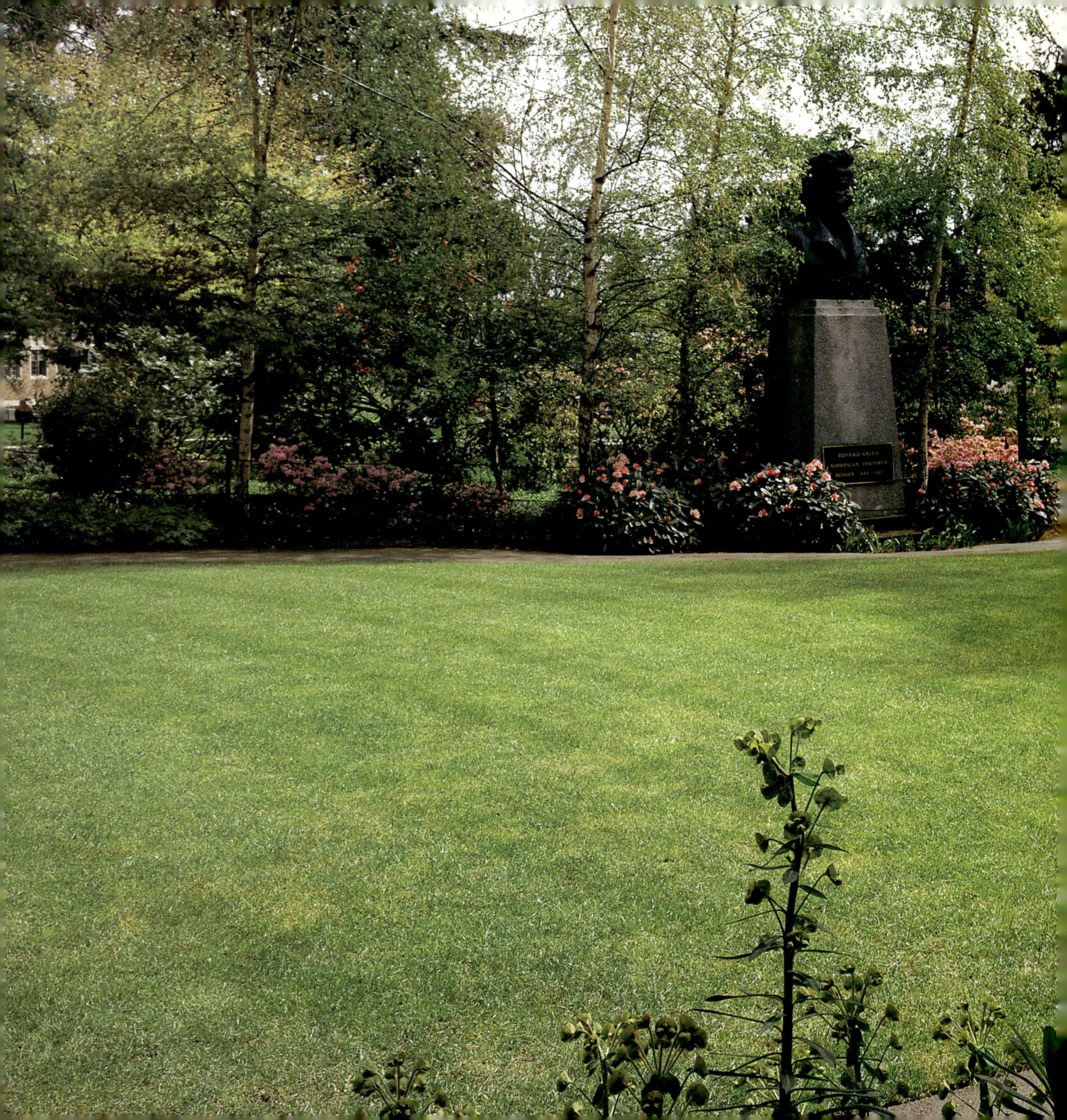
EDVARD GRIEG
NORWEGIAN COMPOSER
BERGEN

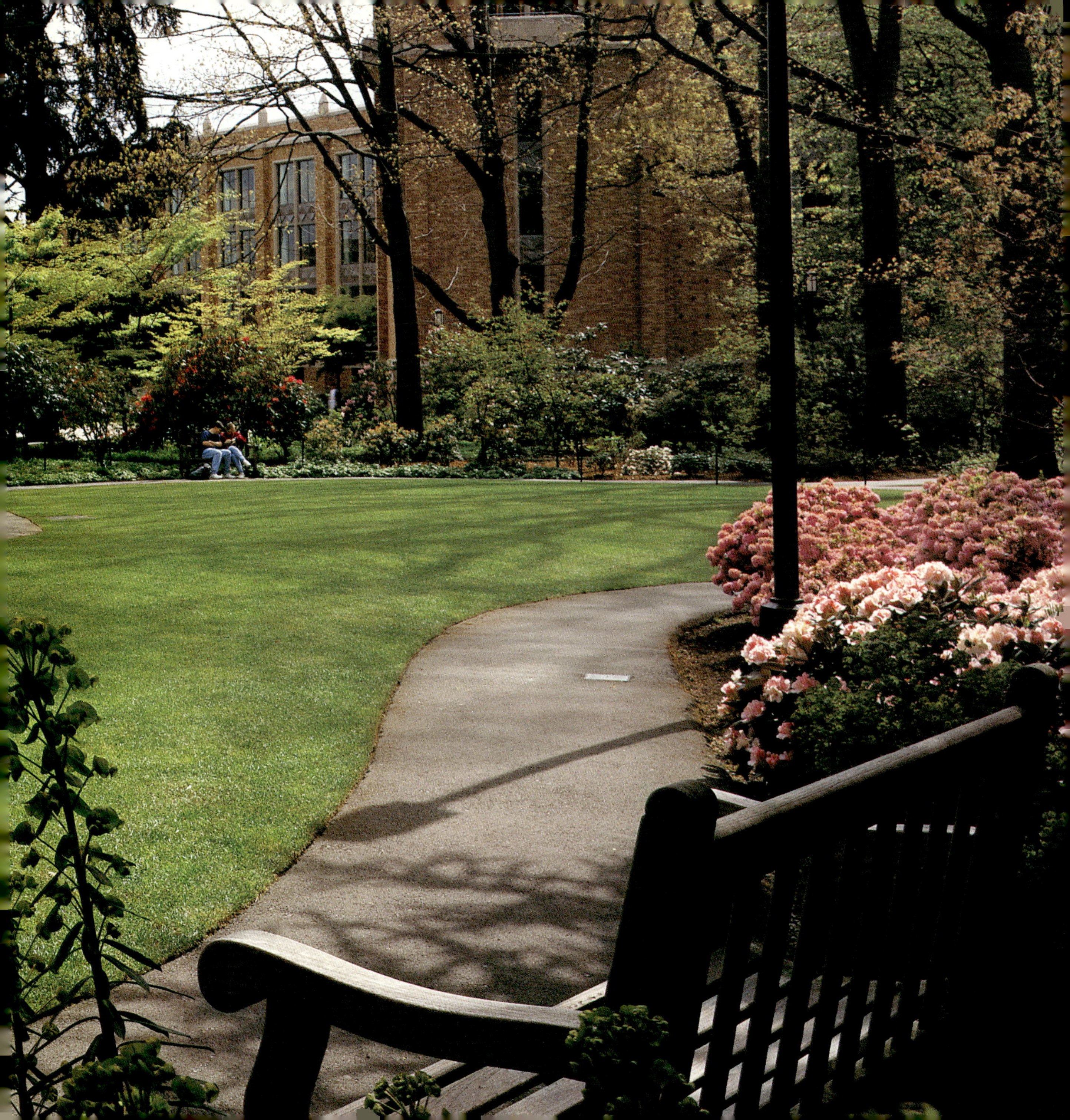

Previous page:
The Grieg Garden, near the HUB, has a statue of the Norwegian composer as its focal point. Once a parking lot, the woodland garden has dozens of varieties of rhododendron and azalea.

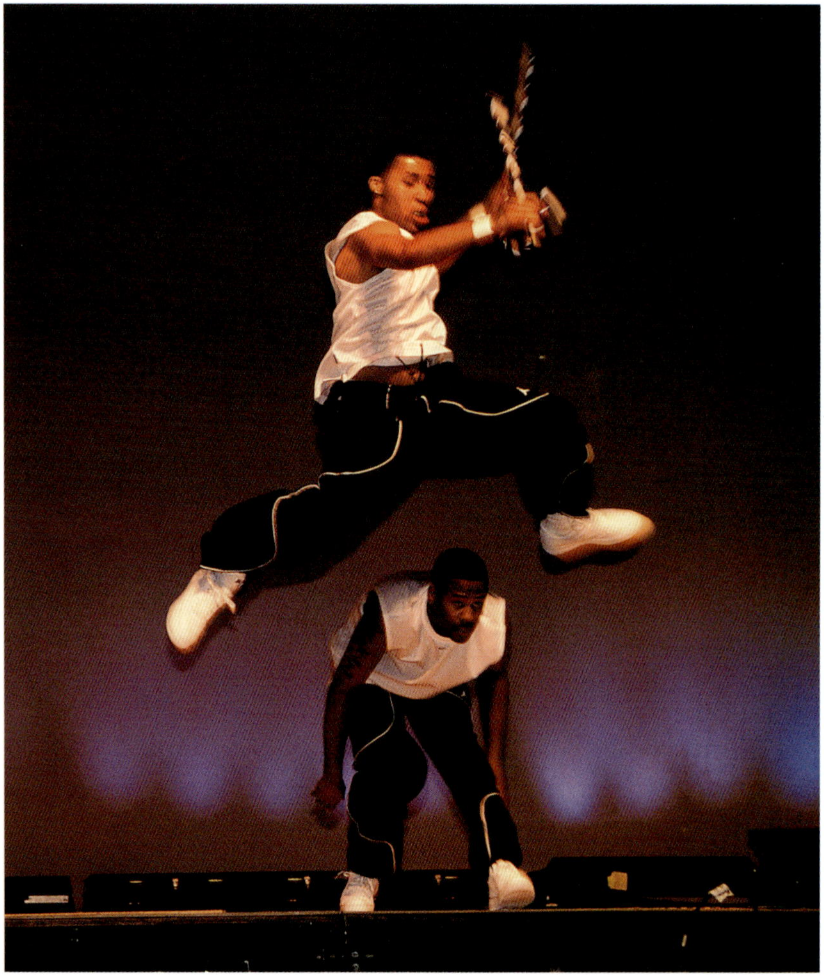

One student leaps over another in the Multi-Greek Emerald City Step Show at Hec Edmundson Pavilion, a tradition among African-American students at the UW.

Dance companies appearing in the UW performing arts center—Meany Hall—range from student groups to professional ensembles.

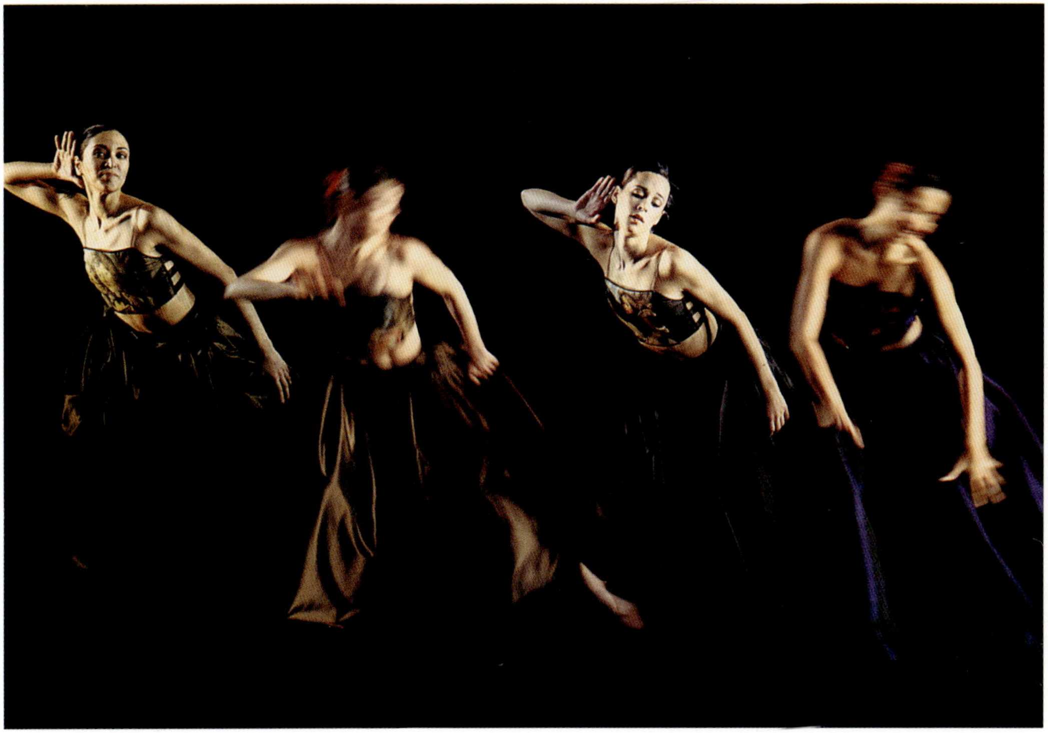

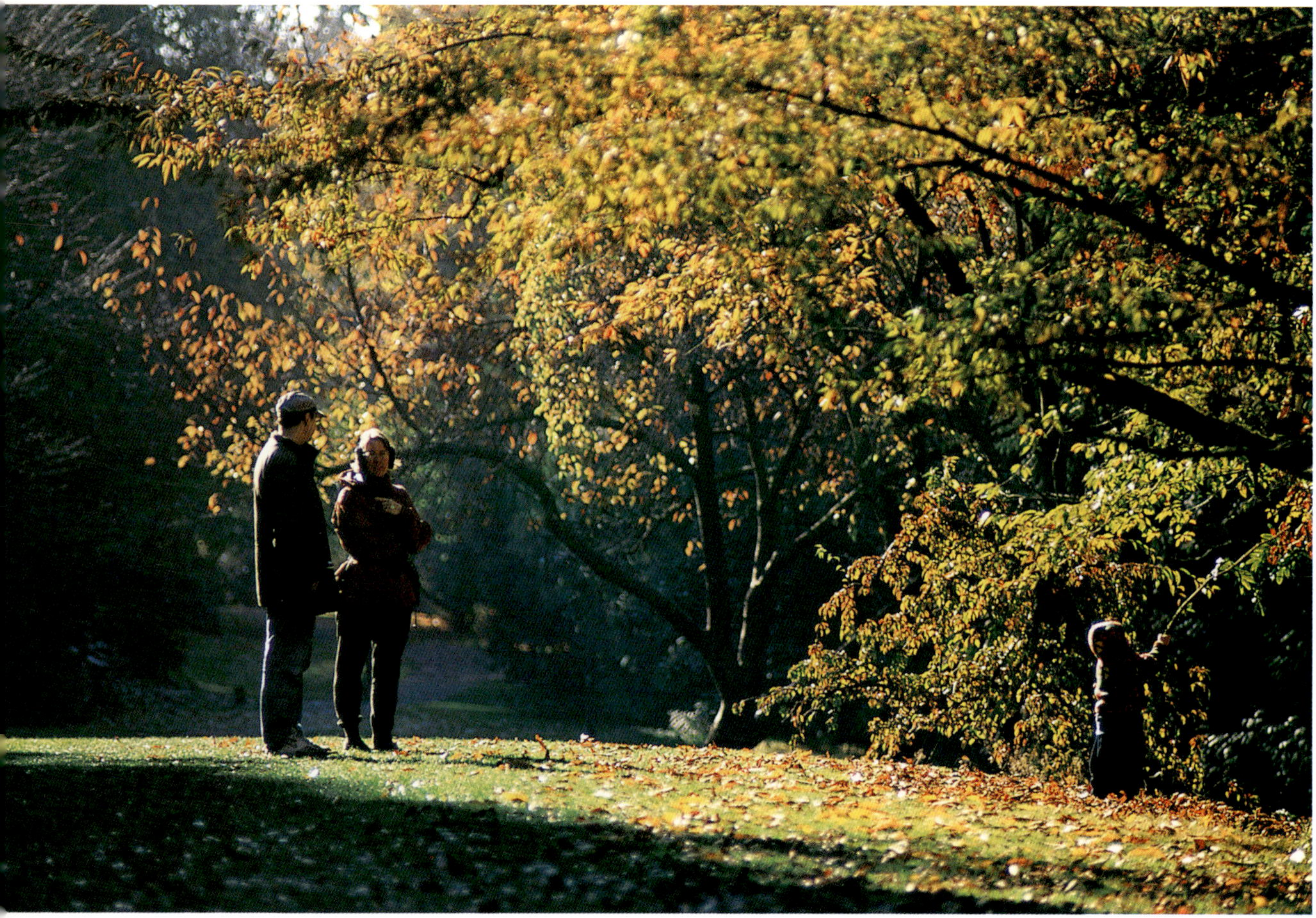

Jogging, biking, boating and walking are some favorite student activities in the Washington Park Arboretum.

Here a preschooler pokes at autumn leaves while his parents chat in the sunshine.

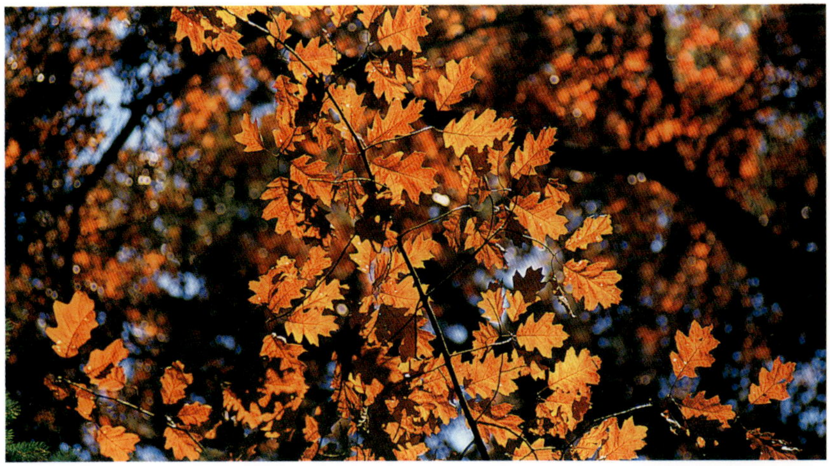

Golden-brown leaves show off one variety of oak in the Washington Park Arboretum. The park features more than 4,600 varieties of trees, shrubs and vines.

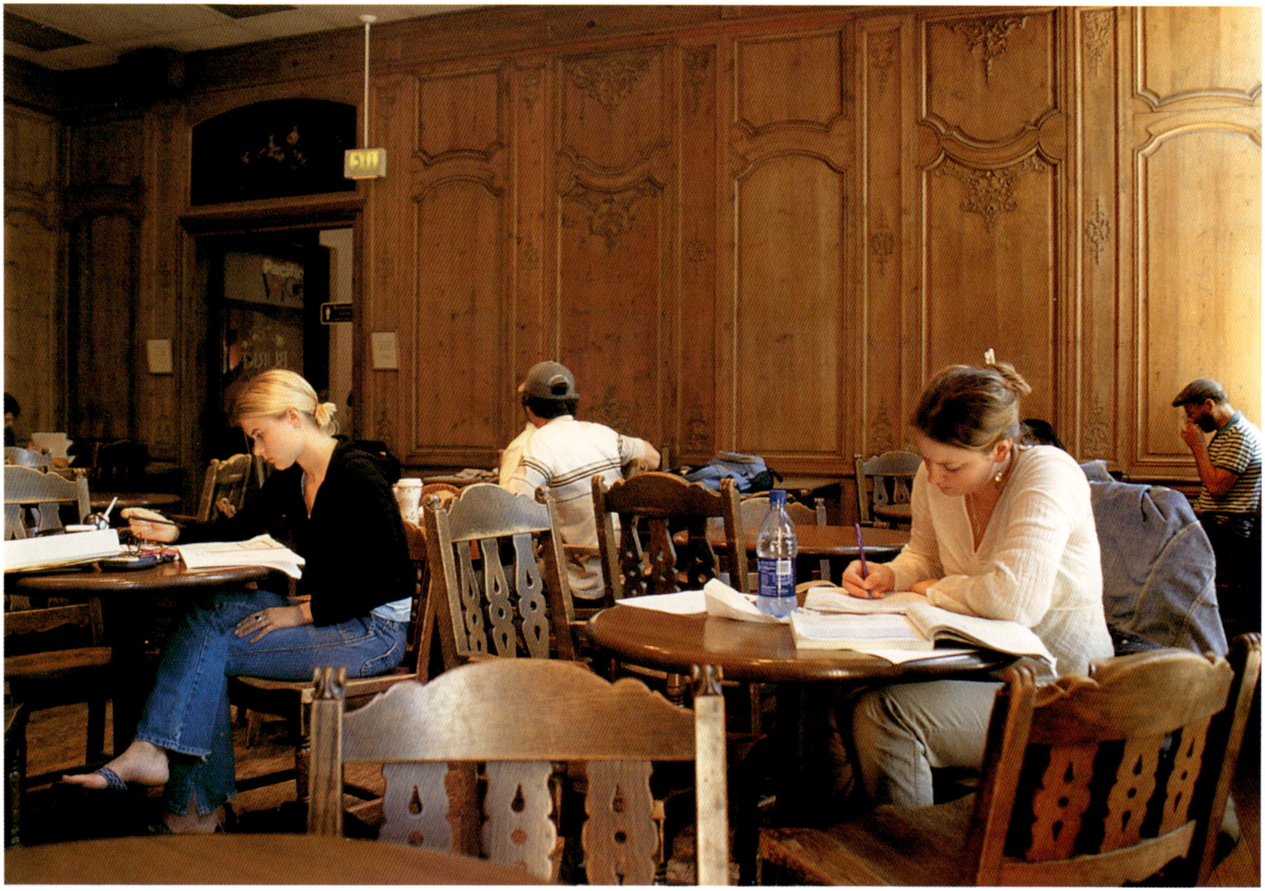

One of the best parts of the University of Washington experience is the many places to study. Here students review their notes amidst the paneled walls of the Burke Museum Café. Older alumni may remember the wooden chairs, which were originally in the Suzzallo Library Reading Room.

Left: A student hits the books in the Allen Library.
Right: The aisles in the Medical Center Library are carpeted: perfect to sit on when you find the right book.

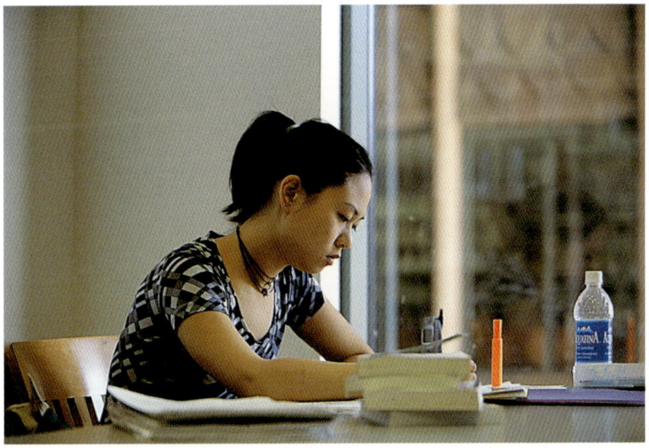

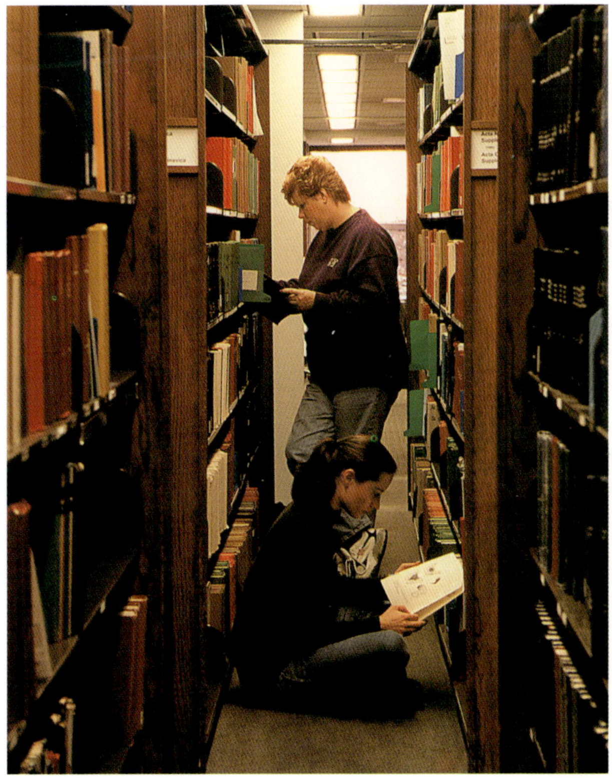

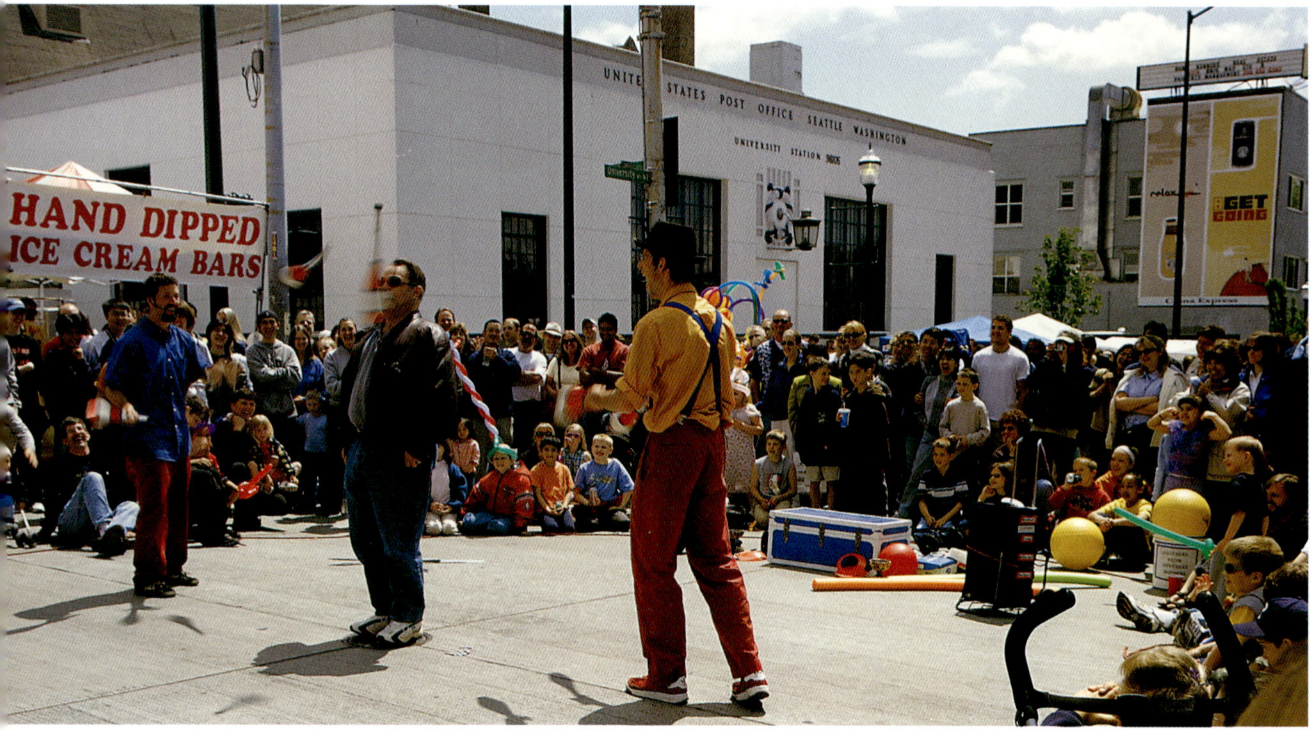

With great food, music and entertainment, the annual University District Street Fair draws a crowd along "the Ave."

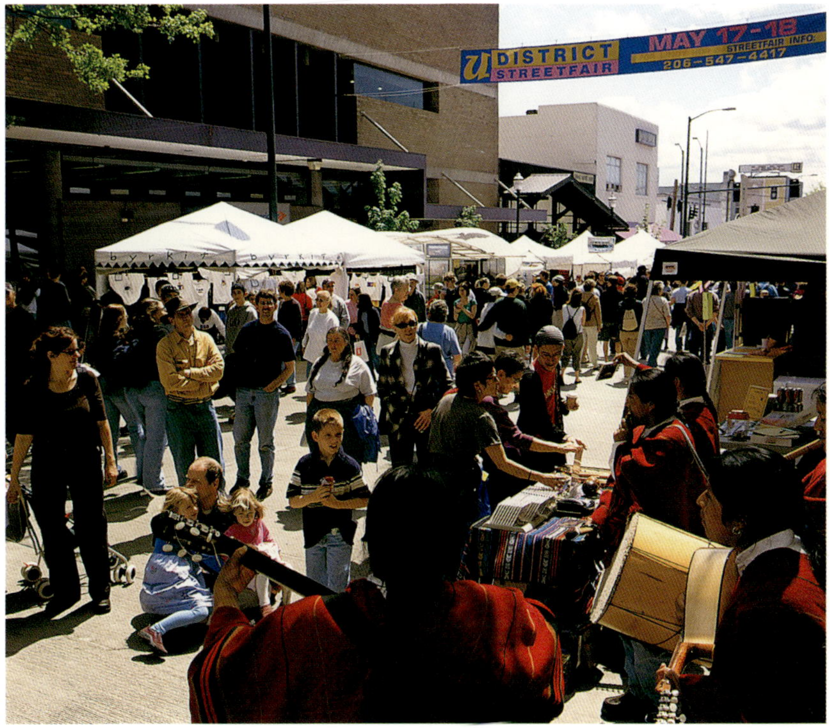
U DISTRICT
STREETFAIR
MAY 17-18
STREETFAIR INFO:
206-547-4417

Left: Almost every bike rack slot is filled along Bloedel Hall.

Right: It's a part of almost every UW student's experience—the Montlake parking lot in the rain.

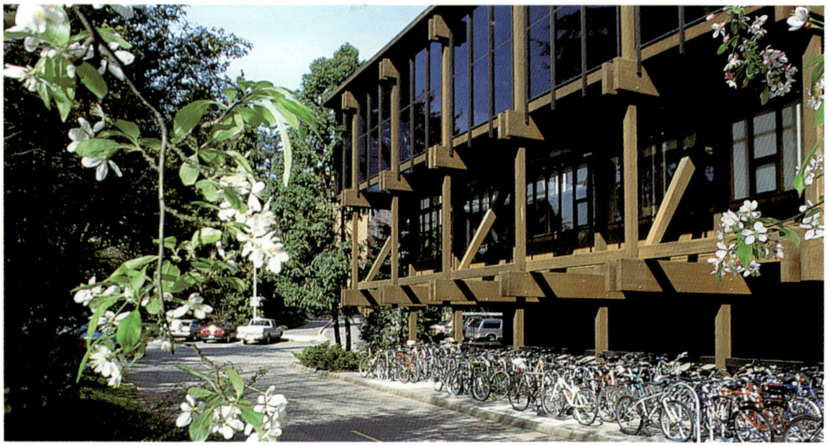

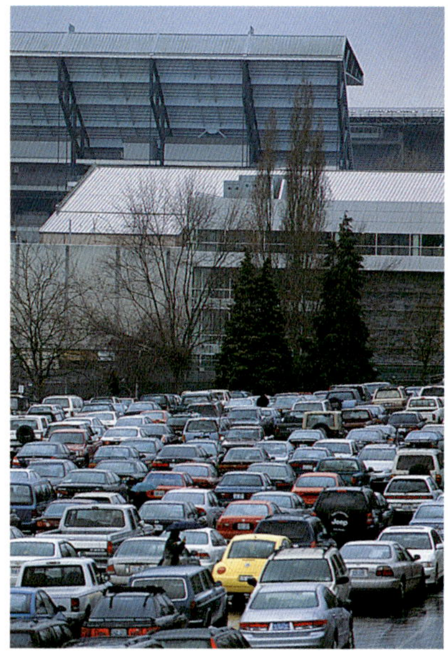

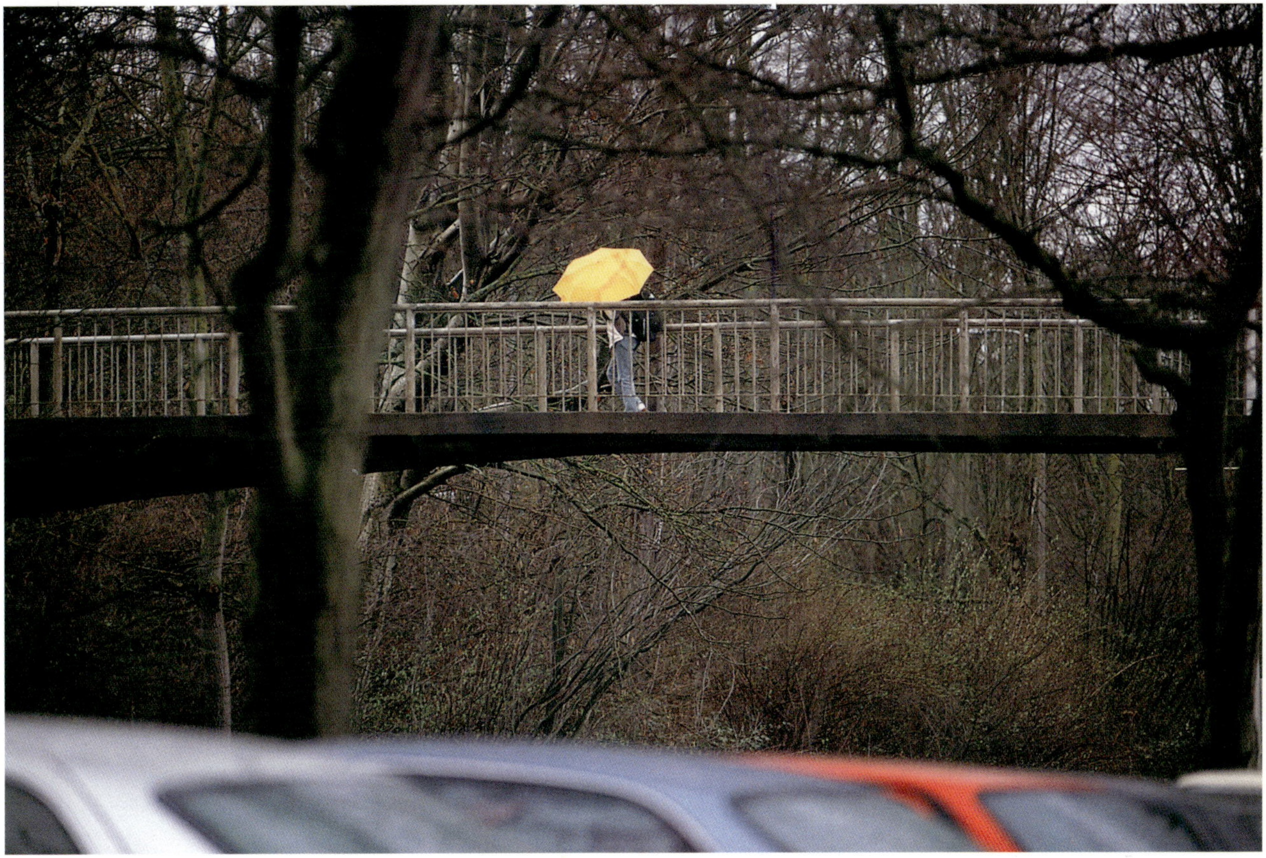

An umbrella shelters a student as she makes her way on the overpass linking the Montlake lot to campus.

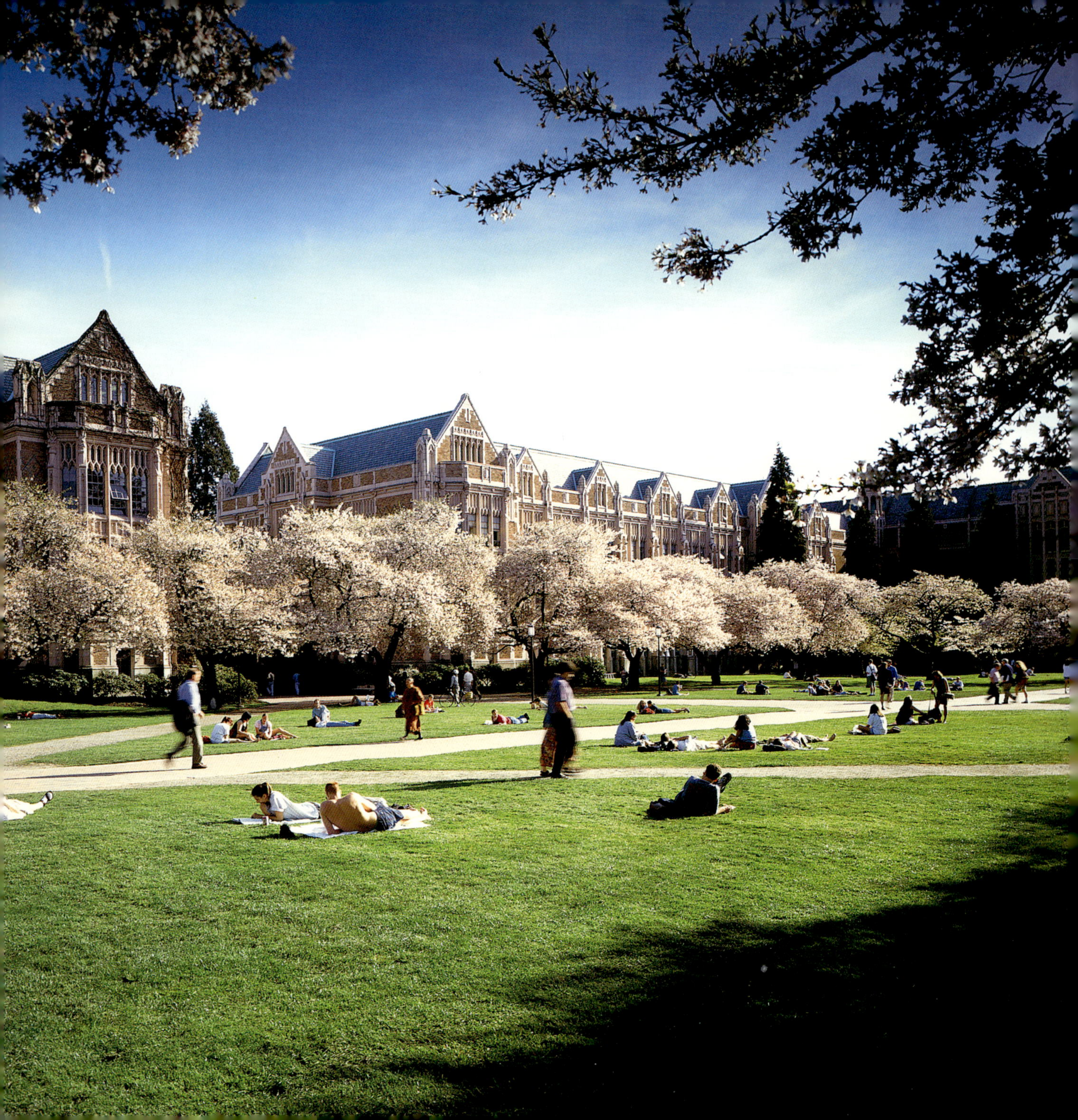

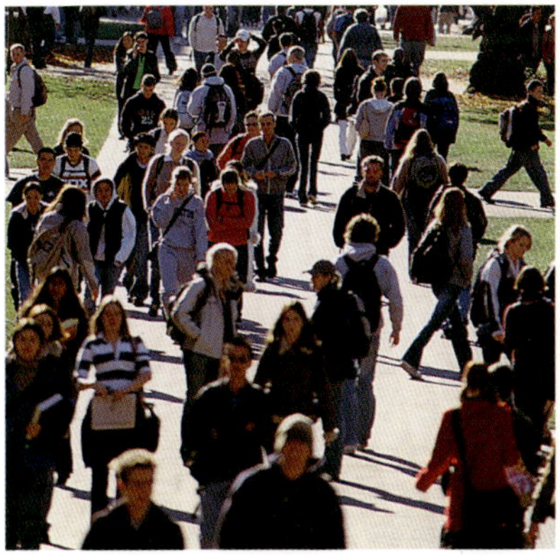

Between classes it seems as if all 39,000 students are on the move.

Opposite page:
The quintessential UW experience is lounging on the Quad while its cherry trees are in bloom.

A solitary student in purple is surrounded by another Husky color—gold.

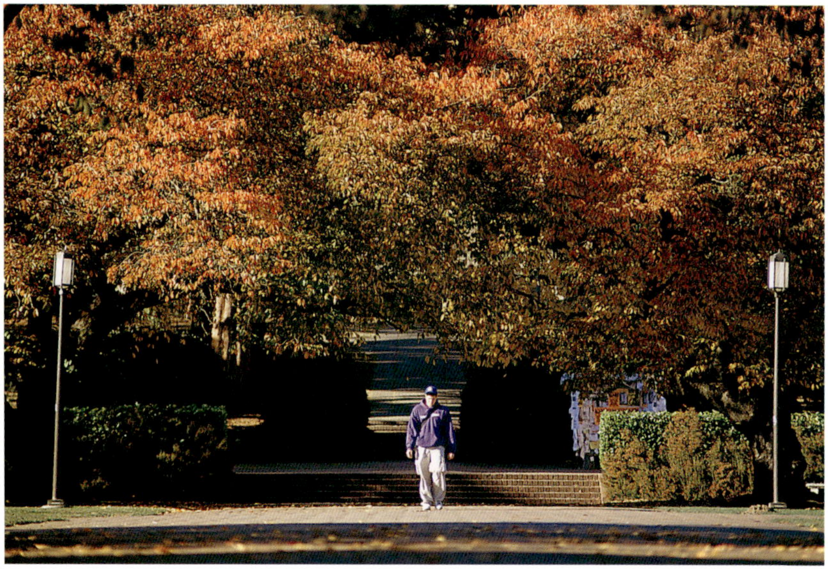

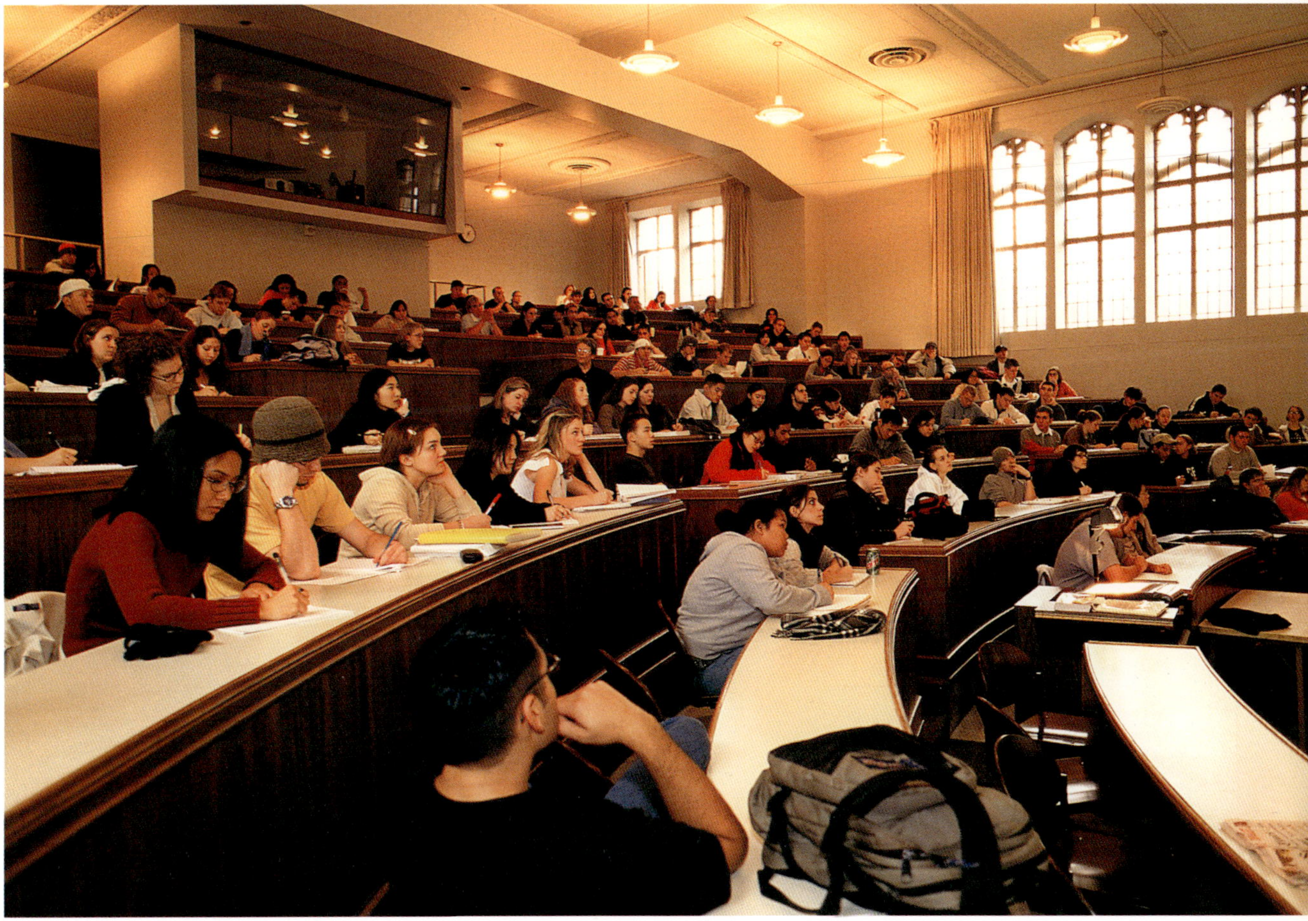

Students in Gowen Hall listen to a political science lecture in what used to be space for the law school.

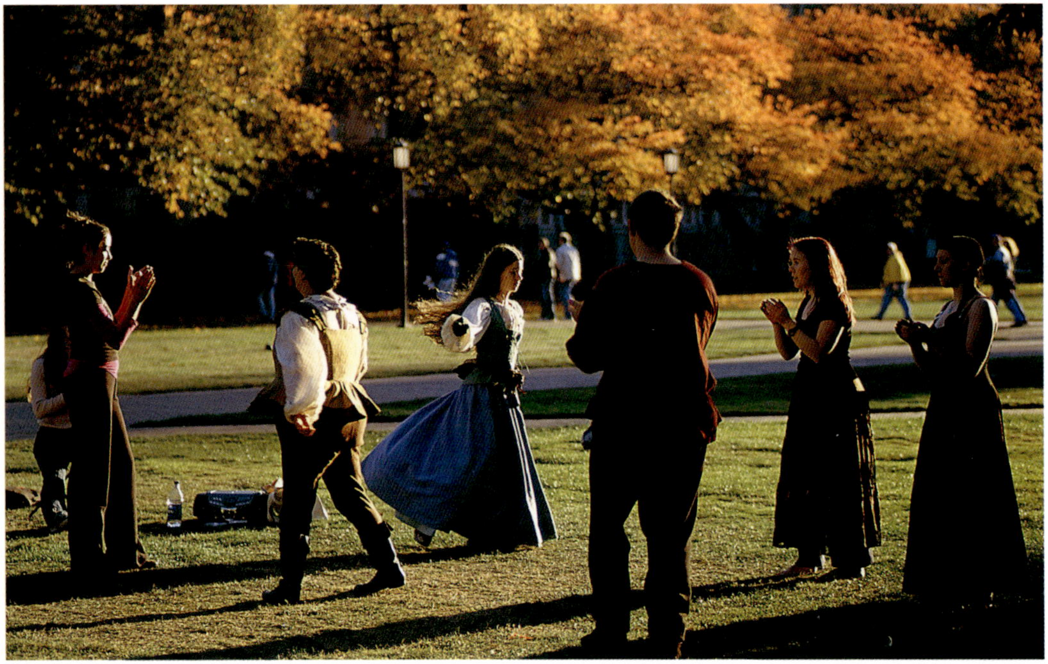

The Quad is a
setting for student
art shows, outdoor
classes and, in
this case, a group
of folk dancers.

Dancers practice on the Quad, which is the setting for several performances during the UW's Summer Arts Festival.

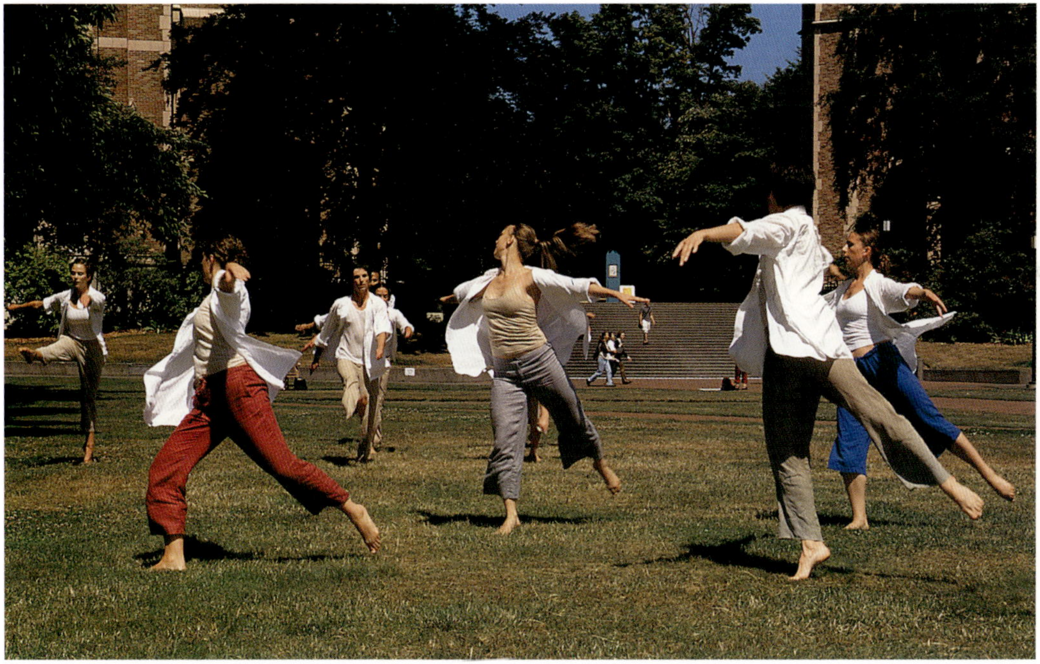

Next page:
The Quad's 30 Japanese Yoshino cherry trees create a pink canopy.

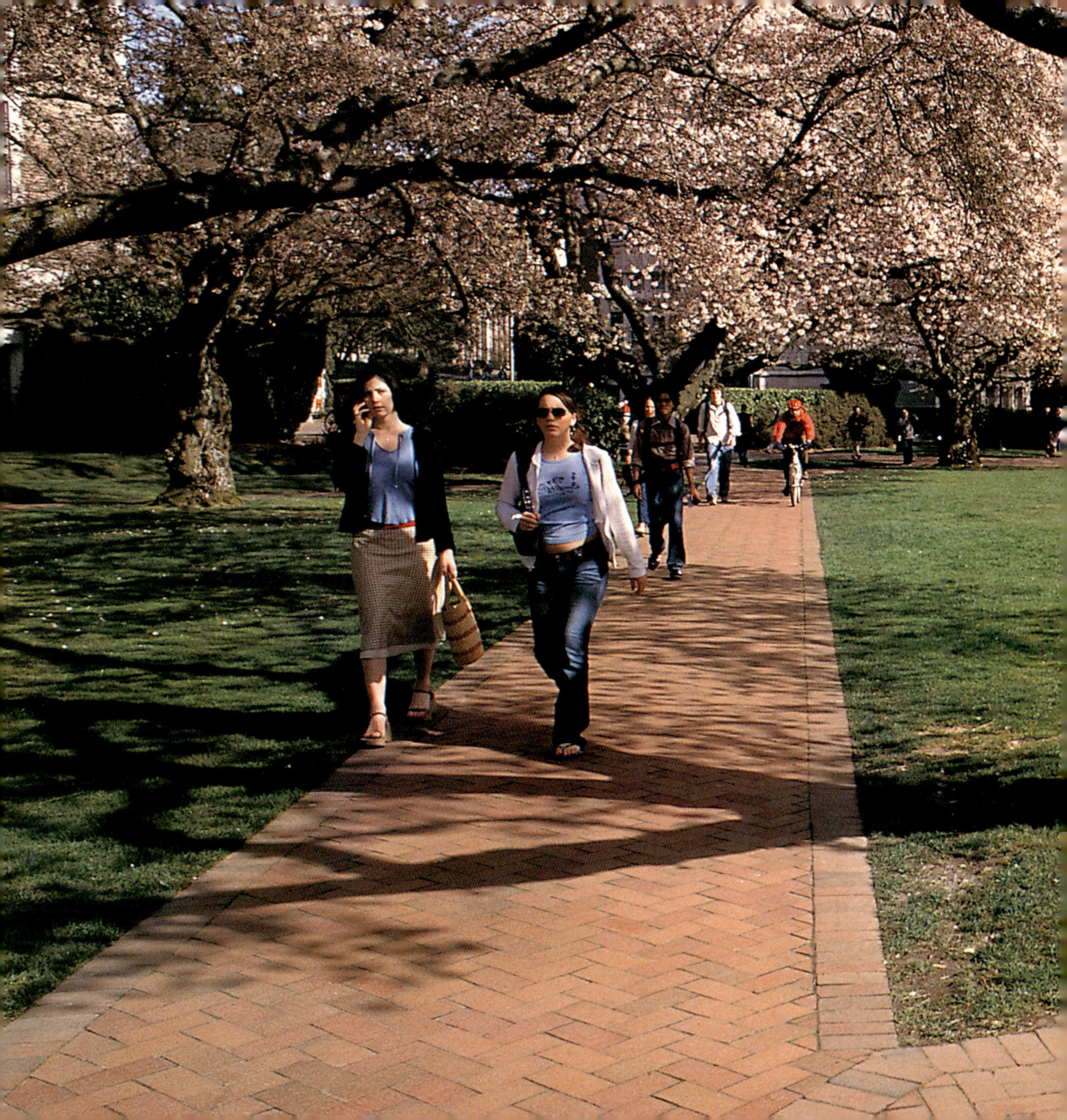

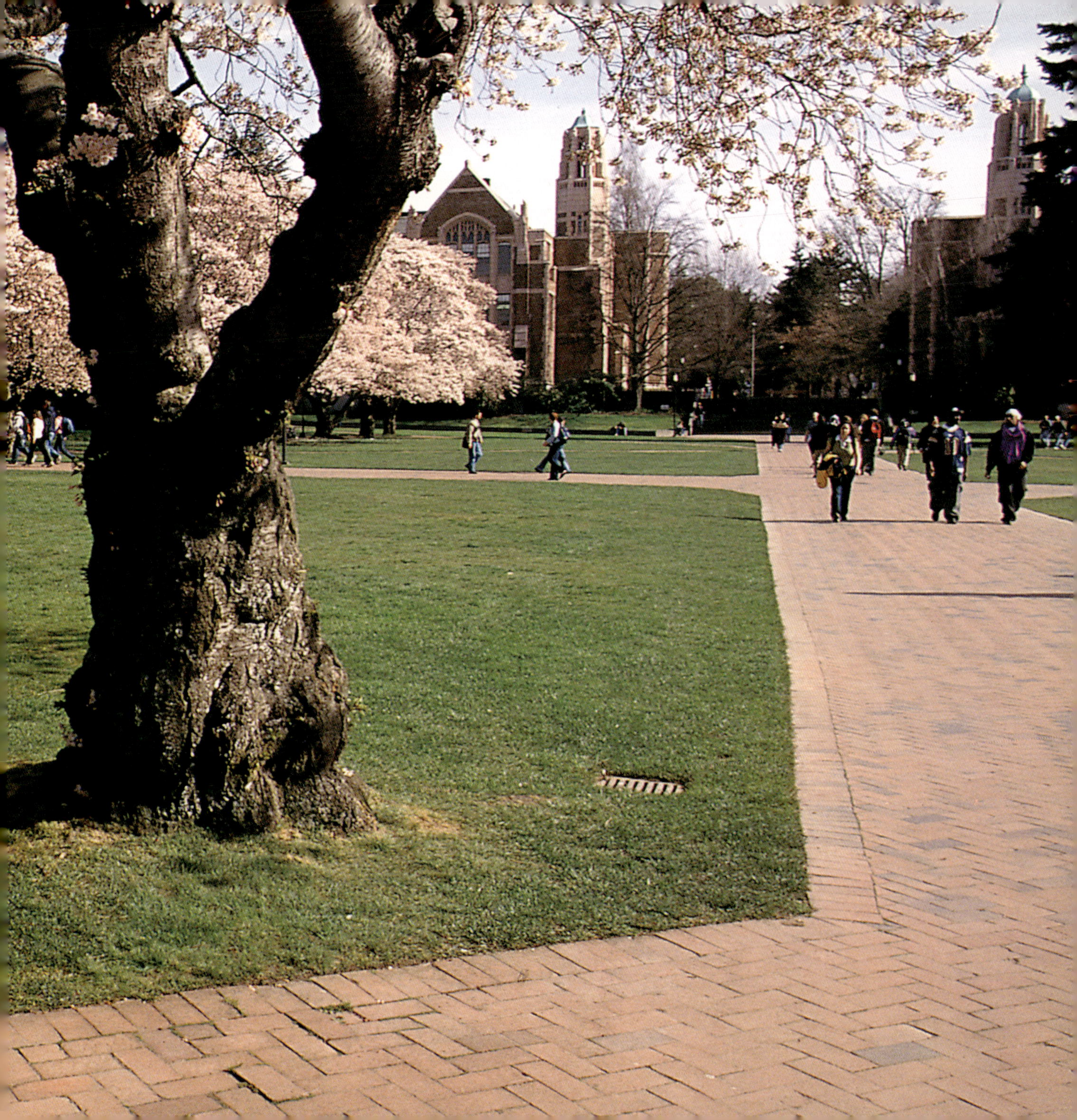

Left: The UW School of Music's ethno-musicology program attracts guest artists from around the world.

Right: This UW music student tries out his French horn in an unusual acoustical setting—the parking garage beneath Red Square.

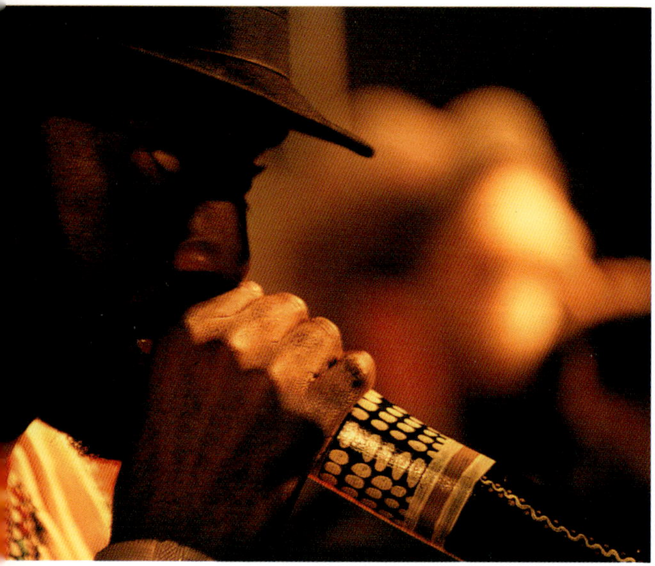

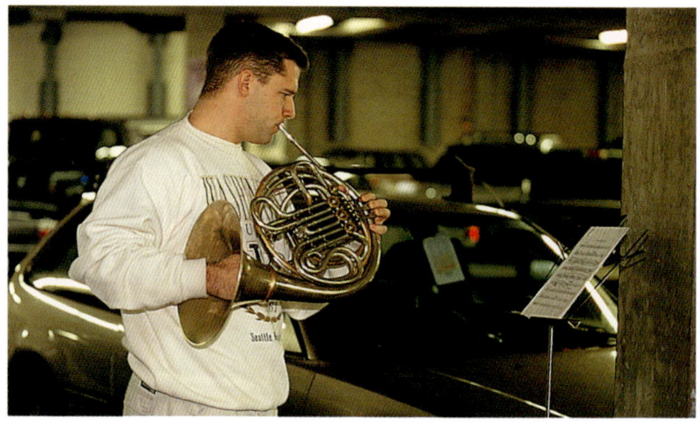

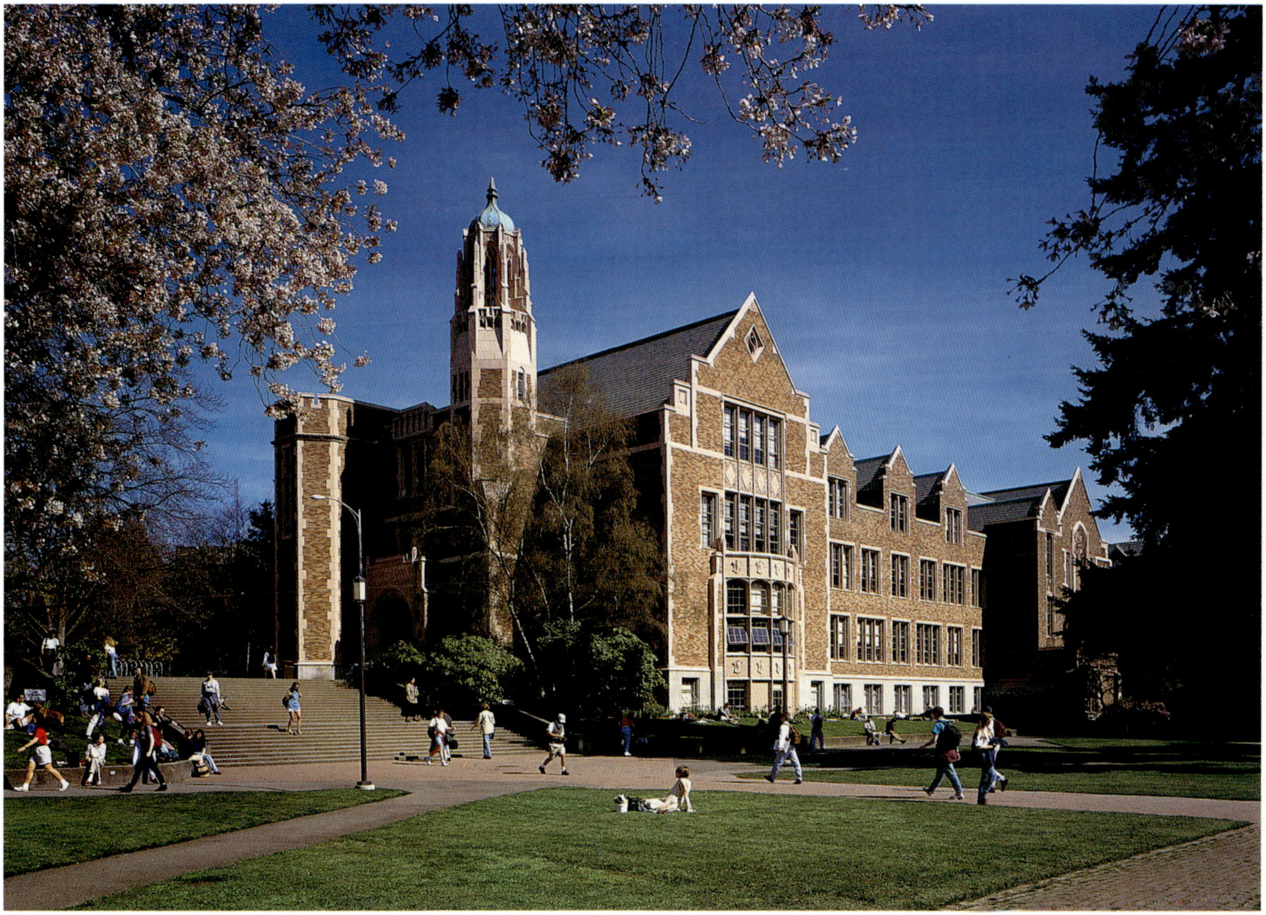

The Music Building, with its ornate tower, follows the classic campus architecture—Collegiate Gothic.

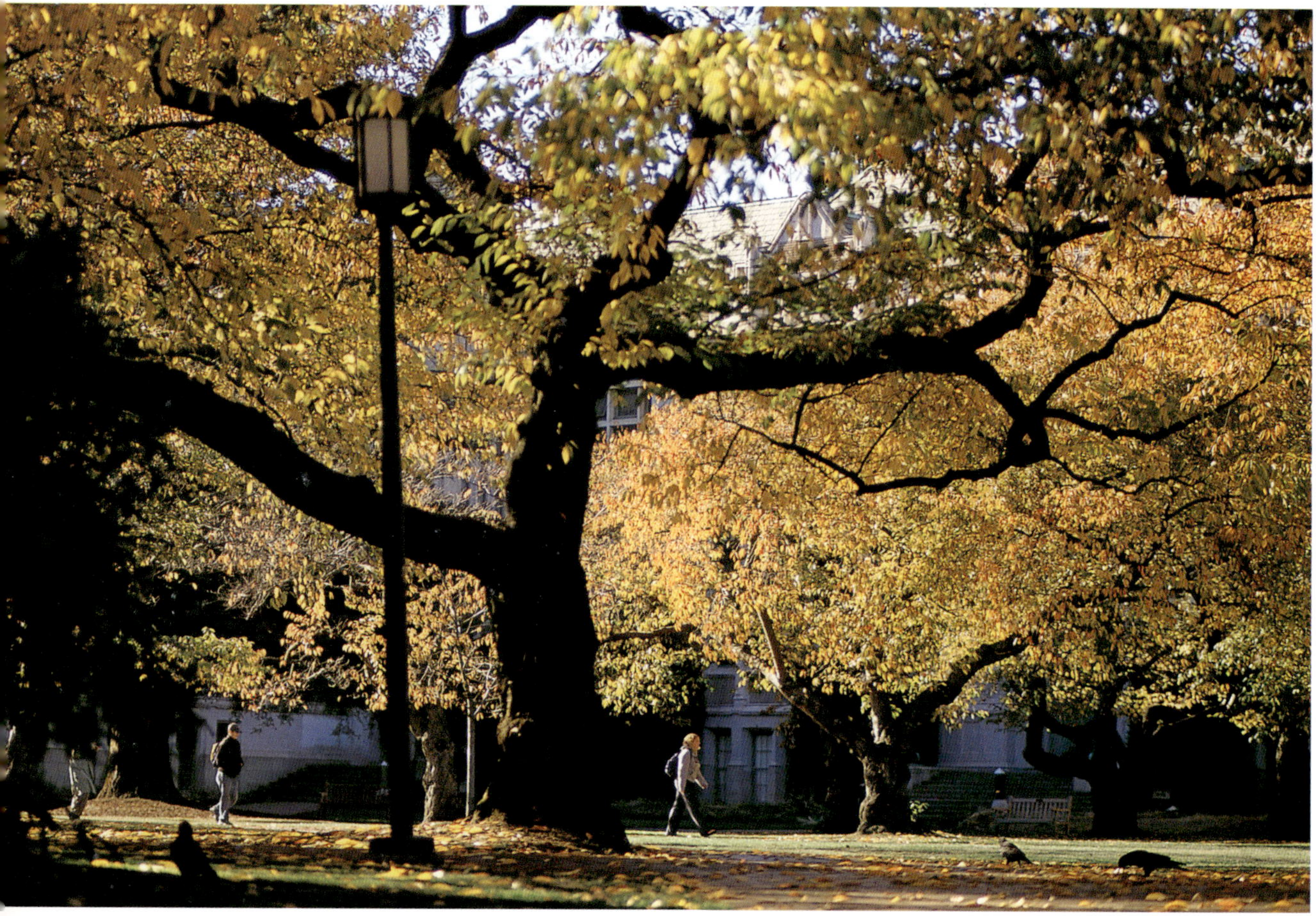

The Quad's cherry trees put on a grand show in the fall too, as their leaves turn to gold and crimson.

Students chat
between classes
along one of the
Quad's walkways.

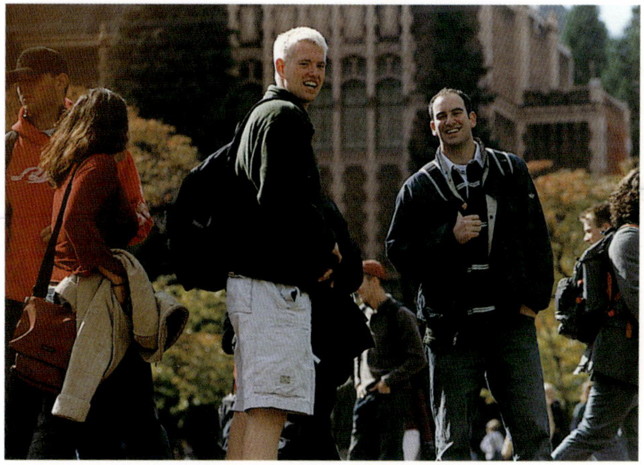

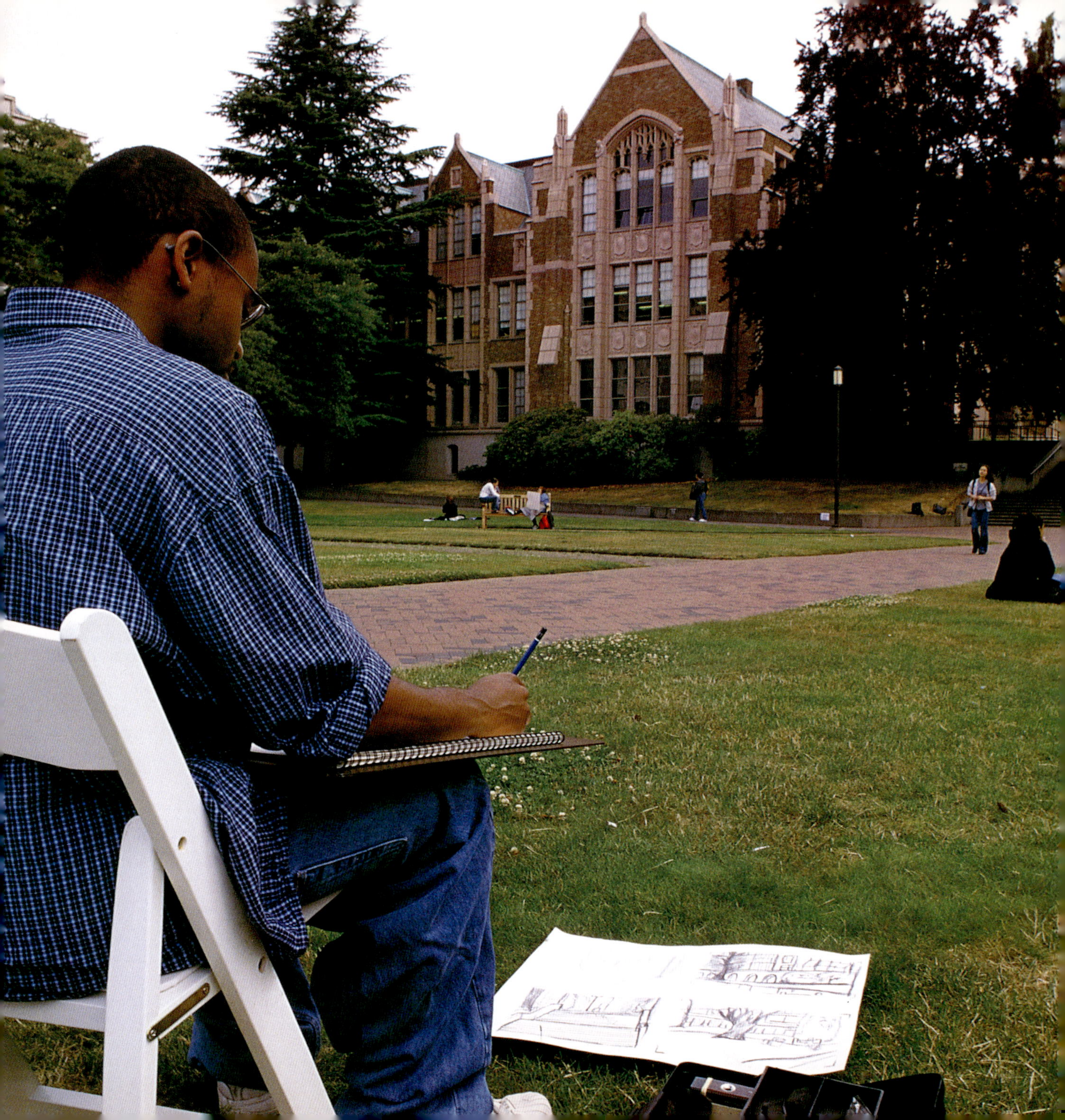

Left: Fall colors inspire a painter.
Right: Art books and journals make an abstract design.

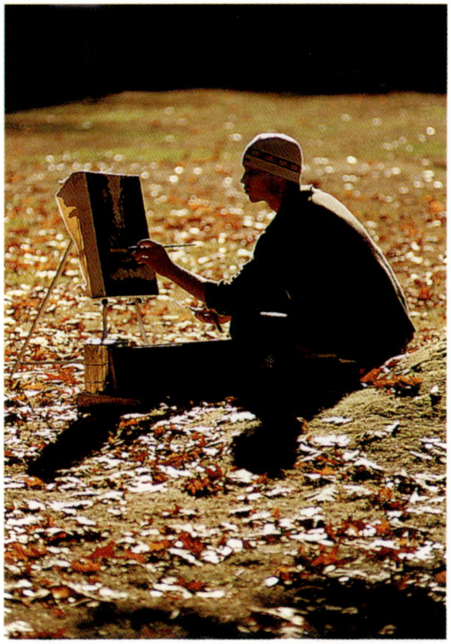

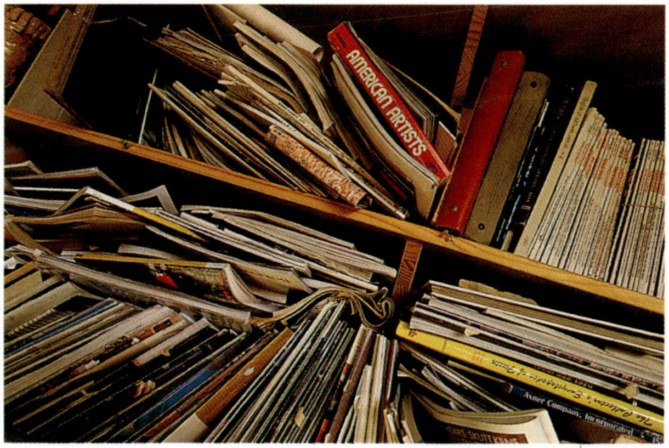

Opposite page:
An art student sketches, with the Art Building in the background.

Left: Art comes in many forms. Here an artist begins to carve a totem pole at the Burke Museum.

Right: A student contemplates a wall of paintings in this art school exhibition.

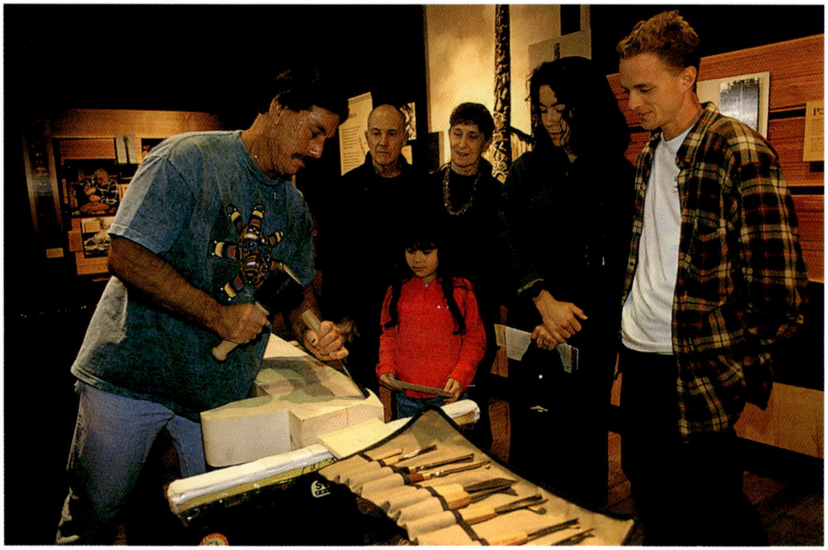

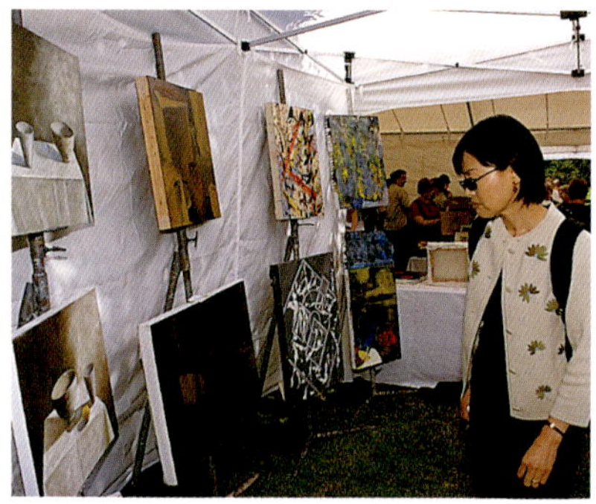

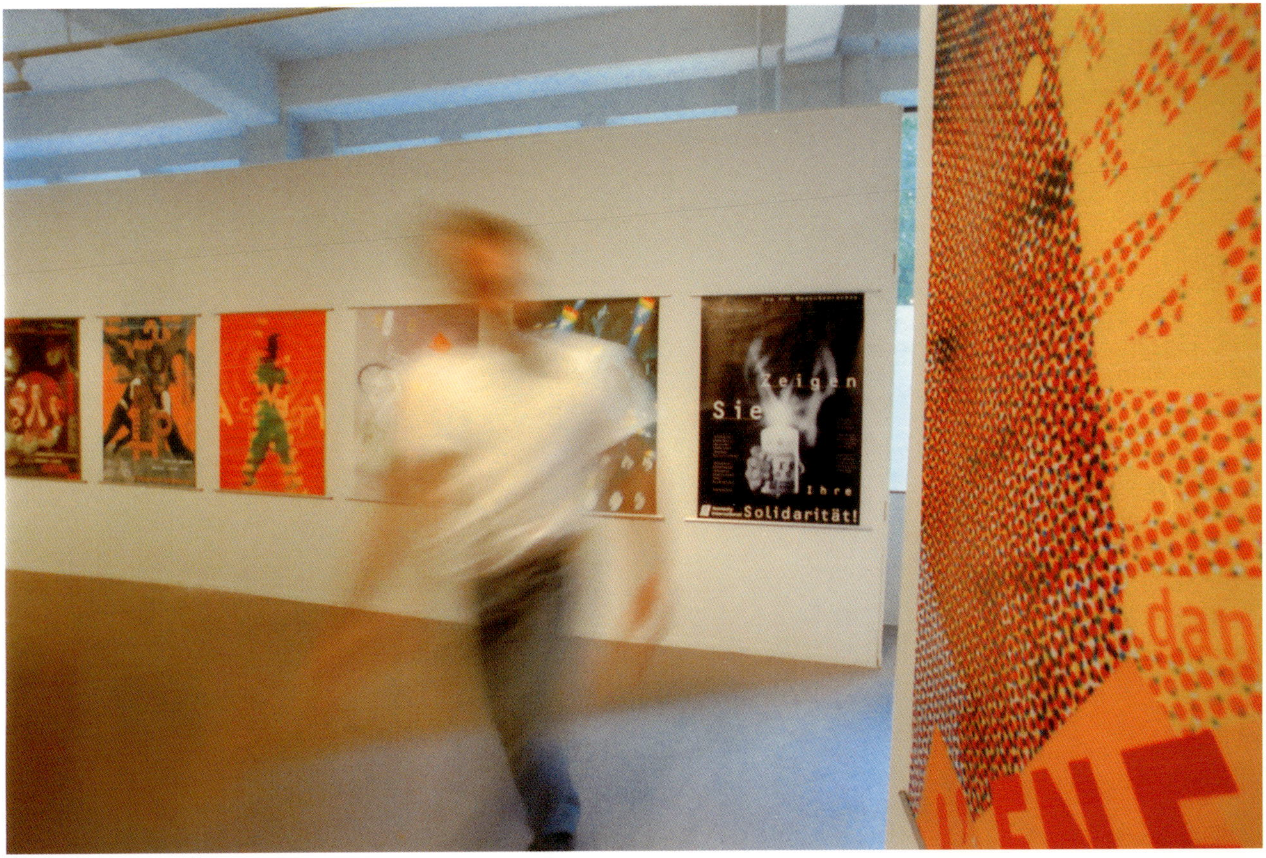

A visitor speeds through an exhibit in the Jacob Lawrence Gallery, the art school's space named for the famous African-American artist, who was on the UW faculty.

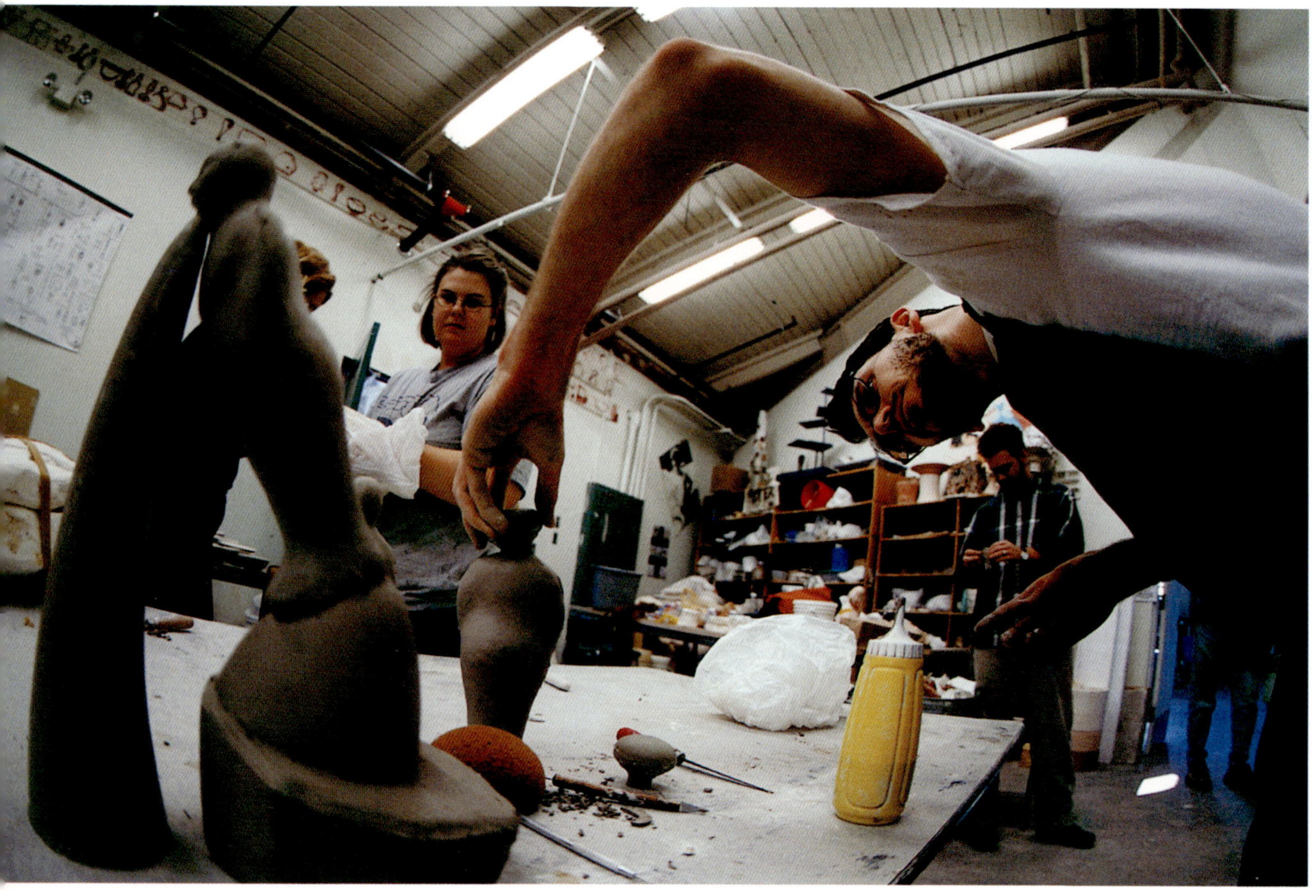

It's a moment for concentration in a ceramics class.

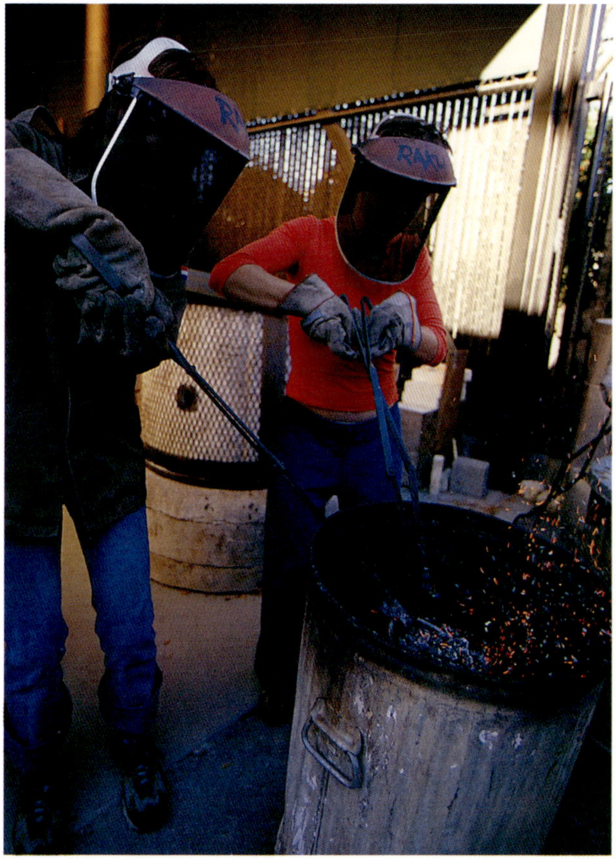

Left: Two students carefully plunge their work into a bucket of ashes as they make Raku pottery. *Right:* Some of the finished pieces cool, while others are still in the ash bucket.

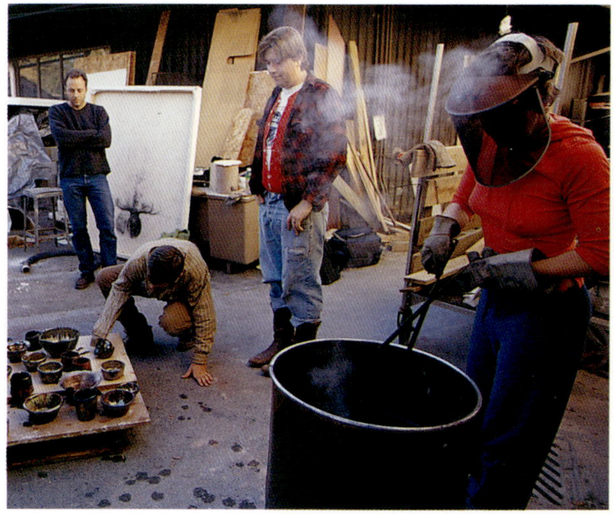

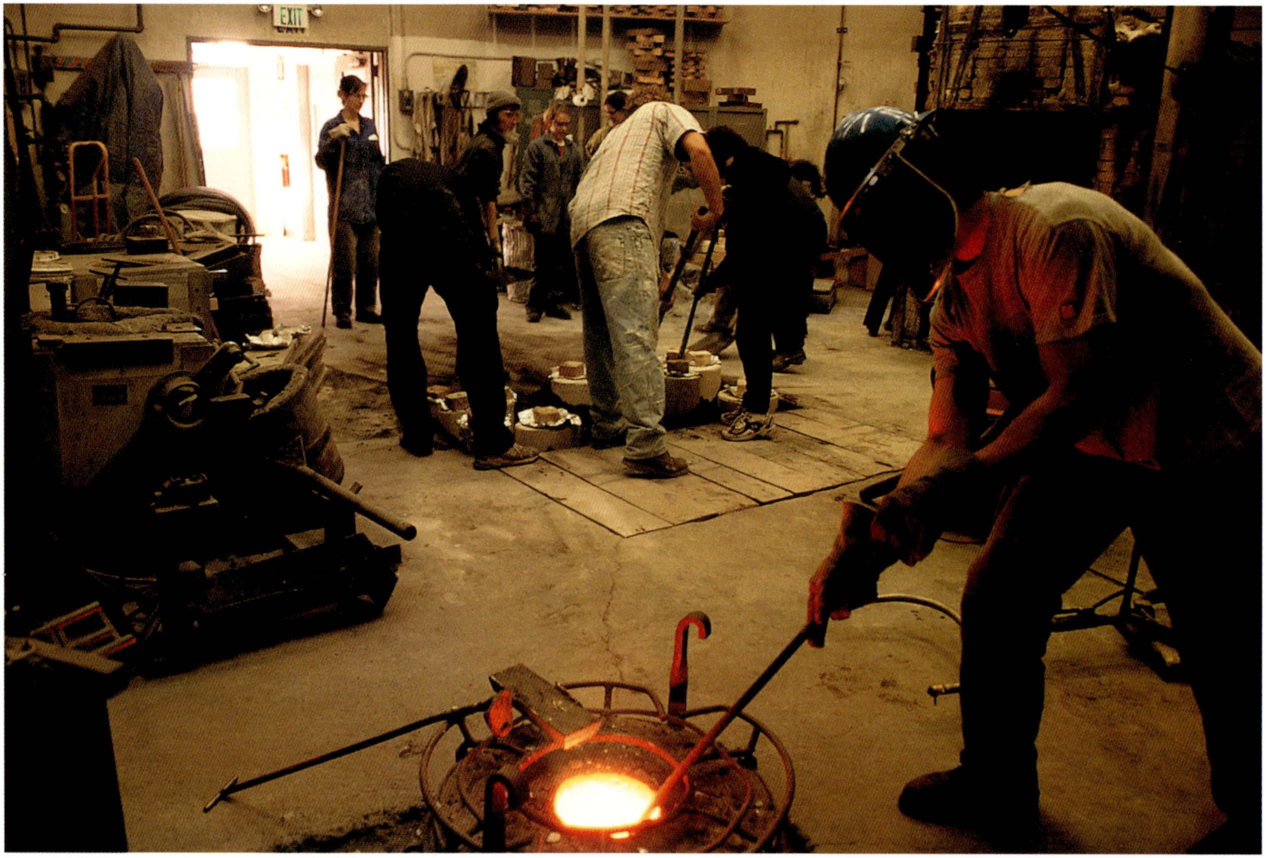

Molten metal throws a red light on an art student preparing to cast a bronze piece.

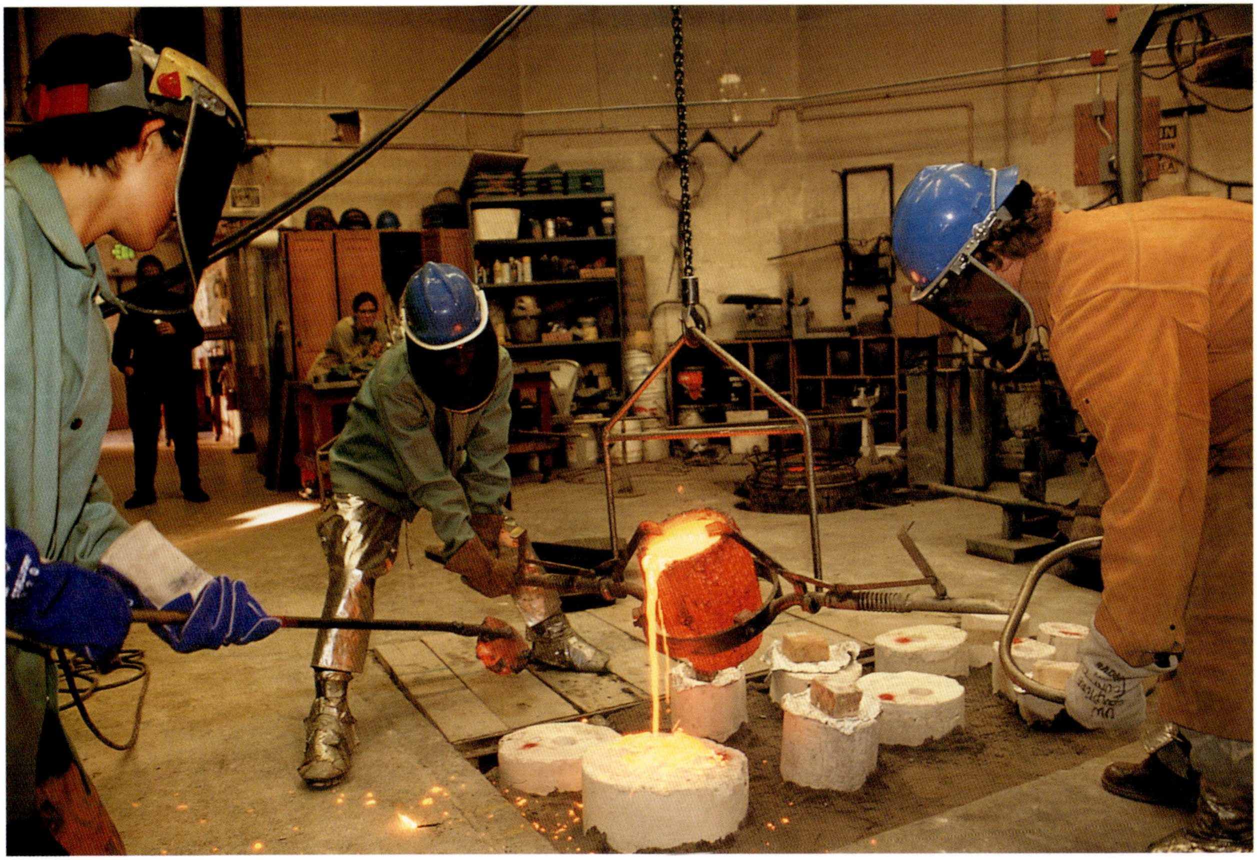

Even with their protective gear, these art students feel the heat as they pour molten bronze into molds.

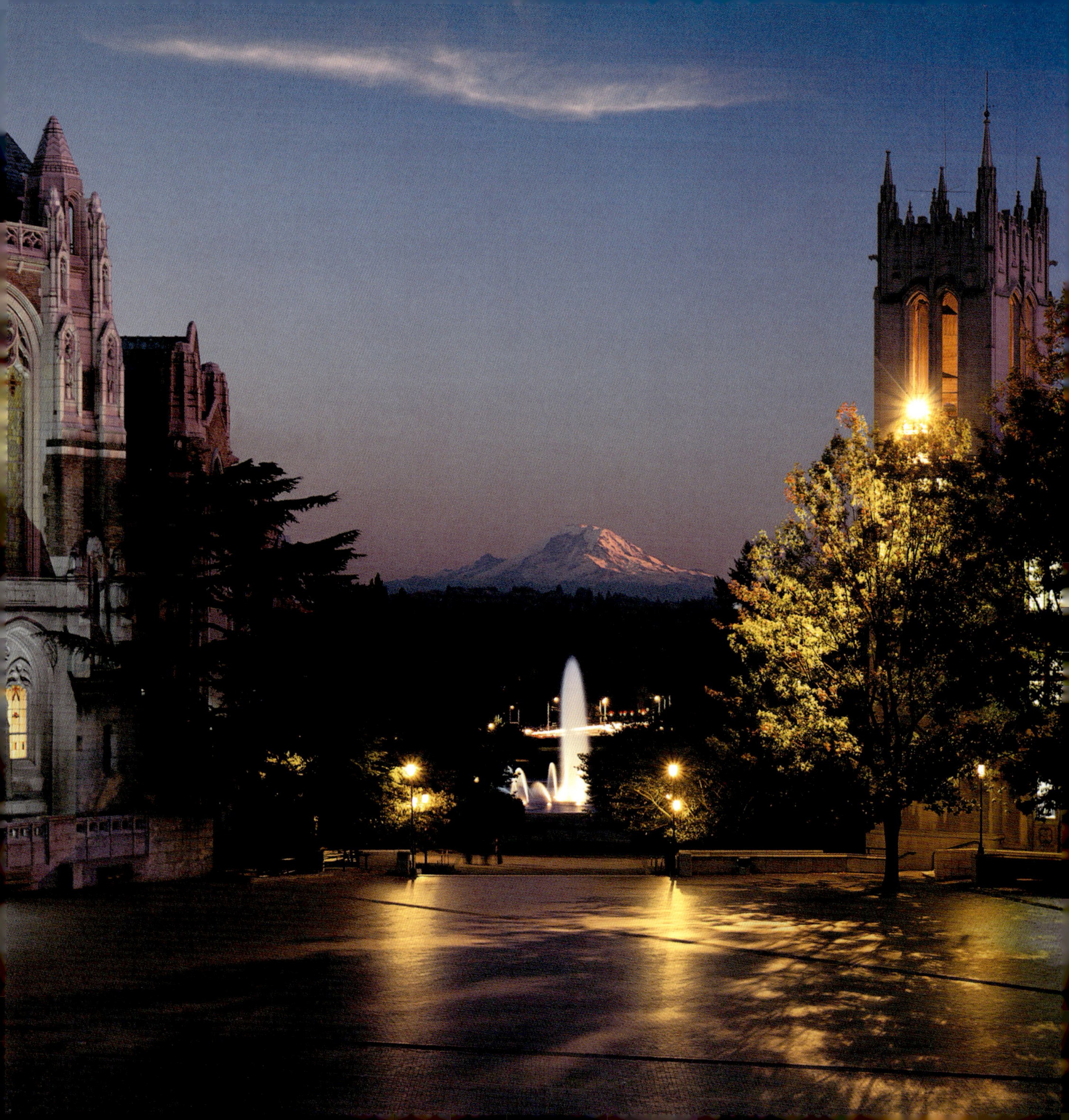

Three vertical square towers serve as a focal point for this approach to Red Square. Designed to evoke the campanile, or bell tower, of an Italian piazza, they are in reality ventilation shafts for an underground parking garage.

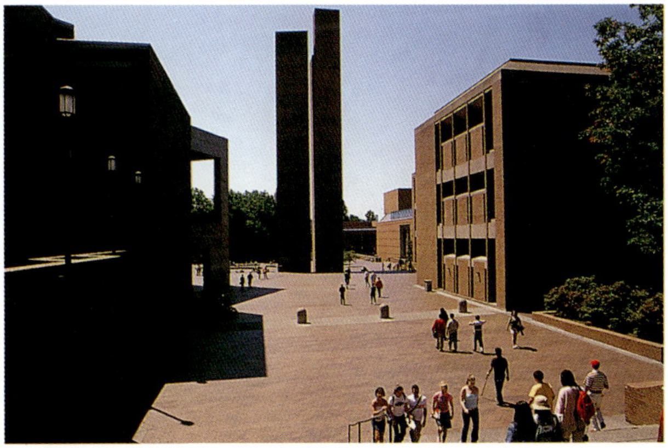

Opposite page:
The setting sun turns Mount Rainier pink in this view from Rainier Vista, one of the best places in Seattle to see the mountain.

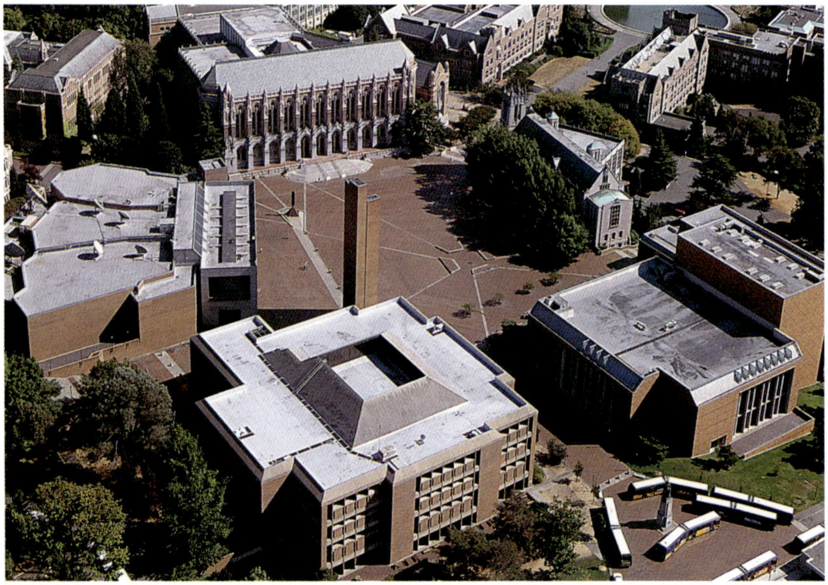

The Central Plaza has the Gothic façade of Suzzallo Library (at top), contrasting with the more modern Odegaard Undergraduate Library (left) and Meany Hall (right). Its unofficial name, Red Square, was the result of a contest in the student newspaper. Other suggestions included The Brickyard and The Prison Yard.

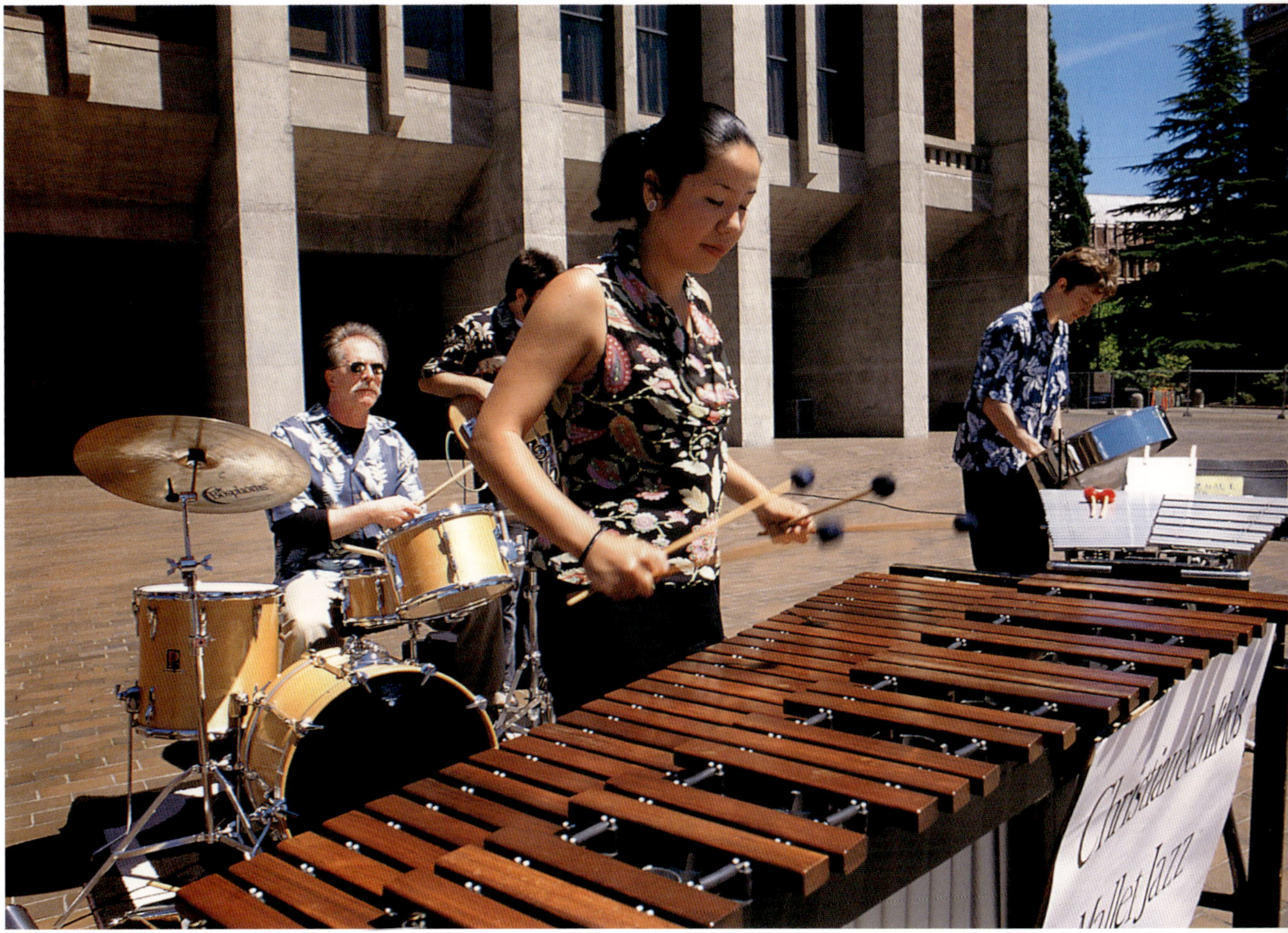

A jazz ensemble
jams on Red Square.

Next page:
Darkness accentuates the glory of Suzzallo Library.

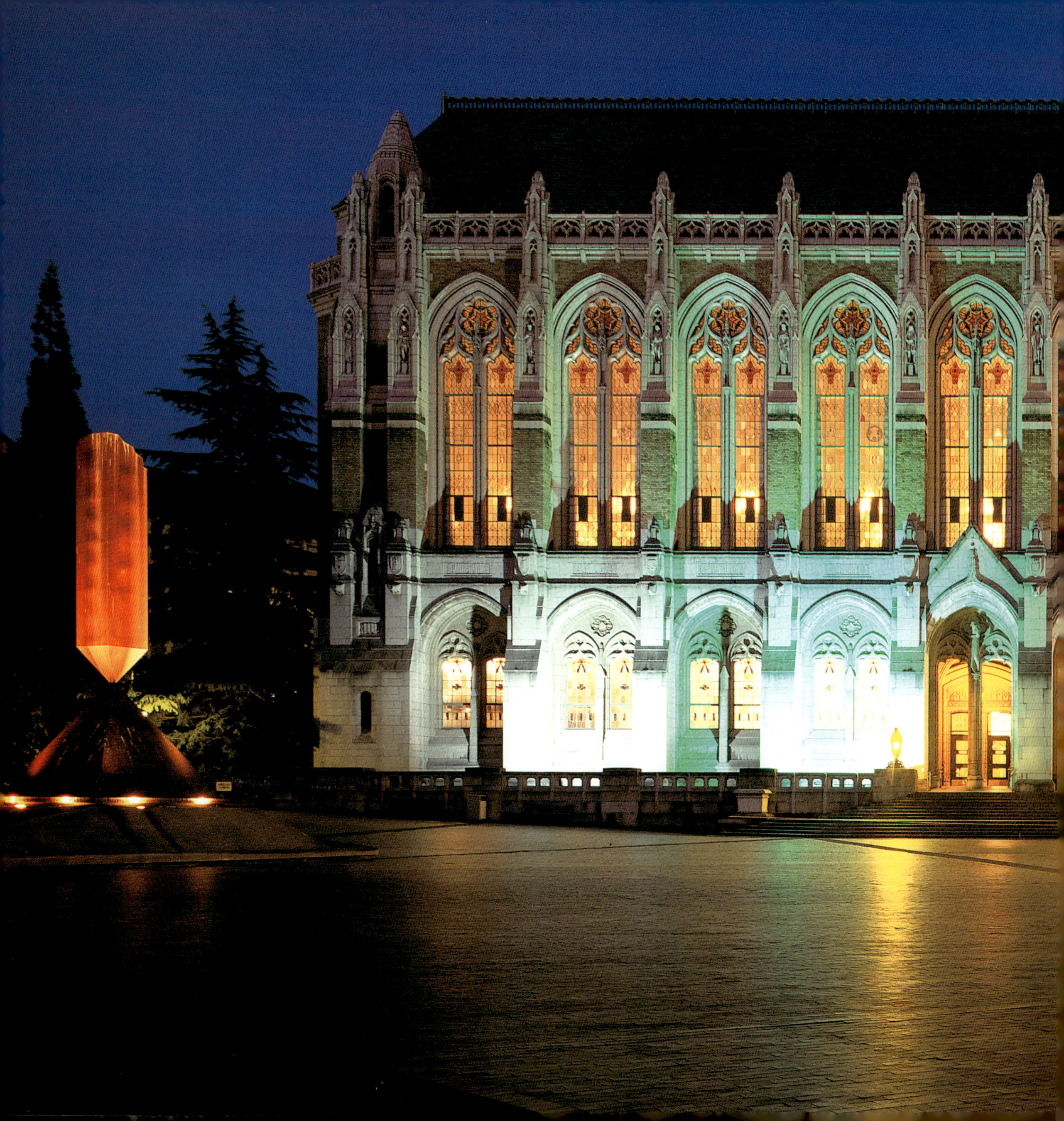

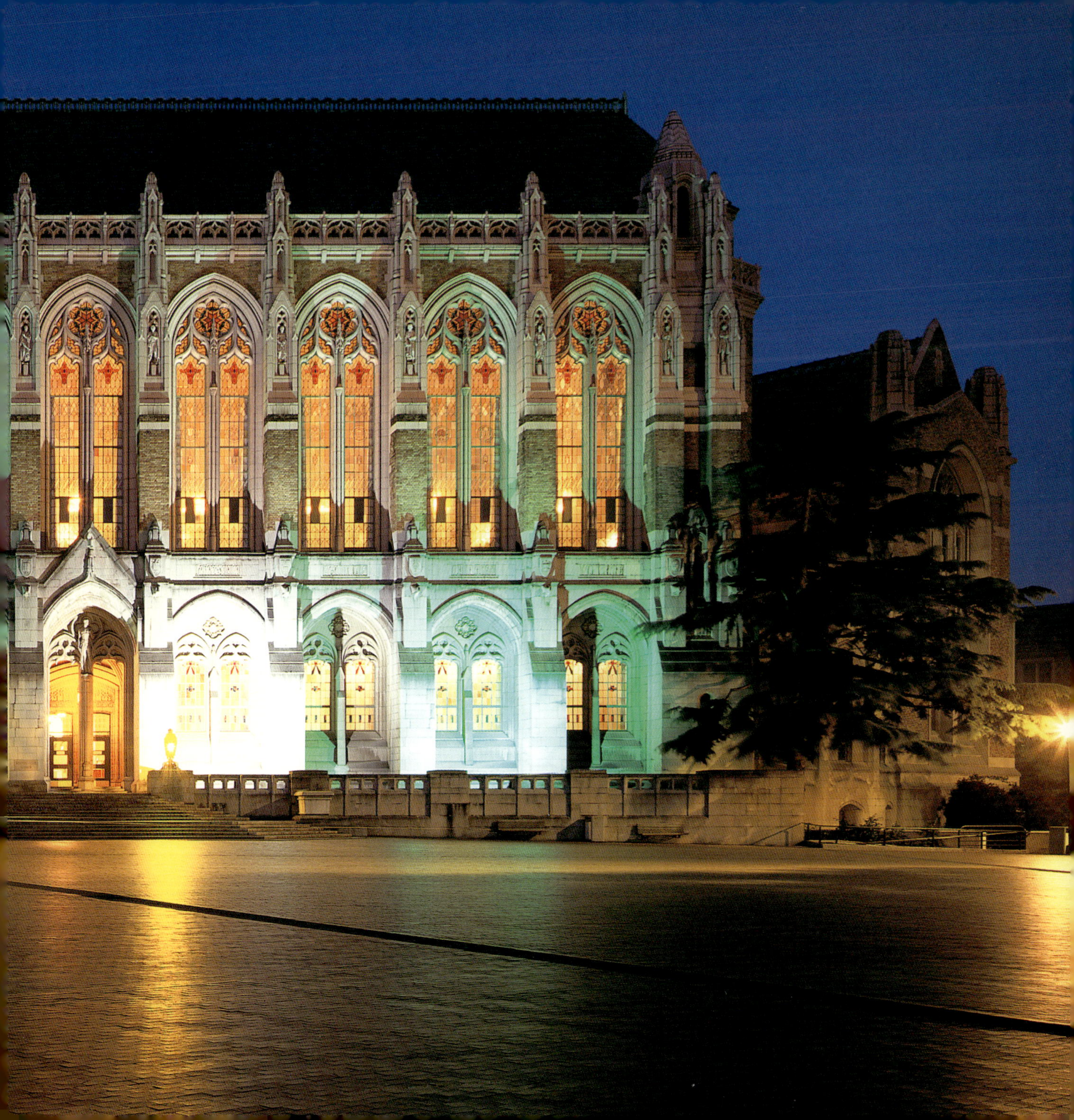

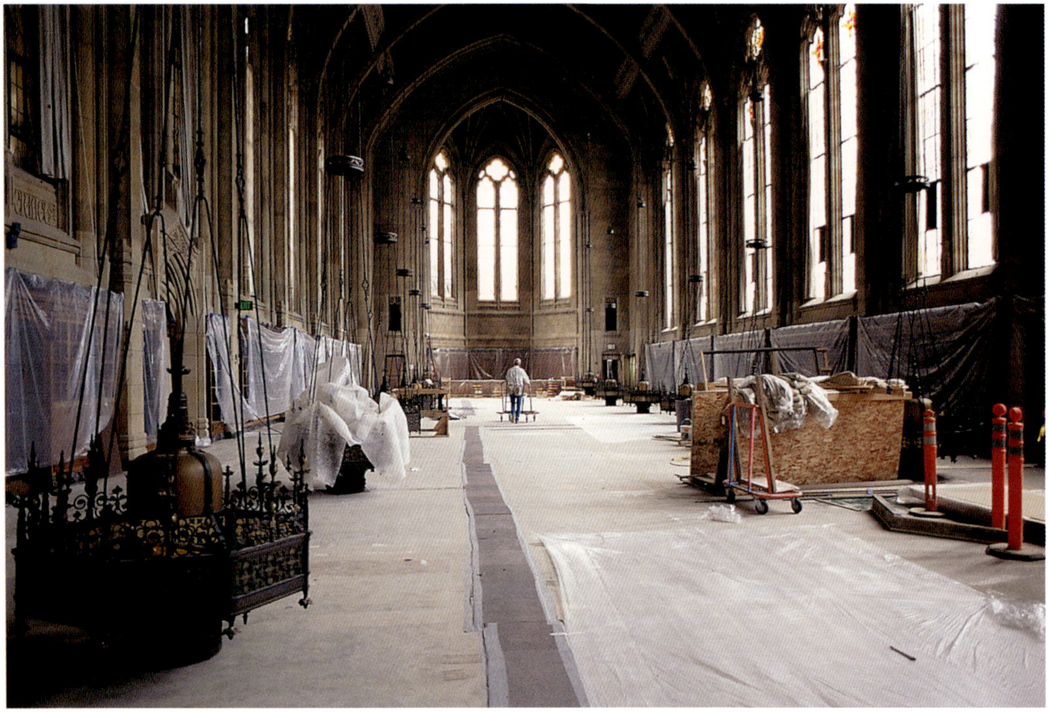

In 2000-02, the original wing of Suzzallo Library was closed for a seismic renovation.

The Reading Room (above) was stripped of its furniture, and even its grandiose light fixtures were modernized.

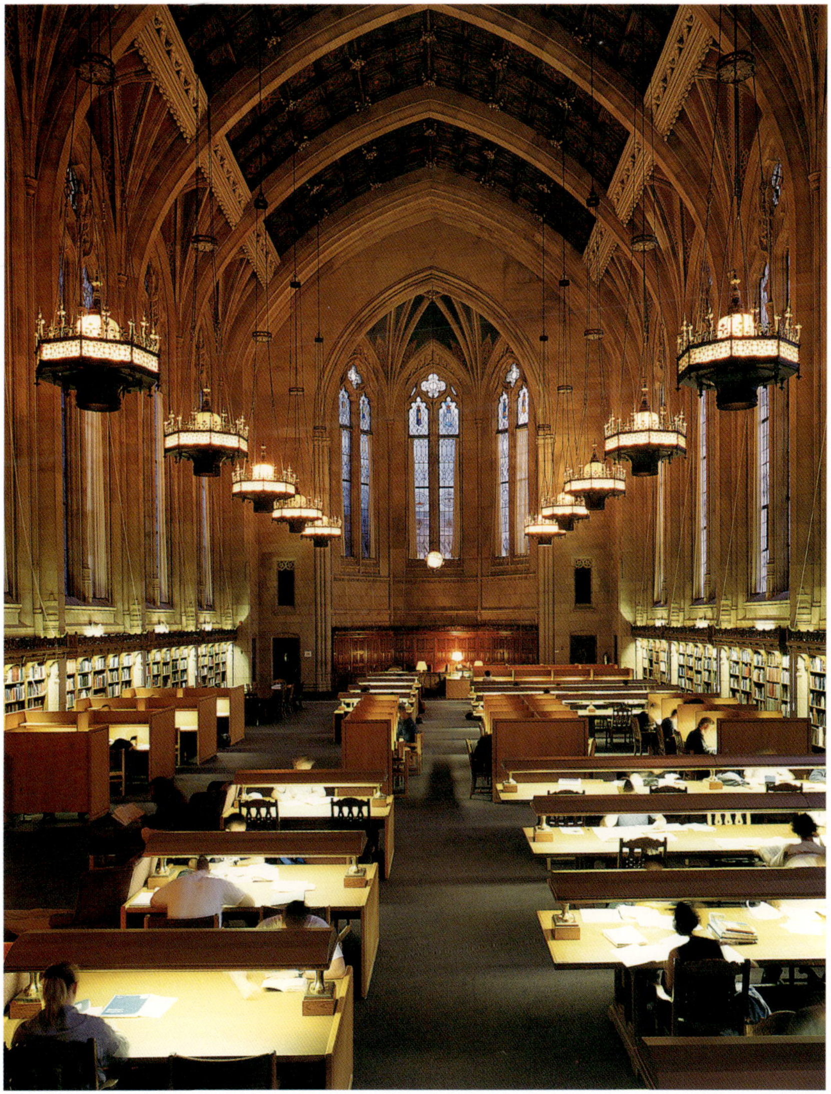

Many students swear they study better in the Suzzallo Reading Room, a true sanctuary for learning. By volume, it is the largest reading room in any library in the United States.

A student curls up to study in the Allen Library. With more than six million volumes, the UW's collection is the 14th largest among U.S. universities.

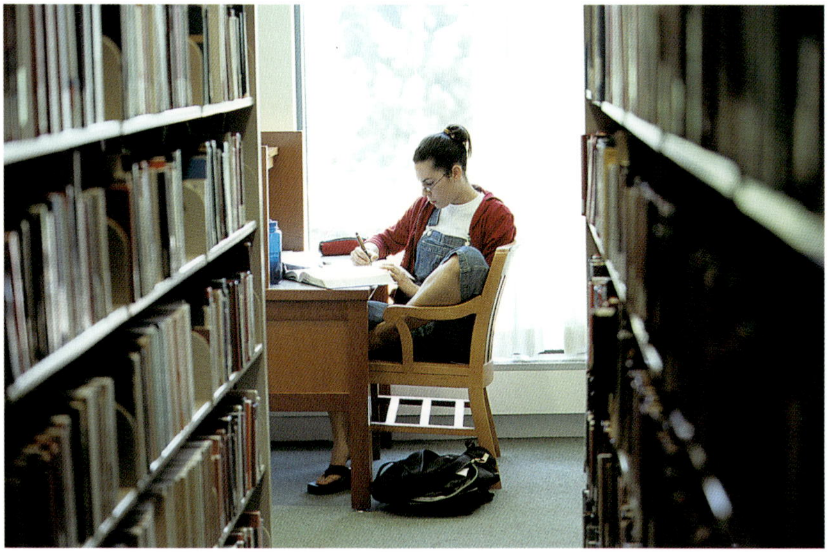

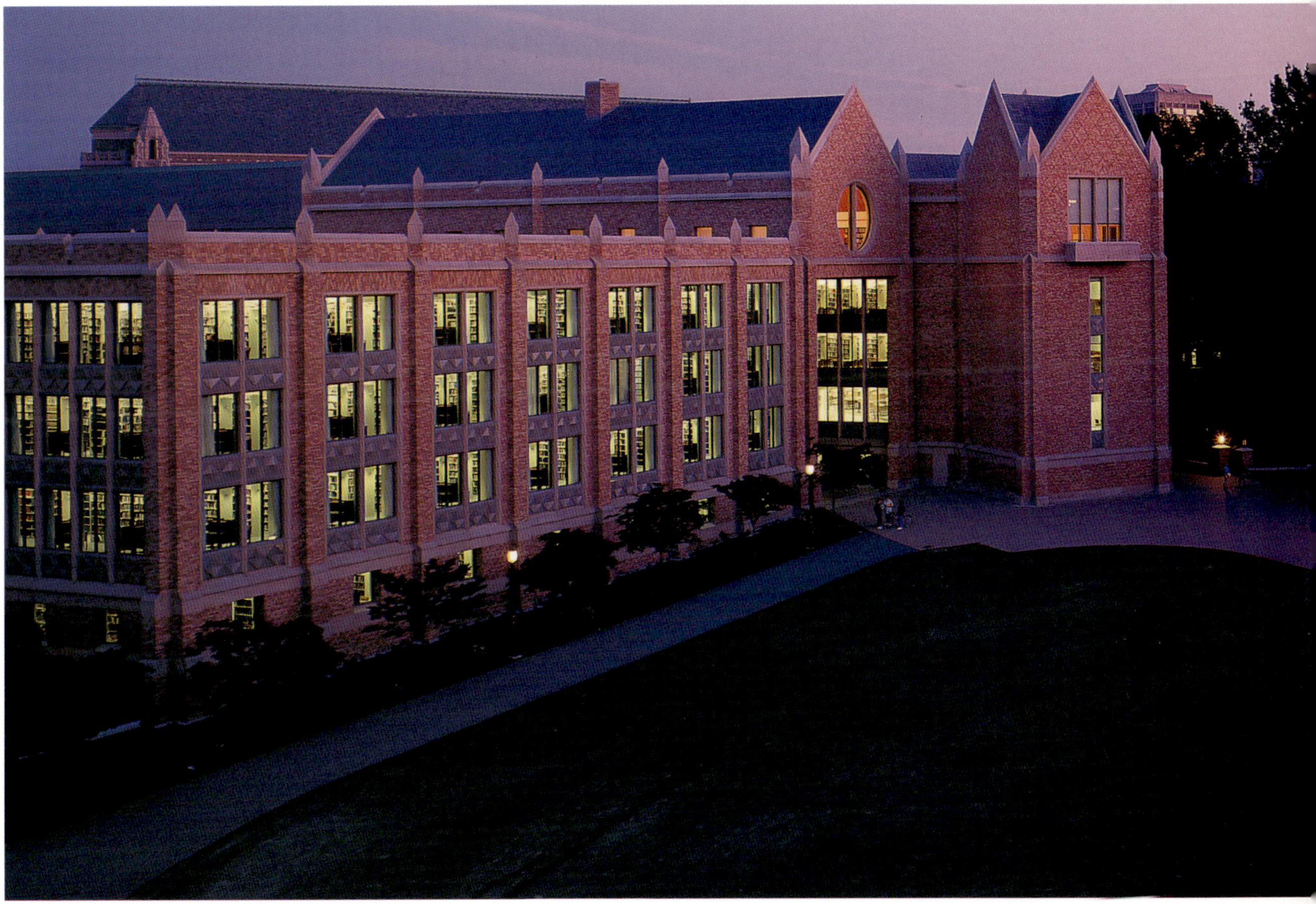

At dusk, the Allen Library shows off its contextual lines, which resemble those of its neighbor, Suzzallo Library.

This 1991 structure is named for UW Libraries Associate Director Kenneth S. Allen, father of Microsoft cofounder Paul Allen.

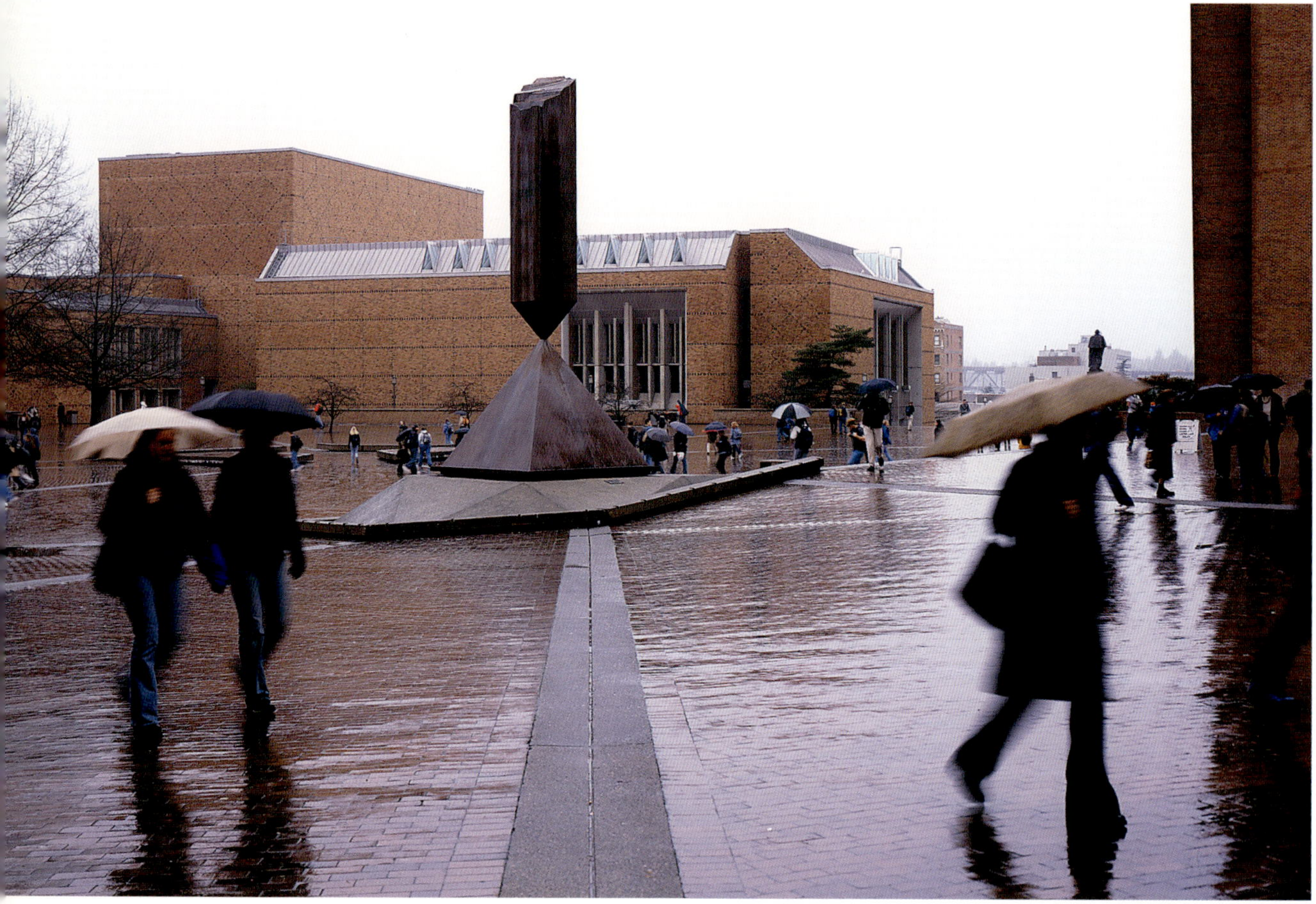

Barnett Newman's *Broken Obelisk* anchors this view of Red Square. Known for his abstract expressionist painting, the late artist rarely worked in three dimensions. Some art experts say this work is the most valuable piece of public art in the state.

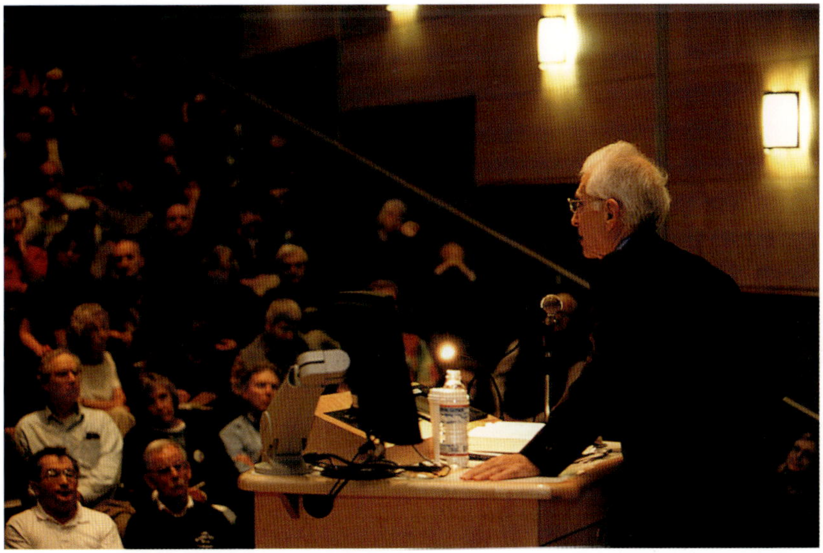

Kane Hall is often the site of evening lectures, such as this book reading with Daniel Elsberg sponsored by the University Book Store.

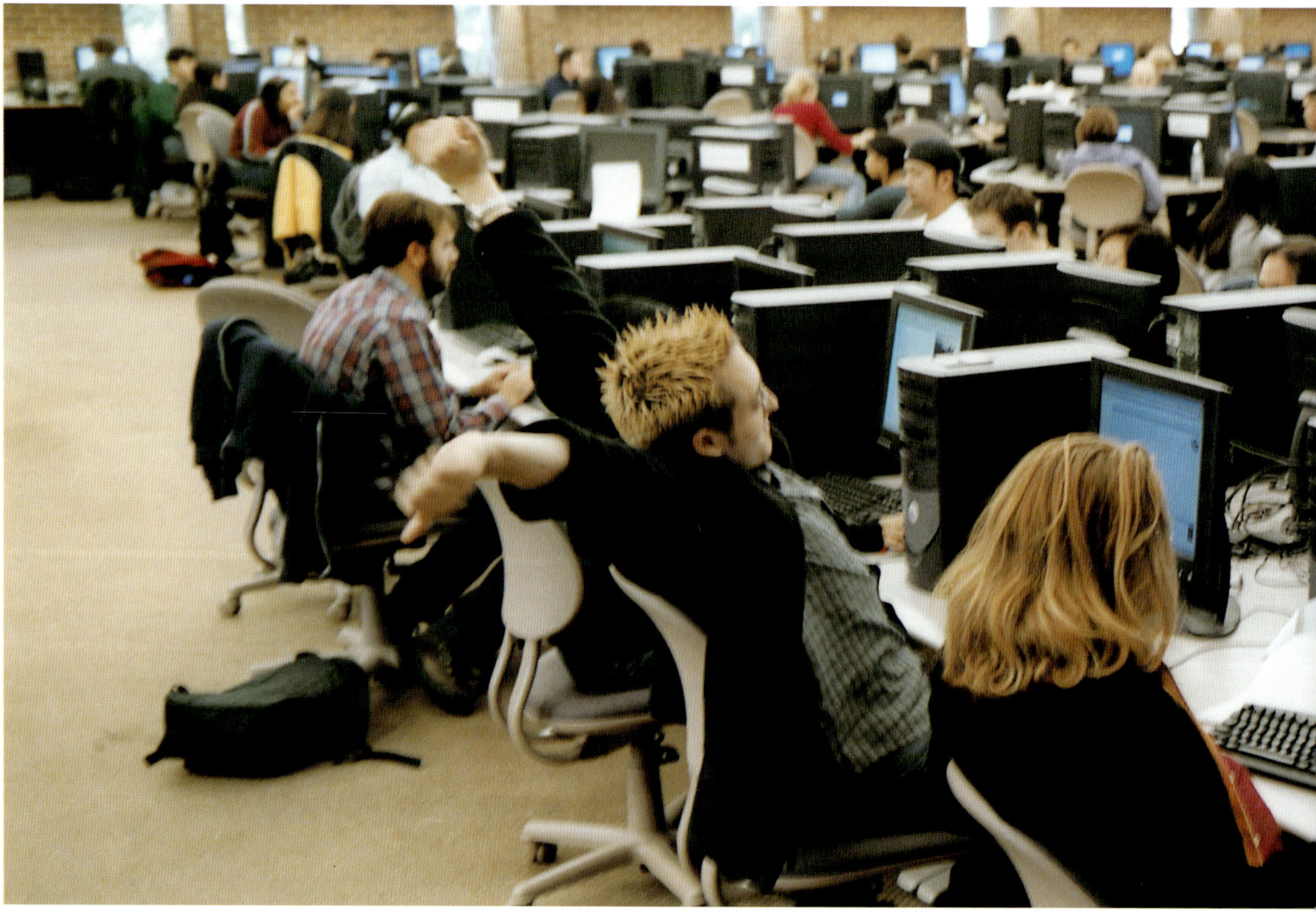

One student takes a stretching break at his workstation in the Odegaard Library computing center. When classes are in session, the library is open 24 hours a day except for Friday and Saturday nights.

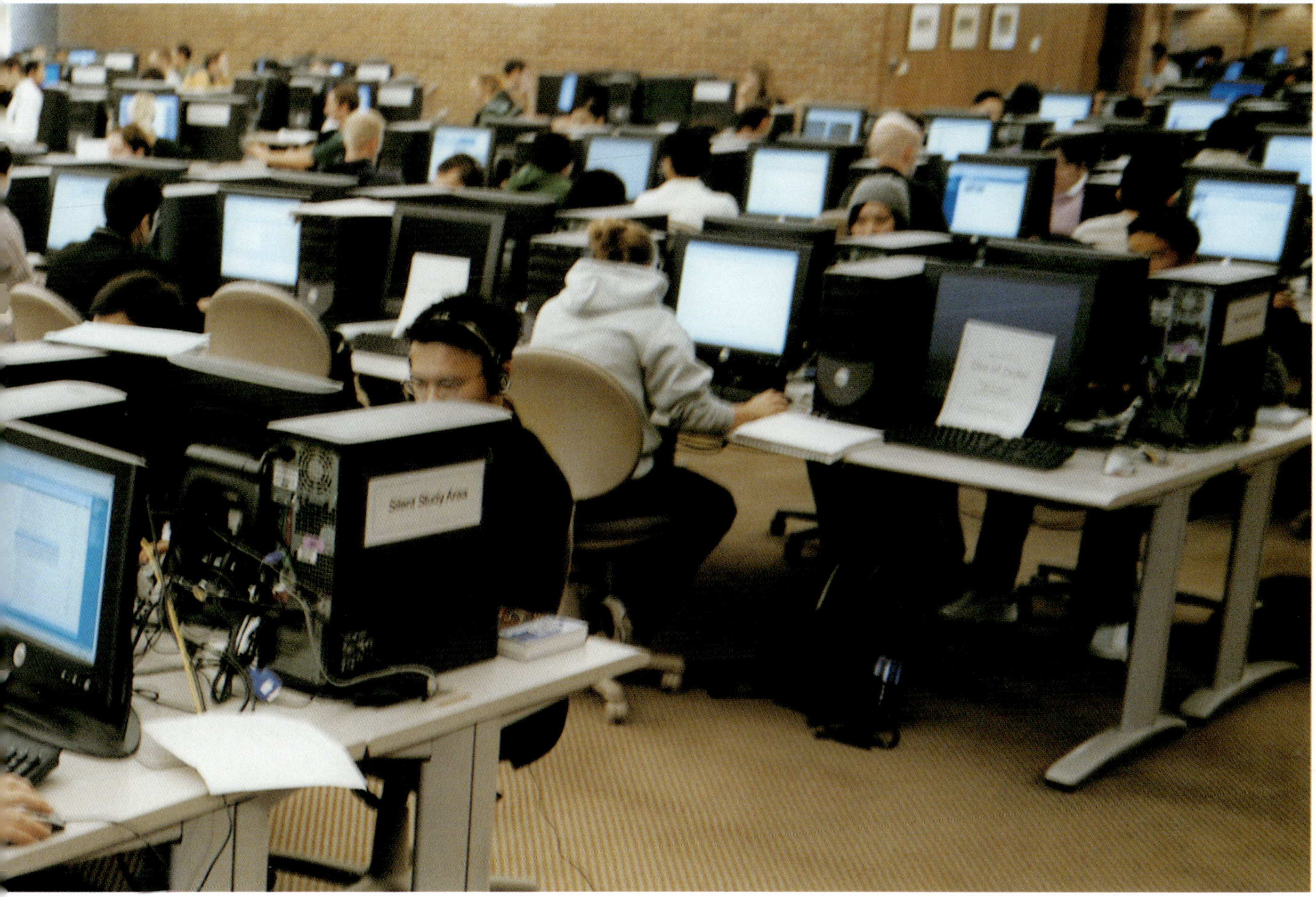
Silent Study Area

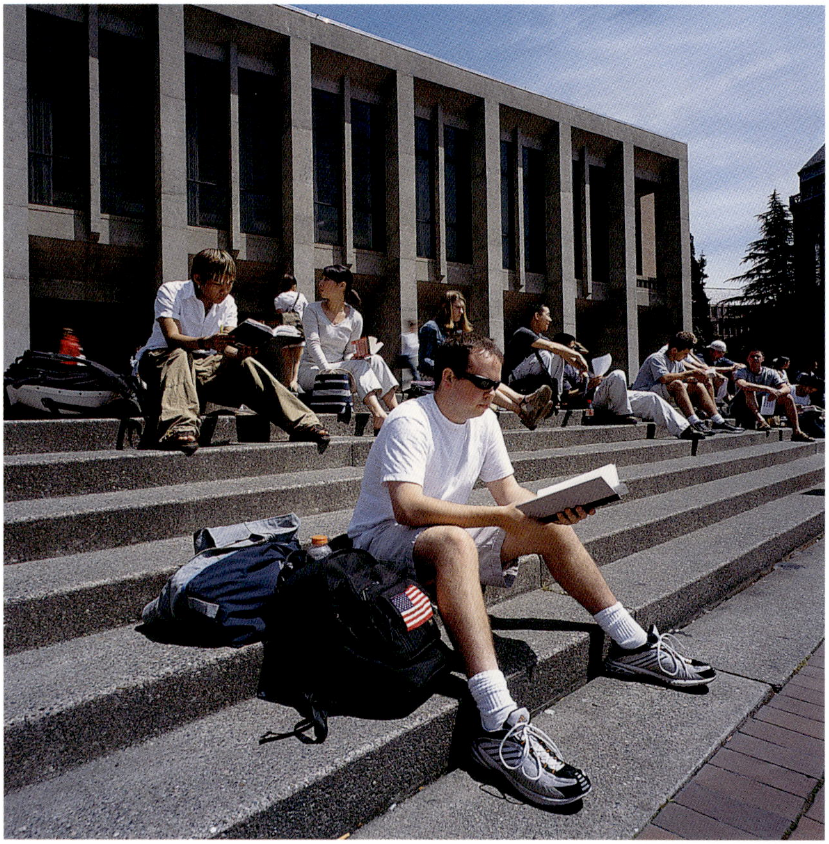

The steps in front of Kane Hall quickly became a student gathering spot after the building opened in 1971. On sunny days, students going into Kane have to weave their way past others enjoying the sunshine.

If the weather is good, you can bet there will be skateboarders, Frisbee addicts and Hacky Sack players in Red Square.

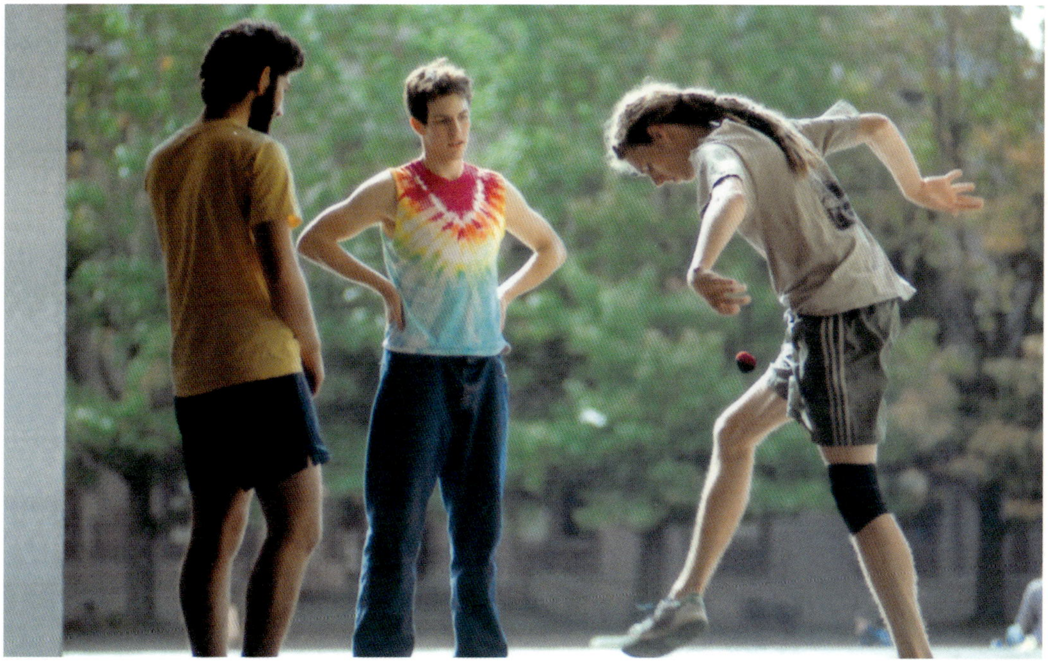

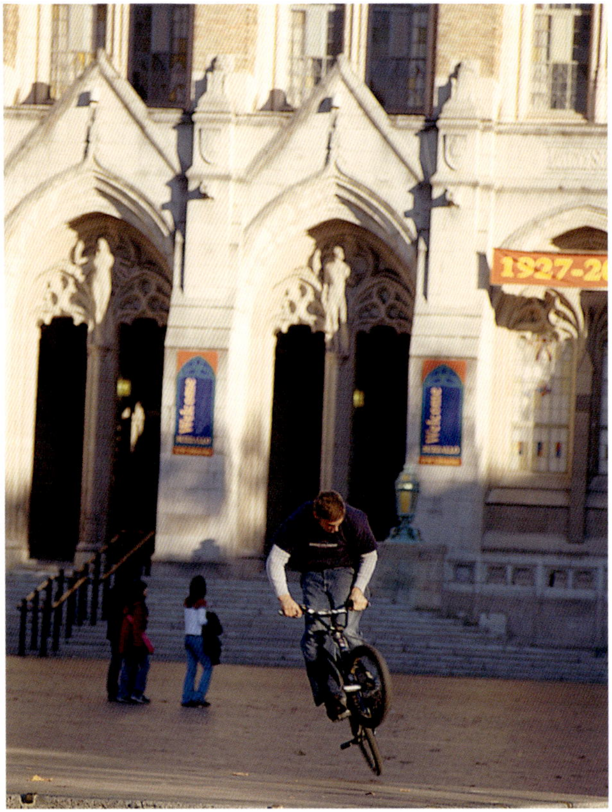

A biker defies gravity in front of Suzzallo Library.

Students cope with a summer shower.

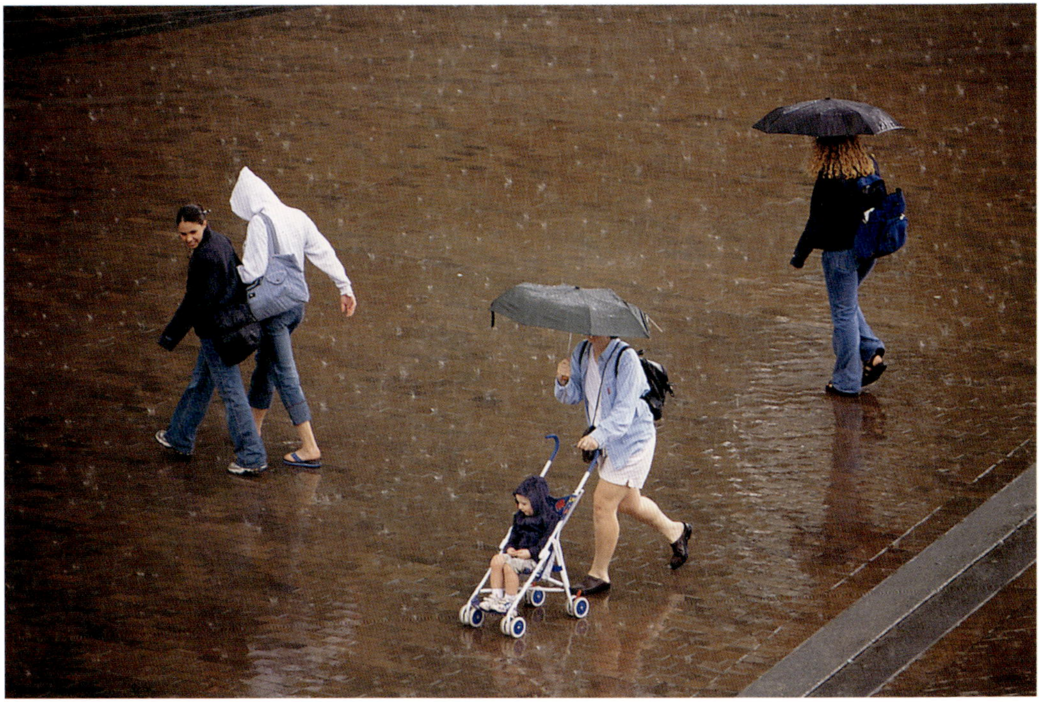

Opposite page:
Museum-goers take in an exhibit at the Henry.

Built into the slope of a hill along 15th Avenue N.E., the modern addition to the Henry Art Gallery includes skylights composed of cubes and pyramids.

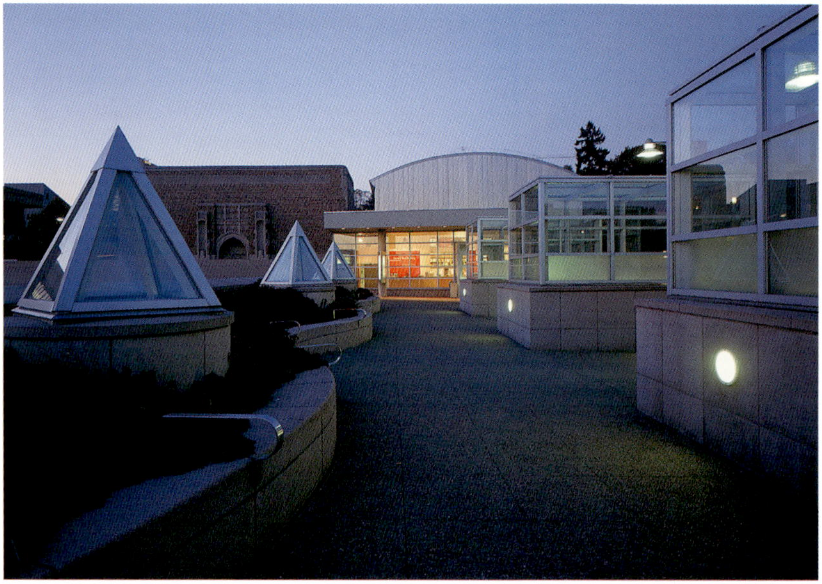

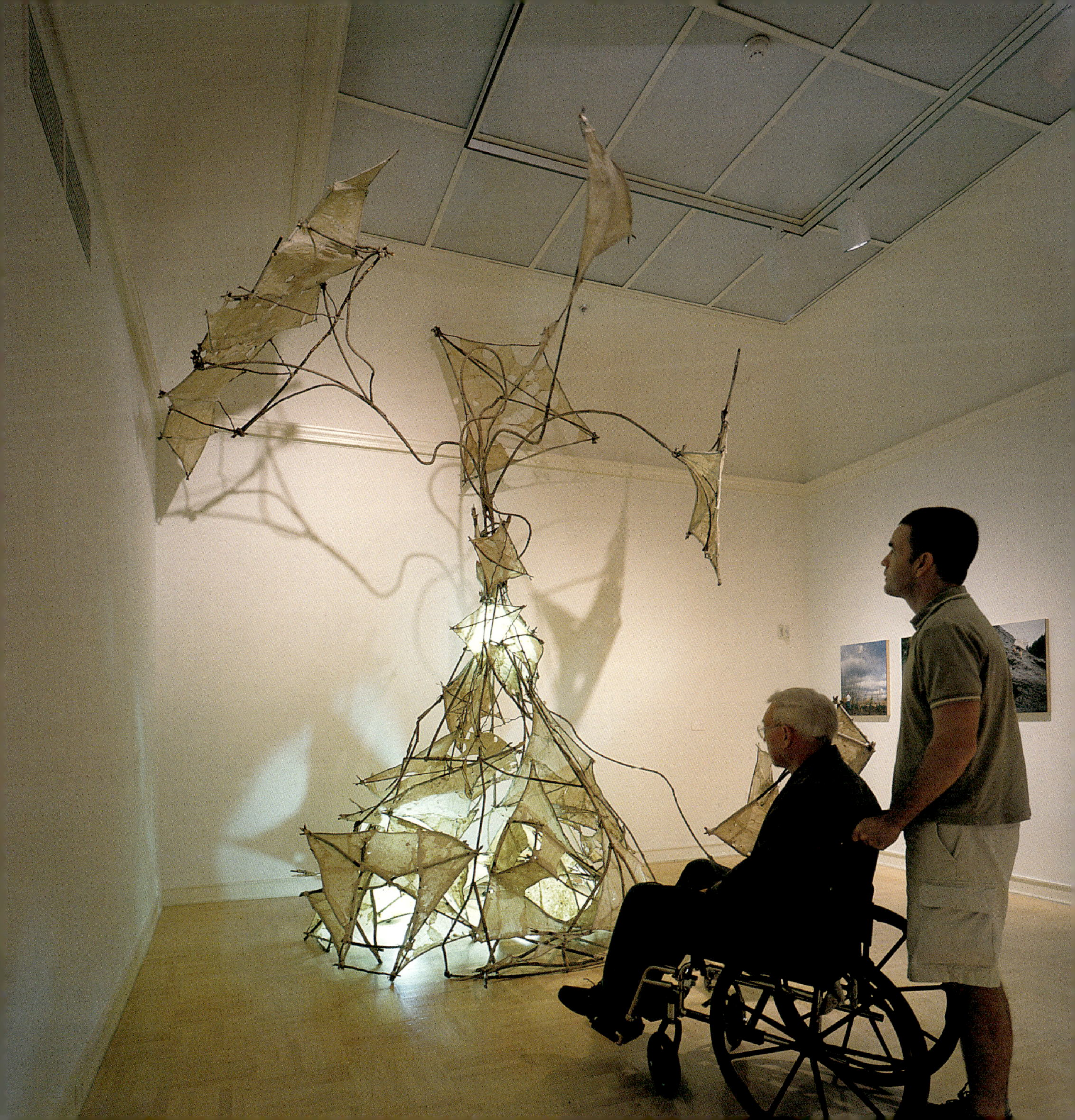

Theater-goers gather for an opening night at Meany Hall. In addition to student and faculty performances, Meany presents touring artists in dance, drama and music.

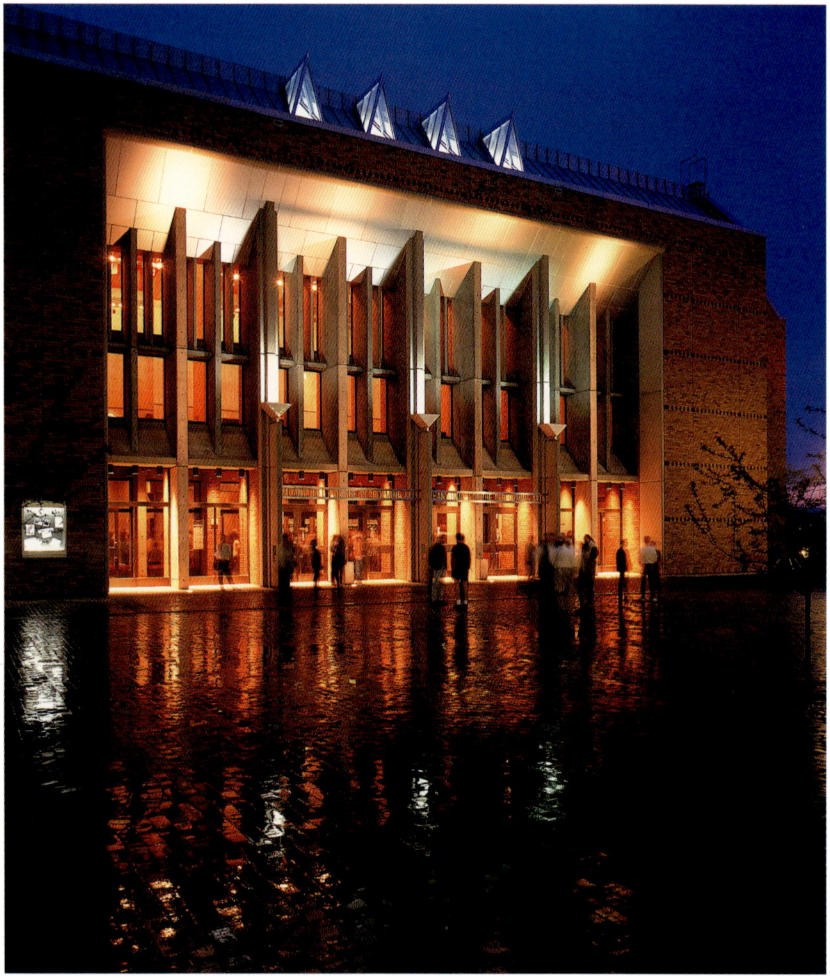

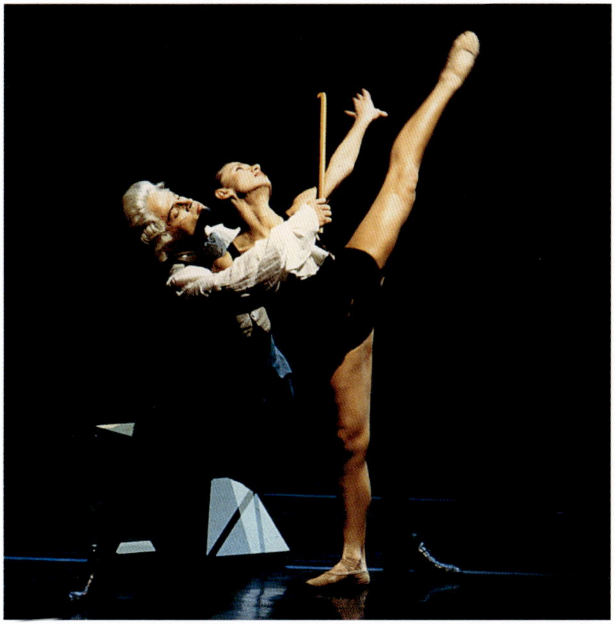

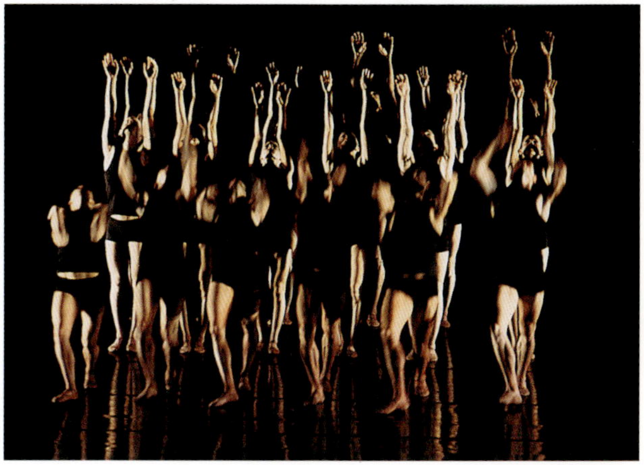

Artists from around the world perform on the Meany stage. Here we see a duet and an ensemble piece from a work celebrating Johann Sebastian Bach, performed by the Compañía Nacional de Danza (the National Dance Company of Spain).

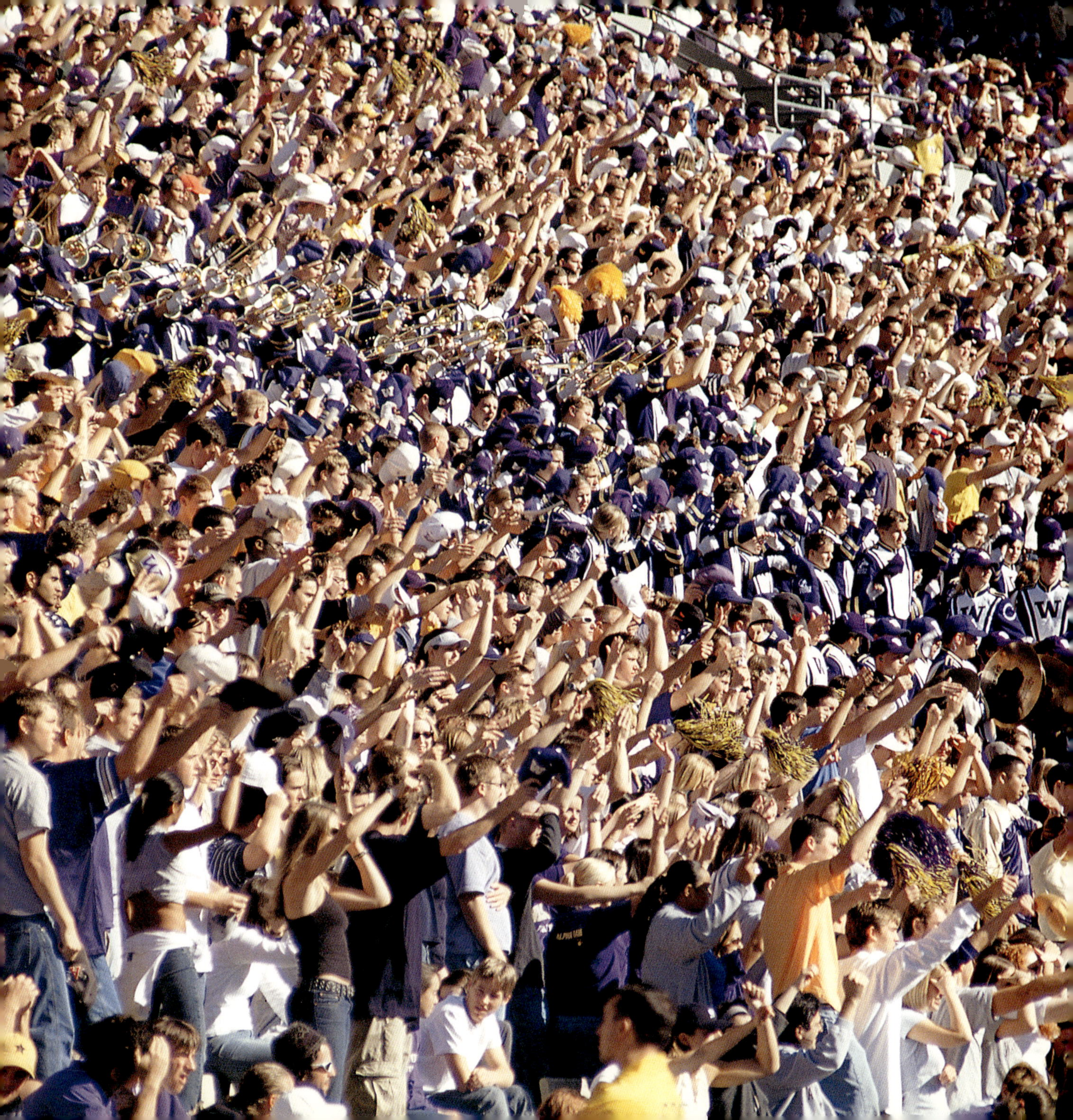

While most Husky regalia is not quite so flamboyant, one fan wears a costume of gold pompoms to show off his UW pride.

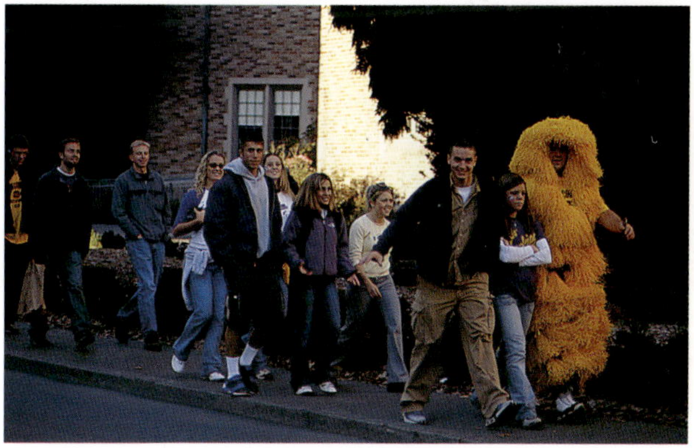

Opposite page:
Students celebrate in Husky Stadium.

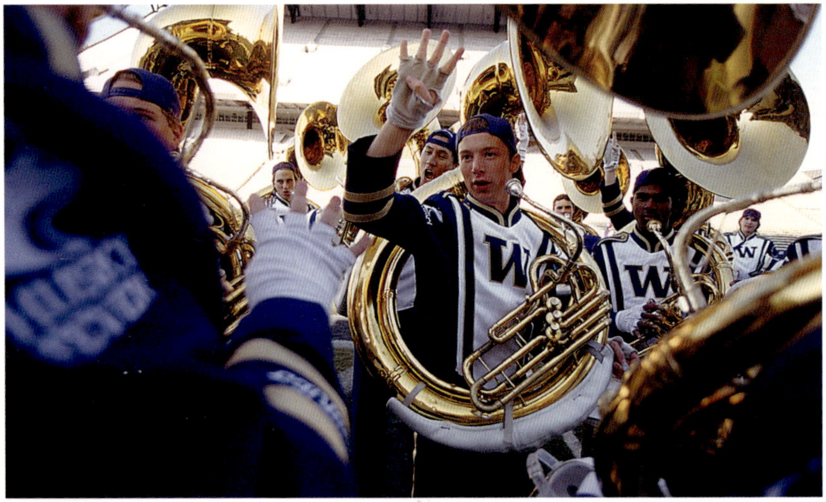

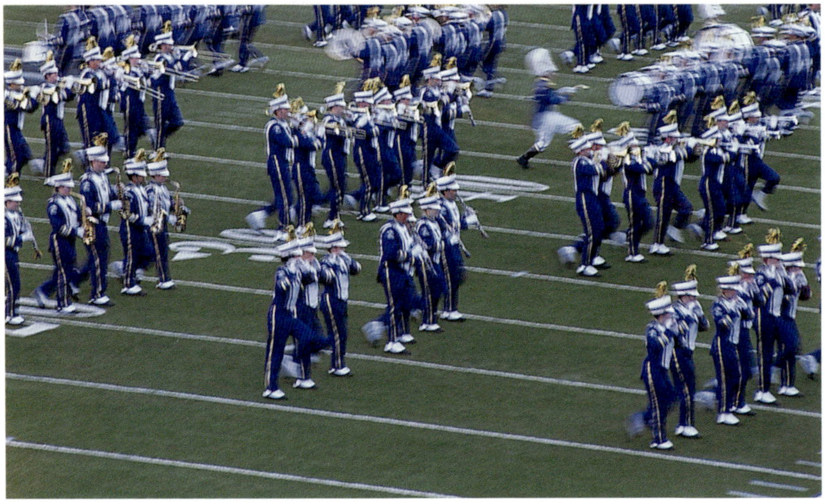

If it is a sunny Saturday afternoon, there will be plenty of pageantry before the game. The Husky Marching Band pumps up the fans.

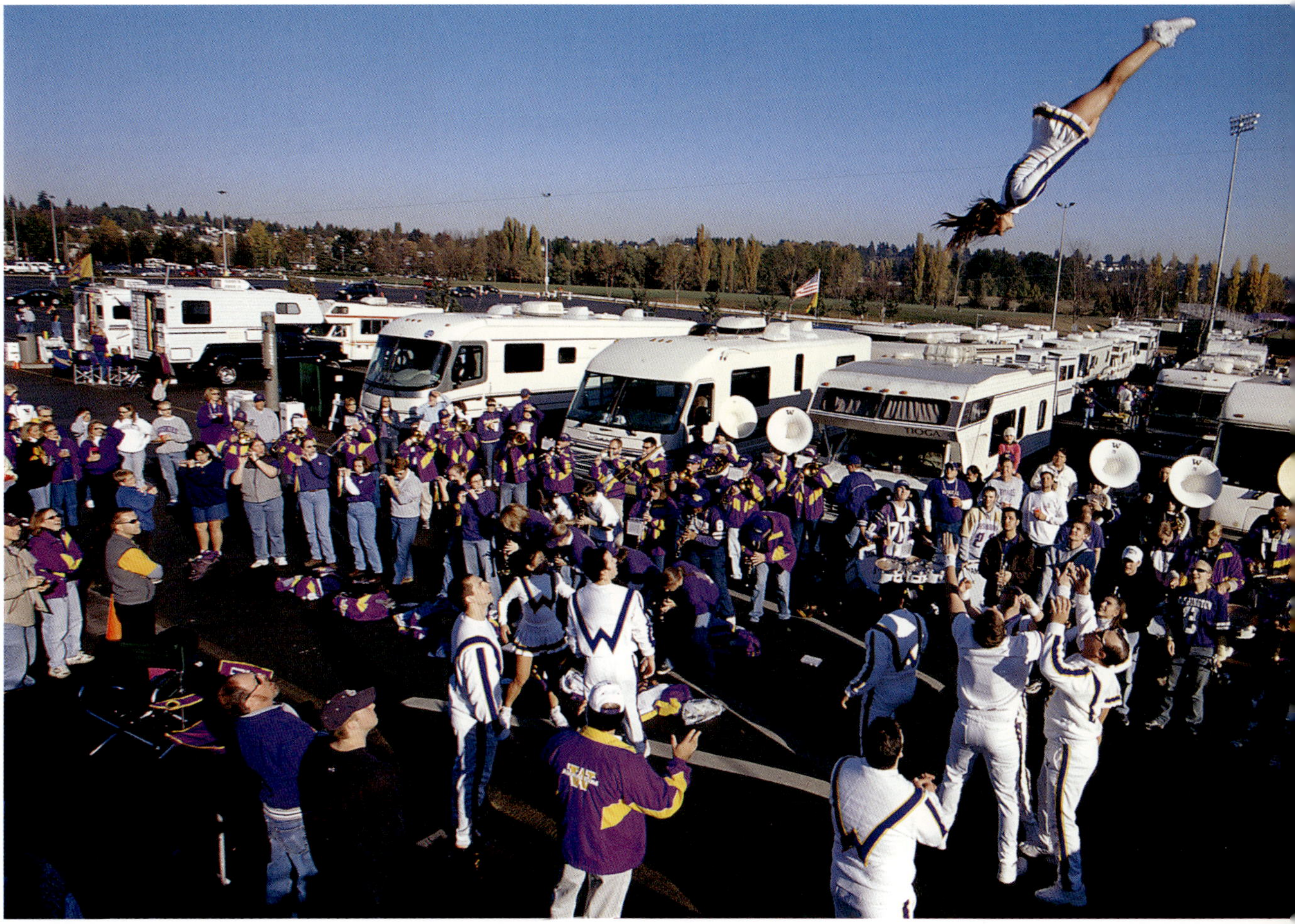

Stunts by the
Husky Cheer Squad
add to the delights
of tailgating
in the Montlake
parking lot.

Next page:
It's a perfect day for
a football game.

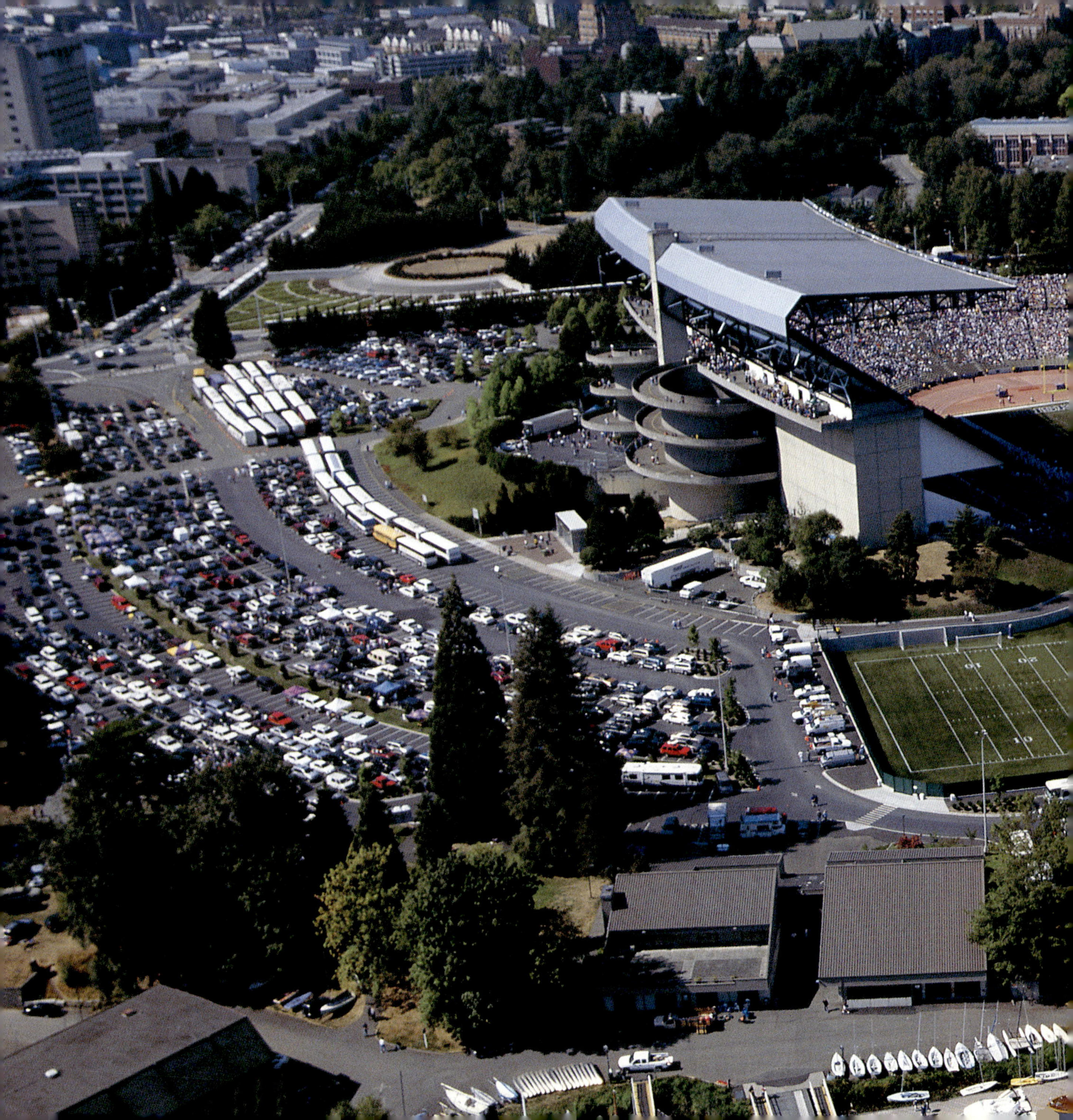

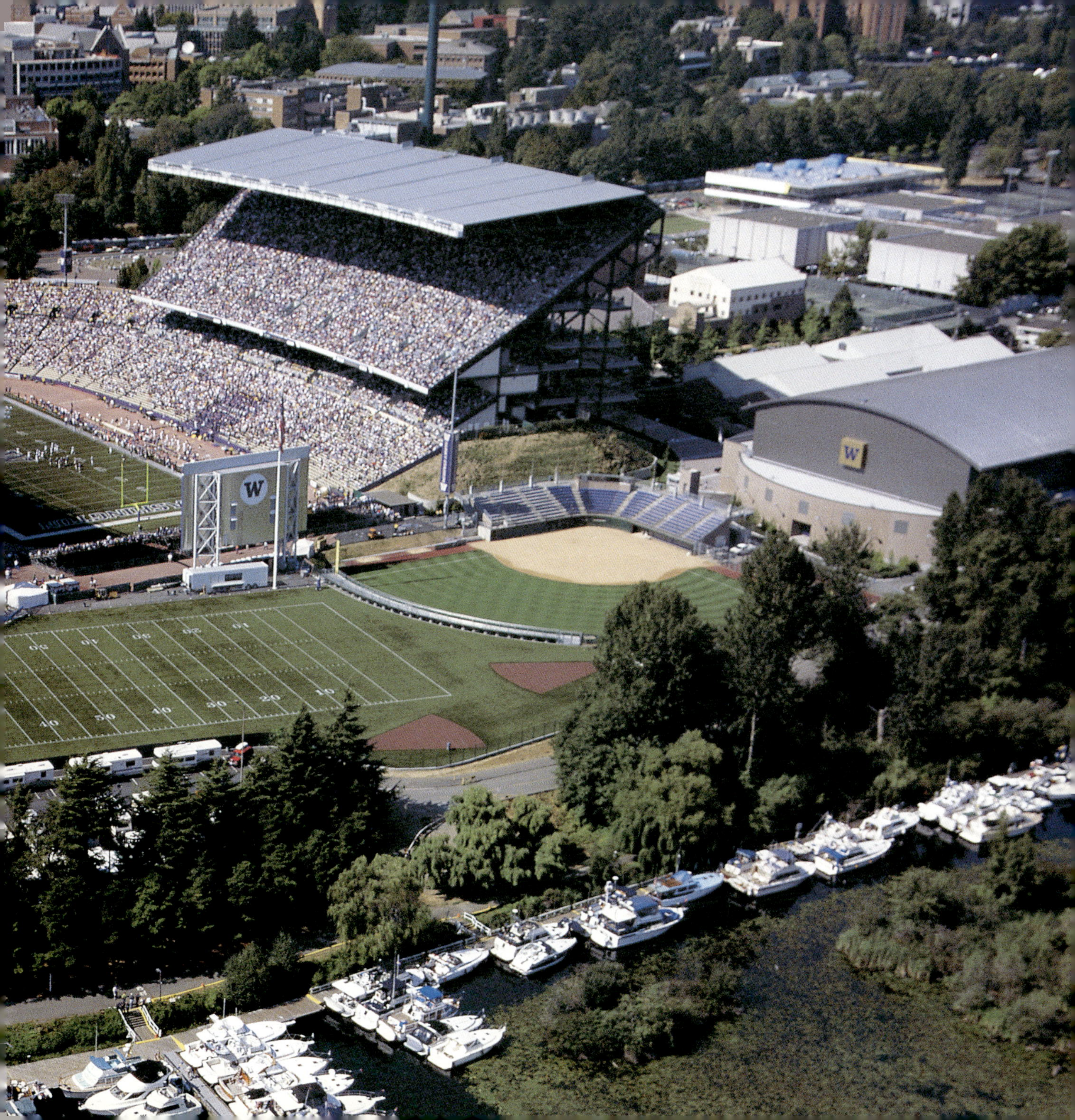

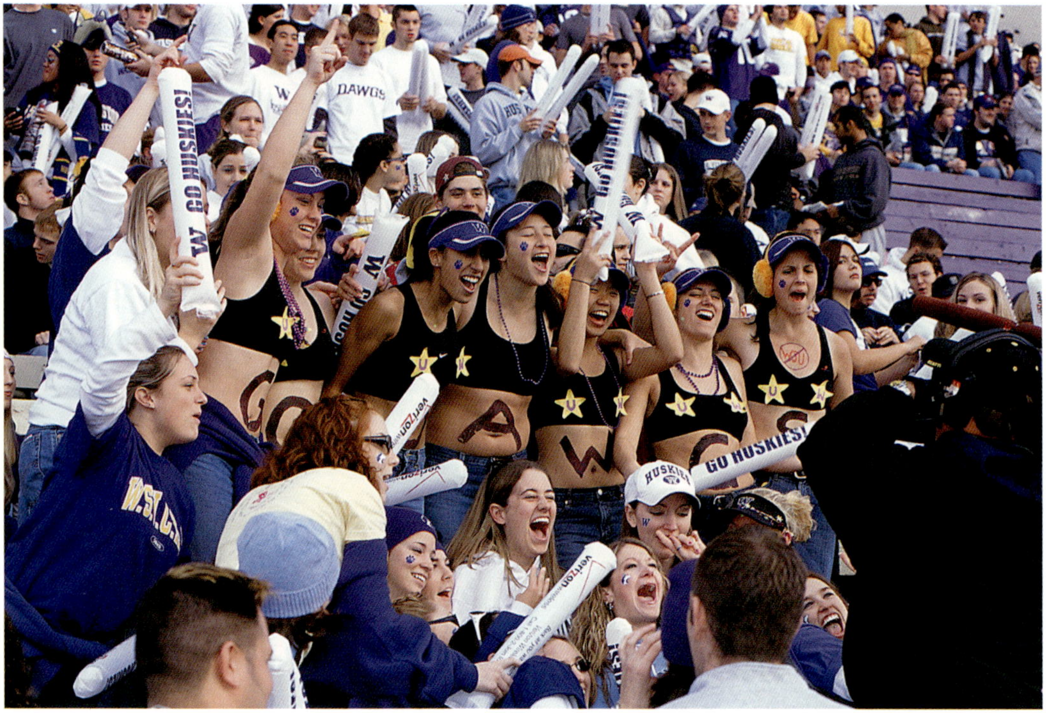

The student section of Husky Stadium can be a spectacle. Here, some UW students show that their support is barely contained.

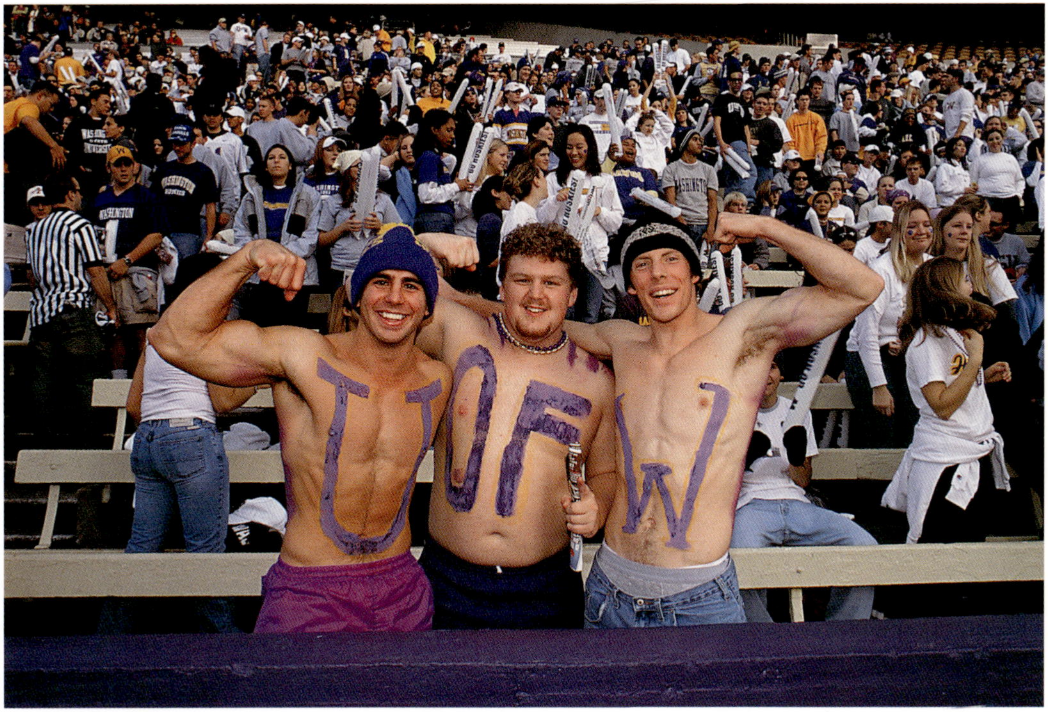

No matter what the
weather, you can bet
that some fanatic
guys will indulge in
chest painting
to show off their
Husky pride.

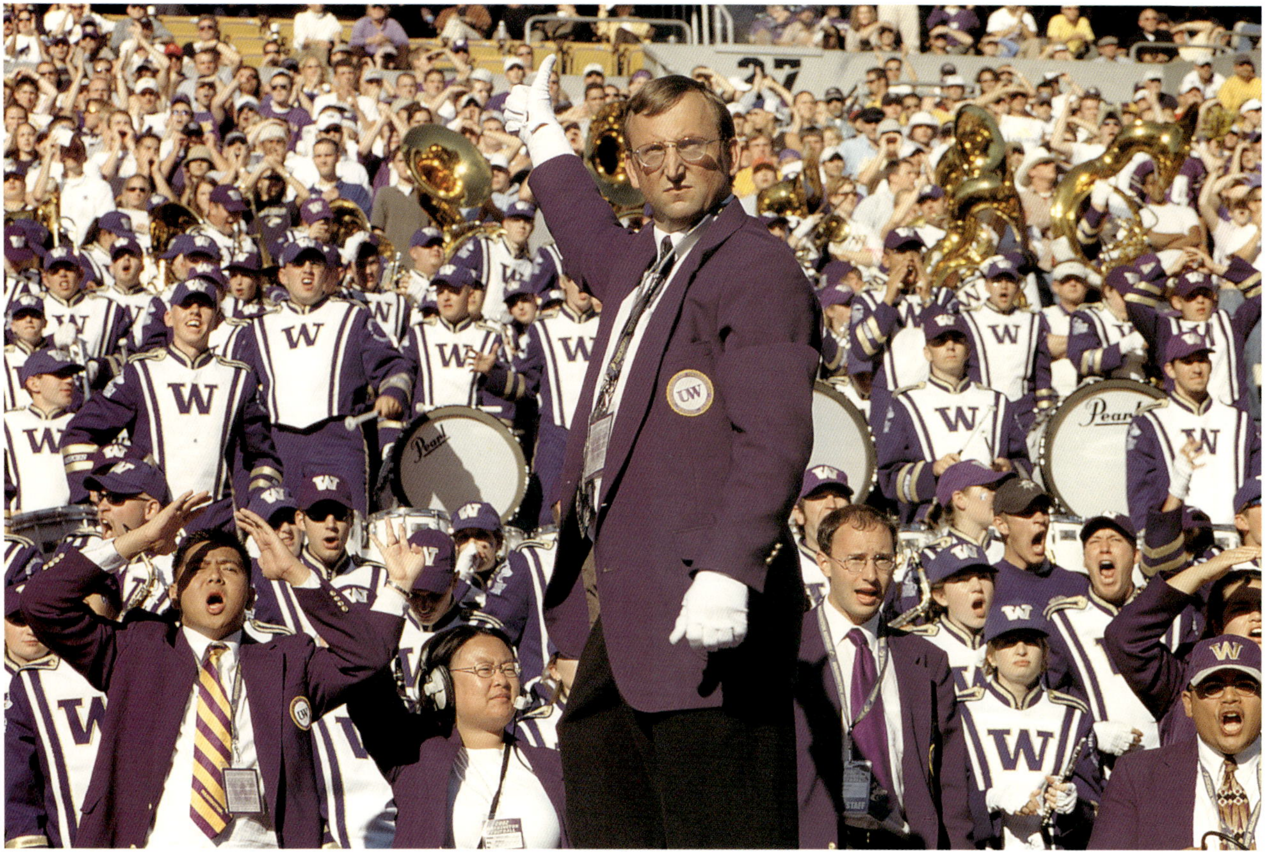

A band director concentrates on the action before signaling the marching band.

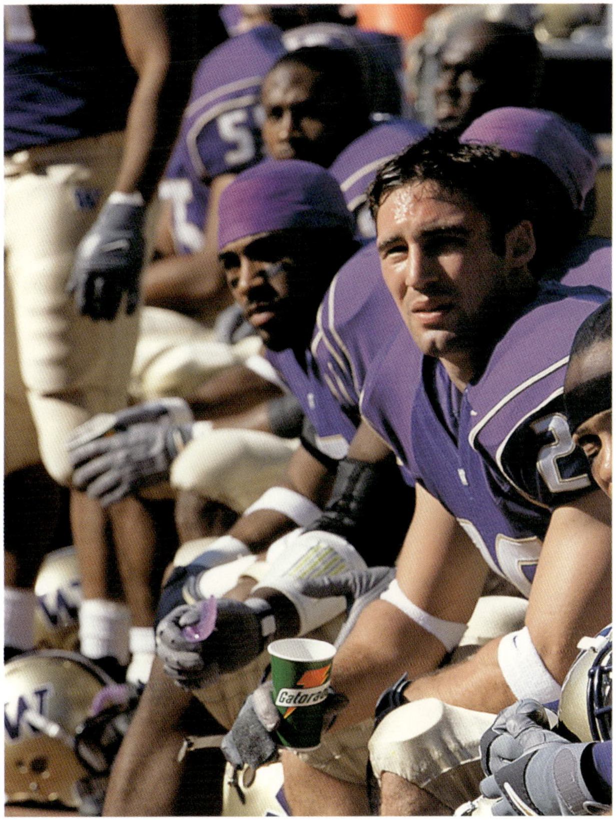

While players focus on the field (left), the Husky Cheer Squad gets the crowd into the game.

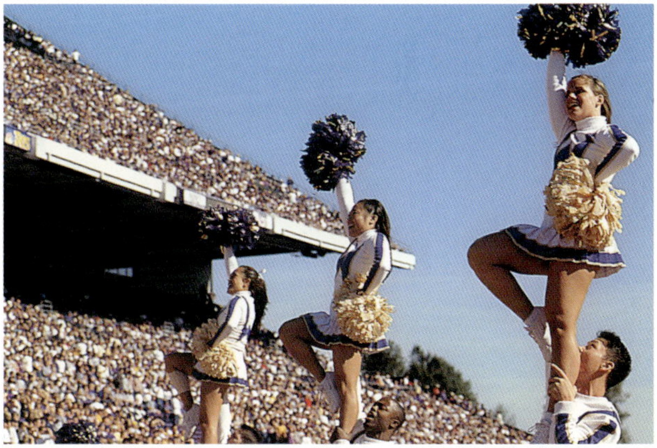

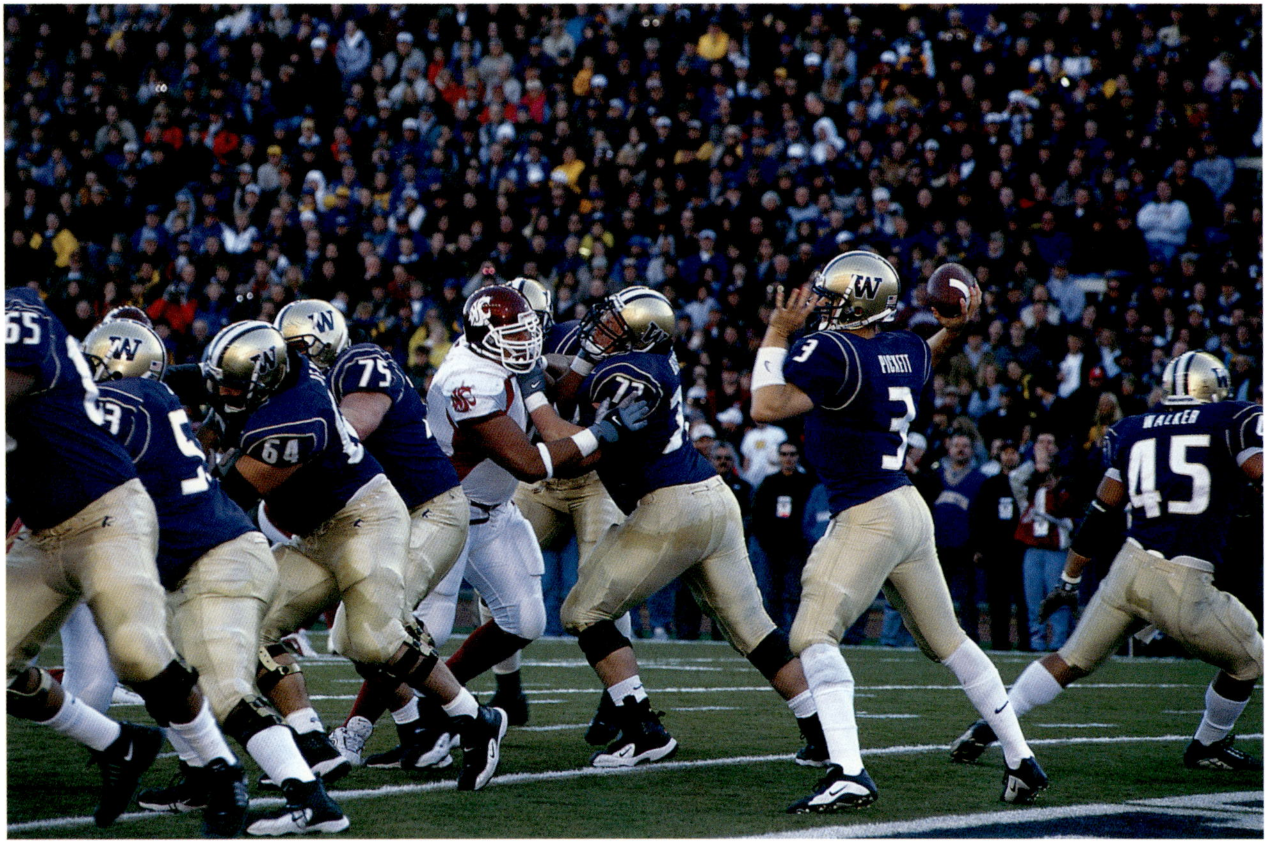

Quarterback Cody Pickett gets ready to connect in this Apple Cup game against WSU.

There's unbridled joy at the moment of a touchdown.

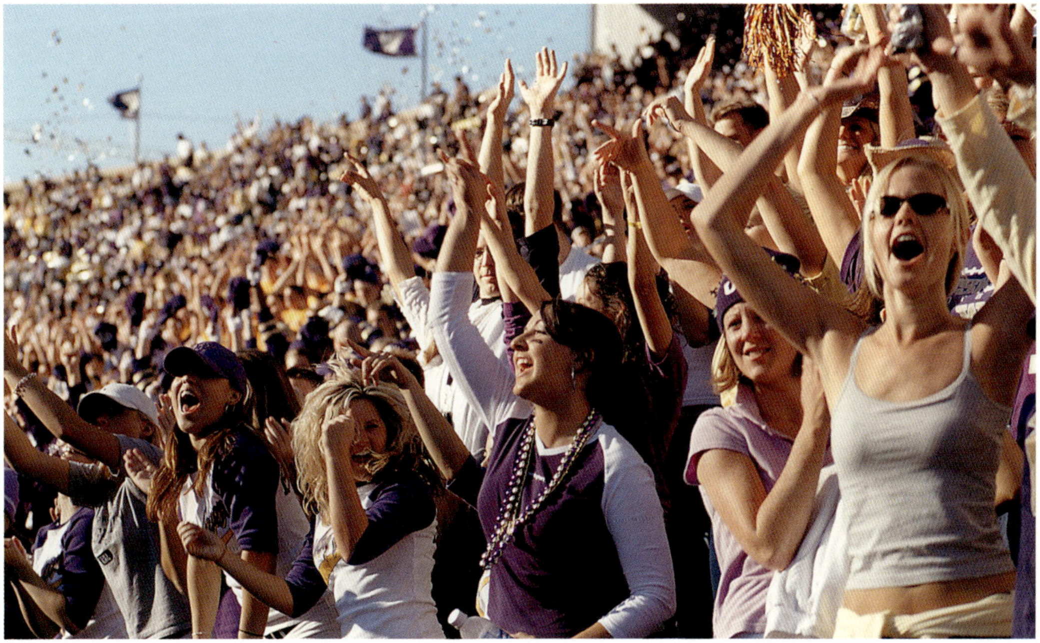

Opposite page:
Happiness is a Husky football game.

It's time for a hug from mascot Harry Husky as UW leads Arizona State.

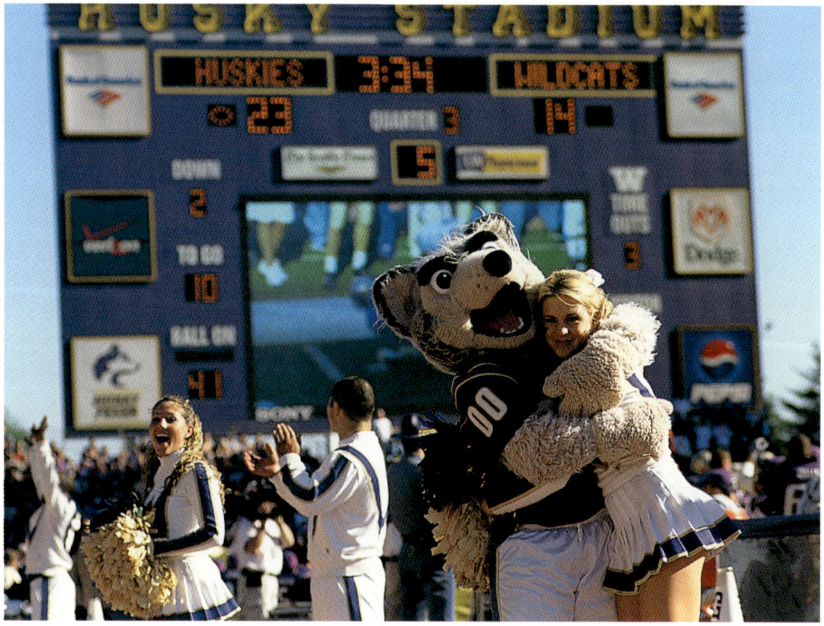

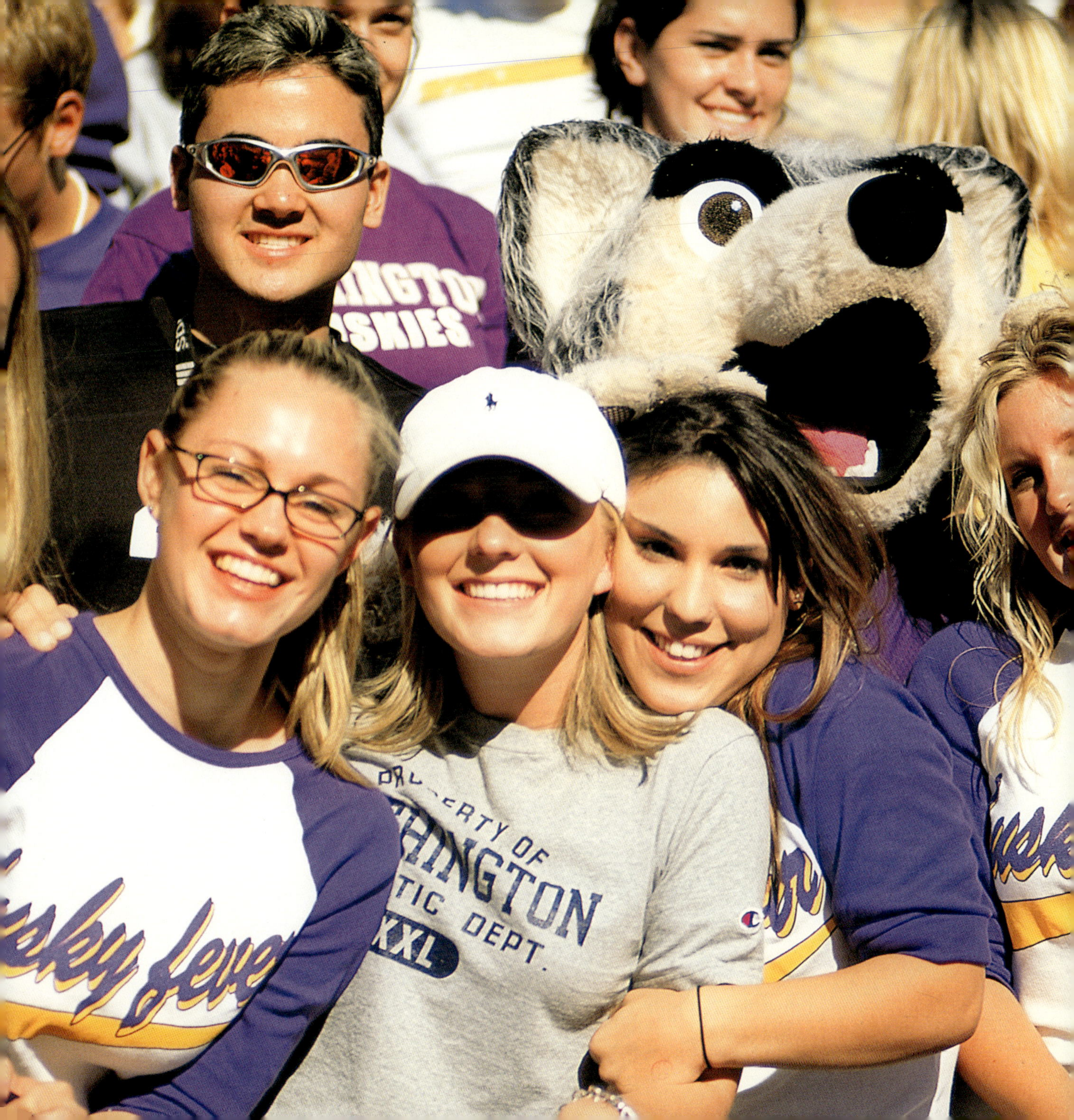
SKIES
HINGTON
TIC DEPT.
XXL

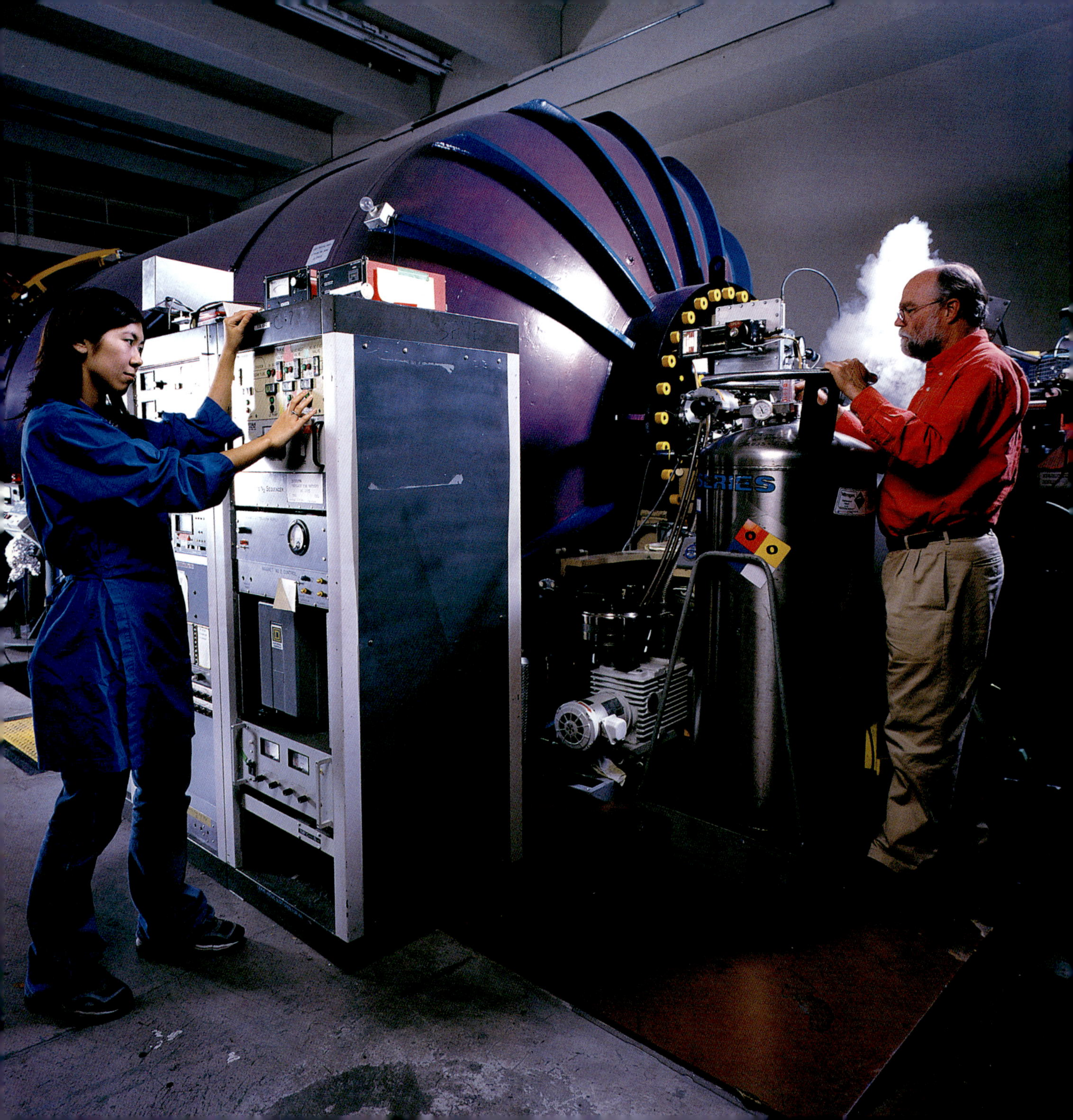
SERIES

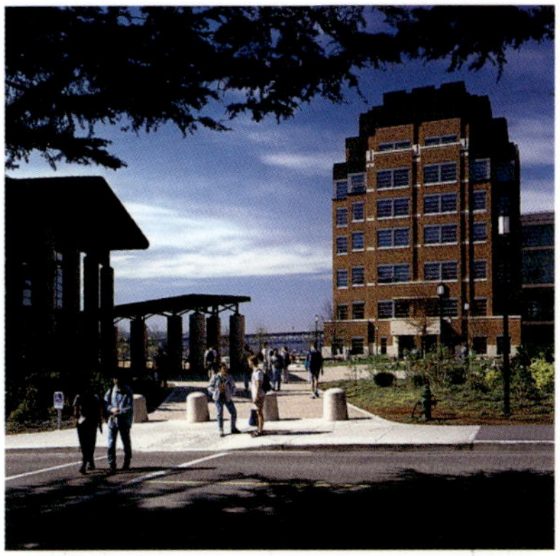

Left: The Physics/ Astronomy Building, designed by renowned architect Cesar Pelli, opened in 1994.

Next page: A flock of Canada geese patrol Drumheller Fountain. In the background is the old Physics Building, now called Mary Gates Hall.

Opposite page: UW physicists adjust the Tandem Van de Graaff Nuclear Accelerator to collect information on nuclear disintegrations and reactions.

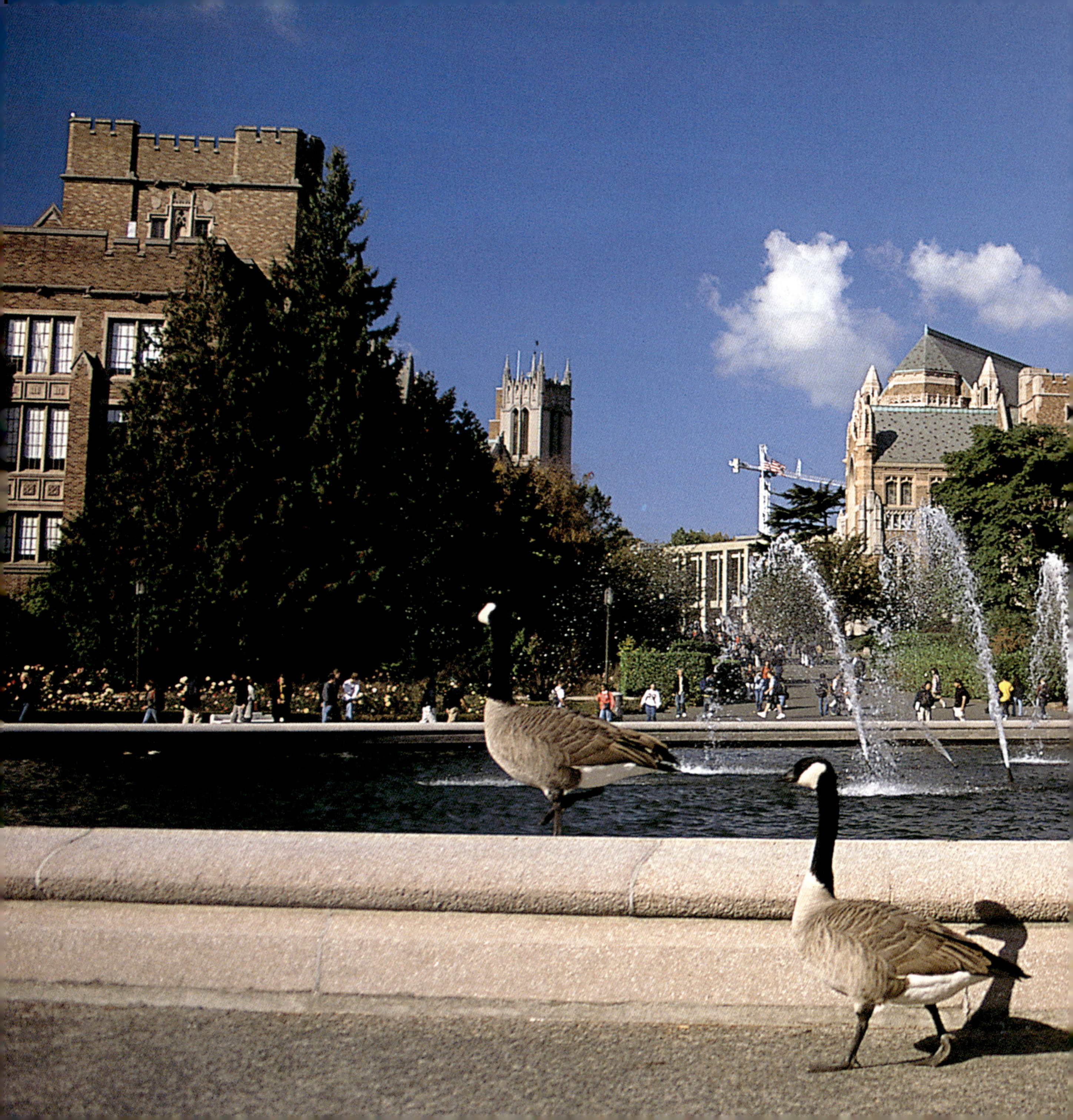

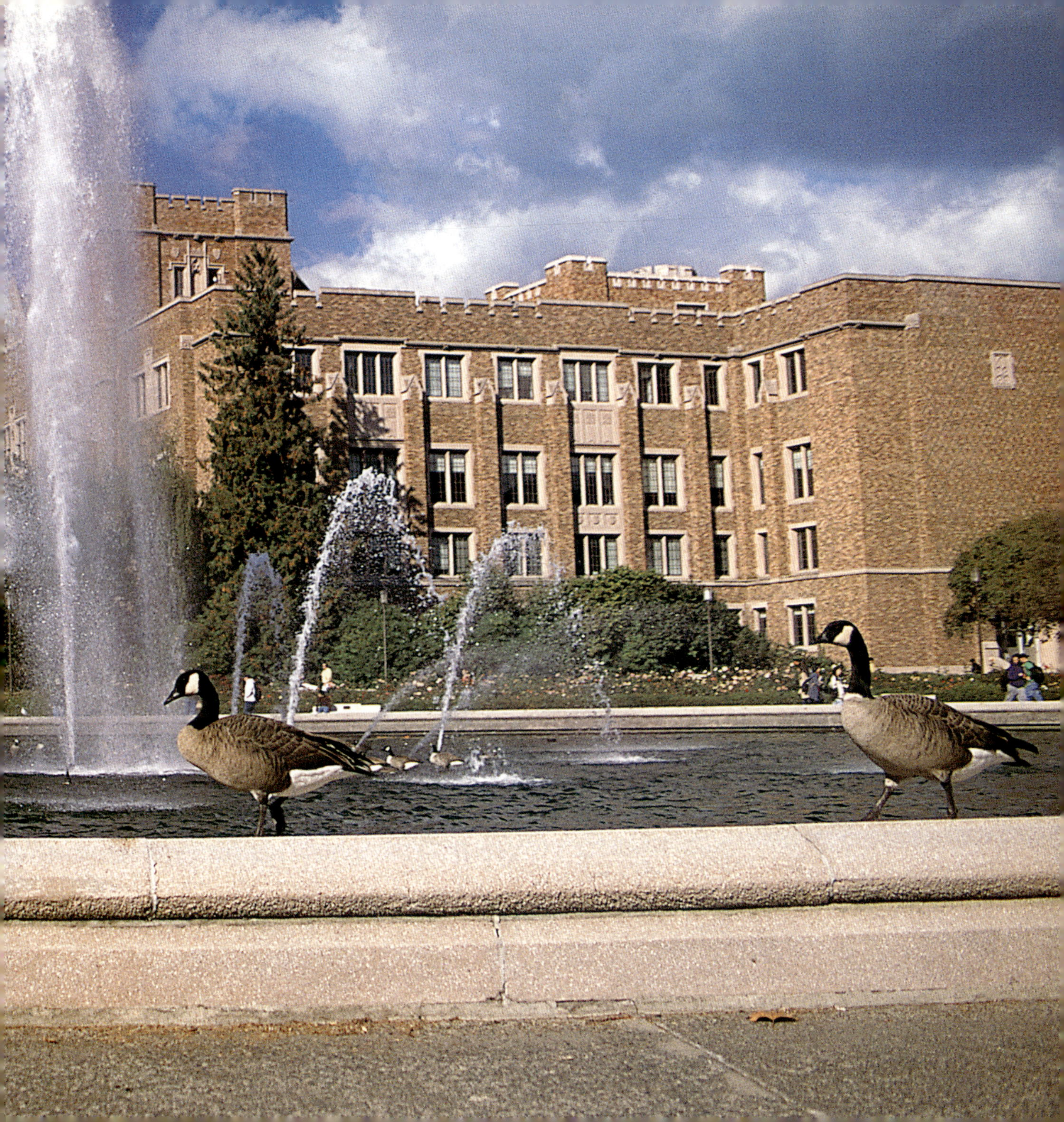

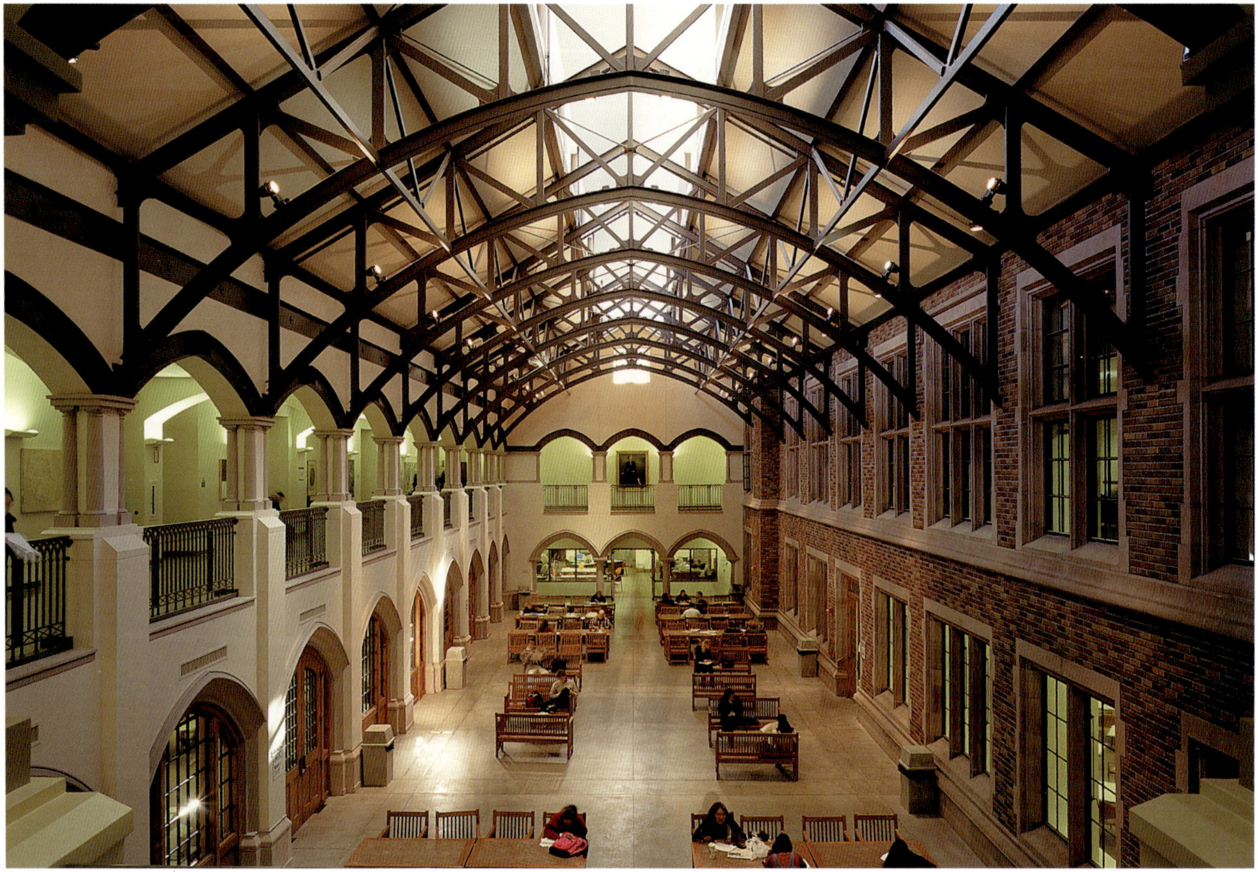

Like Gothic arches, these steel trusses punctuate the ceiling of the Commons, a gathering space in Mary Gates Hall. The wall on the right side of the picture used to be an exterior wall of the old Physics Building before the UW turned it into a center for undergraduate education.

A job fair in the Commons helps to prepare students for life after graduation.

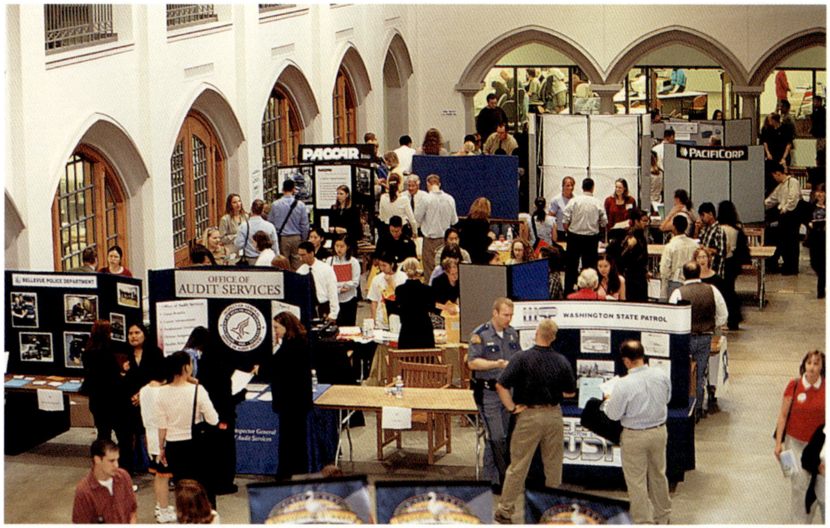

The elaborate entrance to Johnson Hall harks back to Gothic art of the Middle Ages, but inside, 21st-century science is practiced by the Department of Earth and Space Sciences.

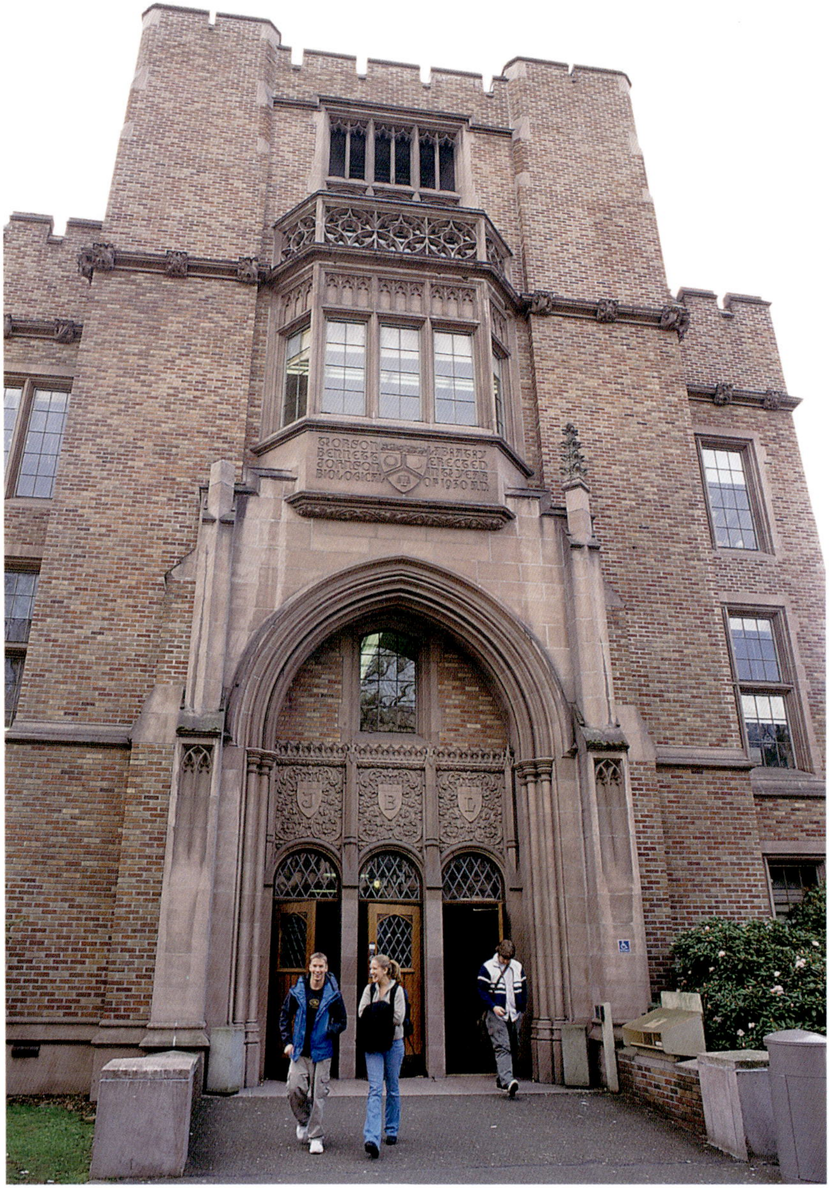

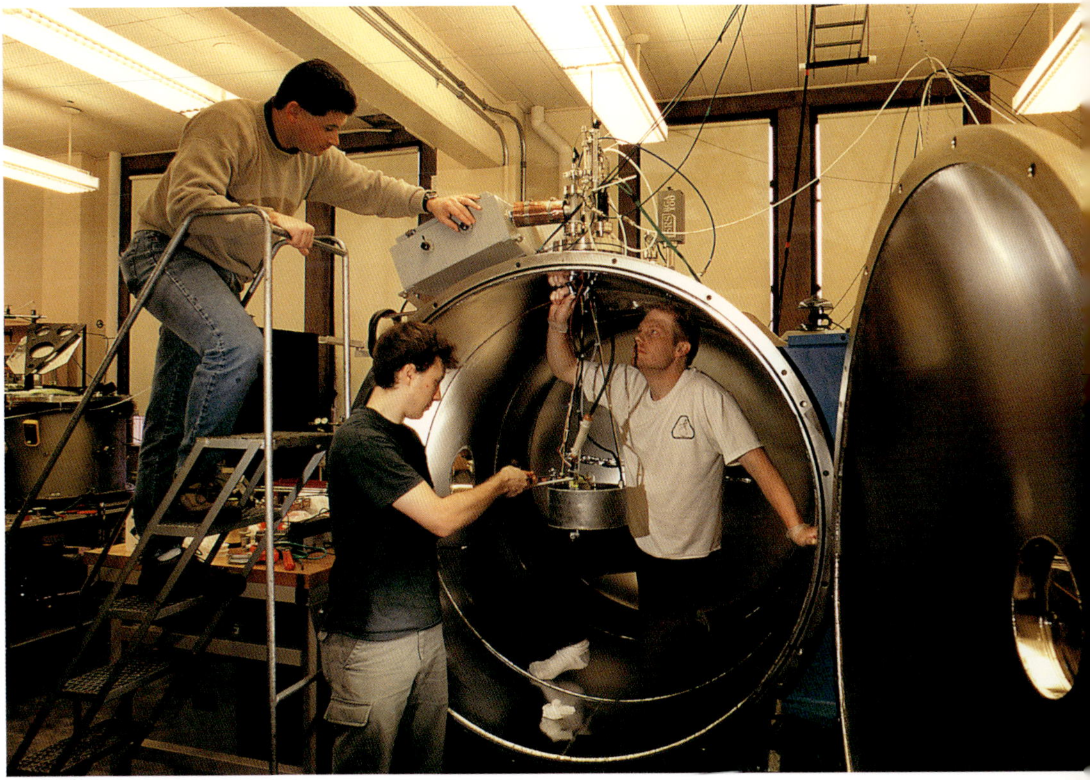

Earth Science graduate students adjust a stainless-steel vacuum chamber during an experiment on plasma propulsion systems for spacecraft in Johnson Hall.

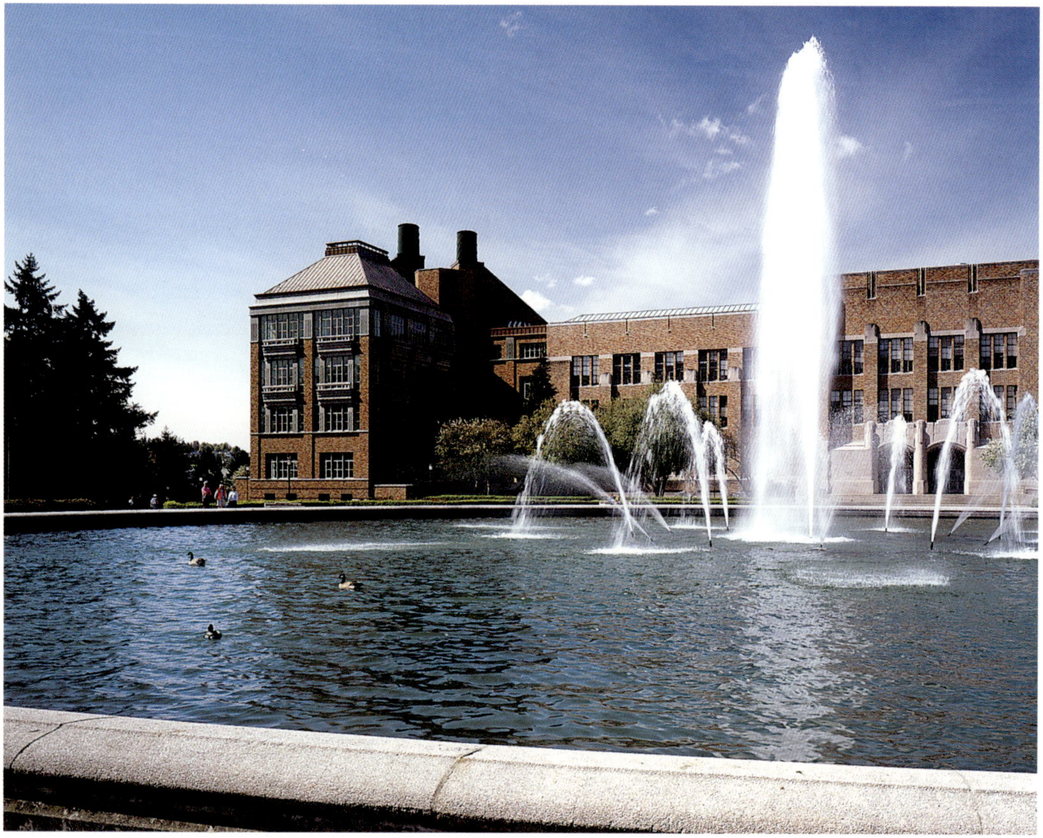

The new Chemistry Building (left), designed by Charles Moore, is linked to Bagley Hall (right), home of the chemistry department since 1937.

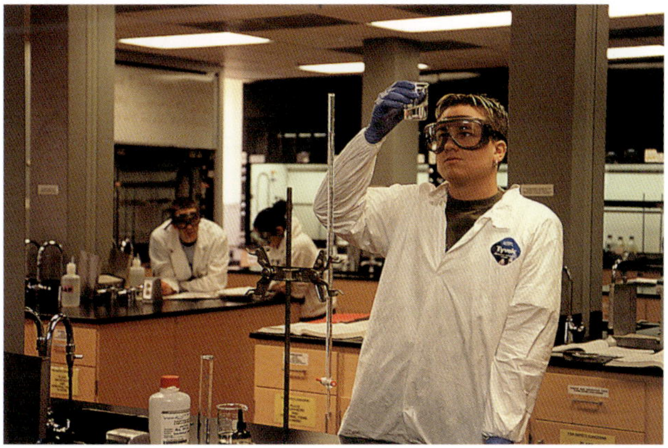

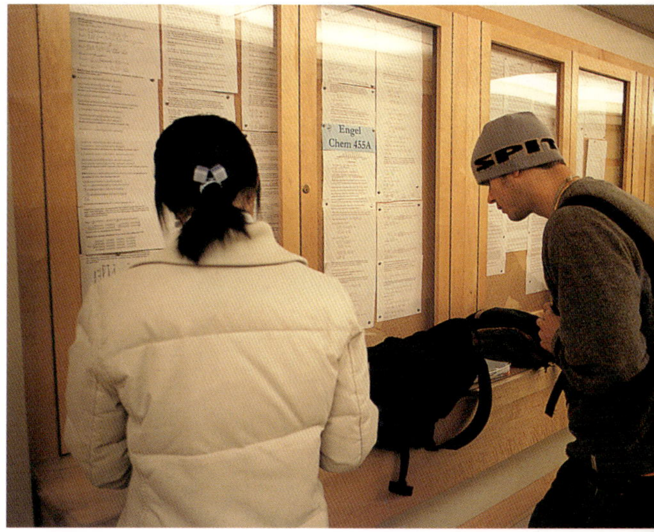

Left: A student works in a new lab in the Chemistry Building.
Right: Grades are posted in the Bagley Hall lobby.

Left: Engineering students are a blur of activity during the Pacific Northwest Regional Robotics Competition, held in Hec Edmundson Pavilion.

Right: The courtyard of Mueller Hall allows light and air into the mostly underground building. In the rear is Roberts Hall.

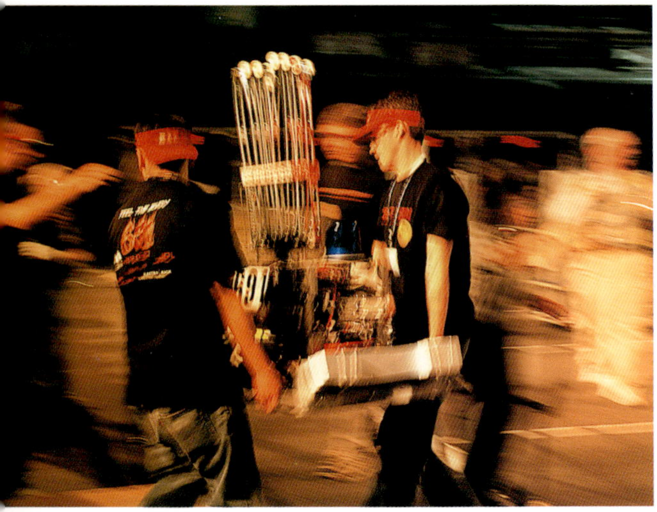

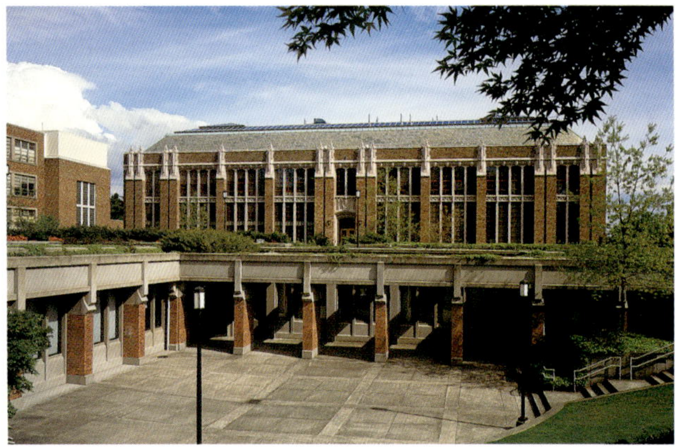

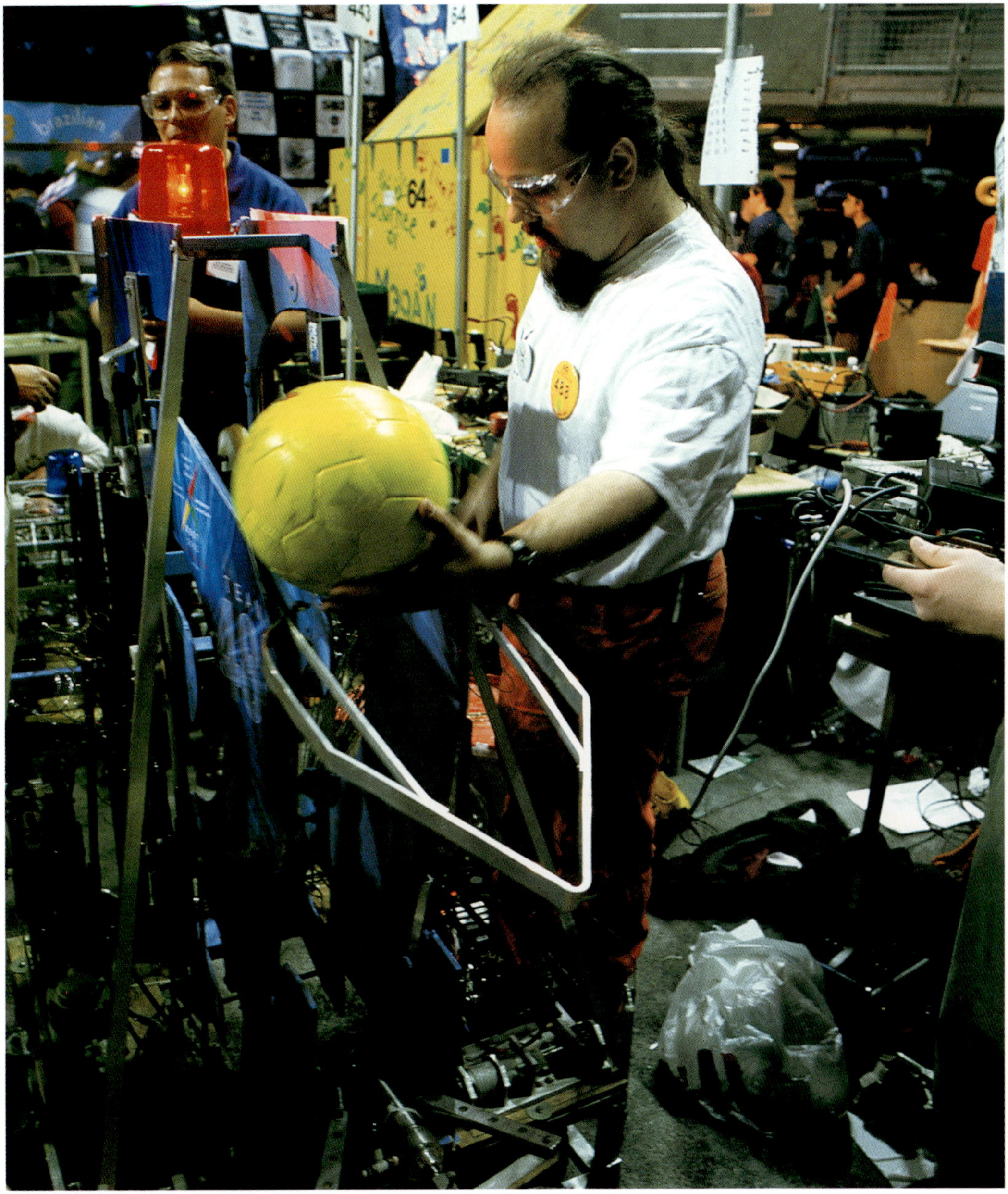

A student cradles a soccer ball while he tests his robot during the robotics competition. Teams had only six weeks to imagine, design and build a remote-controlled 130-pound robot.

Opposite page:
The Kirsten Wind Tunnel, behind Guggenheim Hall, has been a test site for models of most Boeing aircraft, racing yachts, the Space Needle and even Husky Stadium.

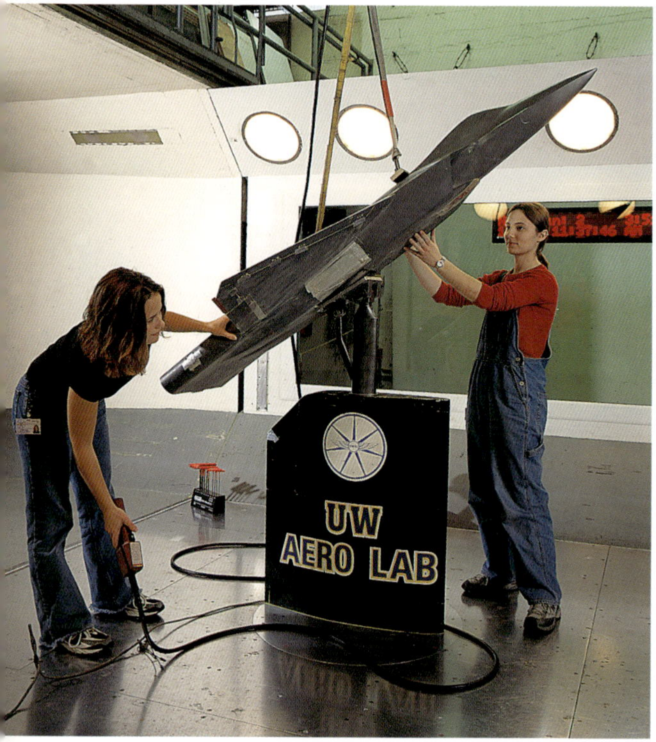

Two engineering students test an airplane model in the Kirsten Wind Tunnel.

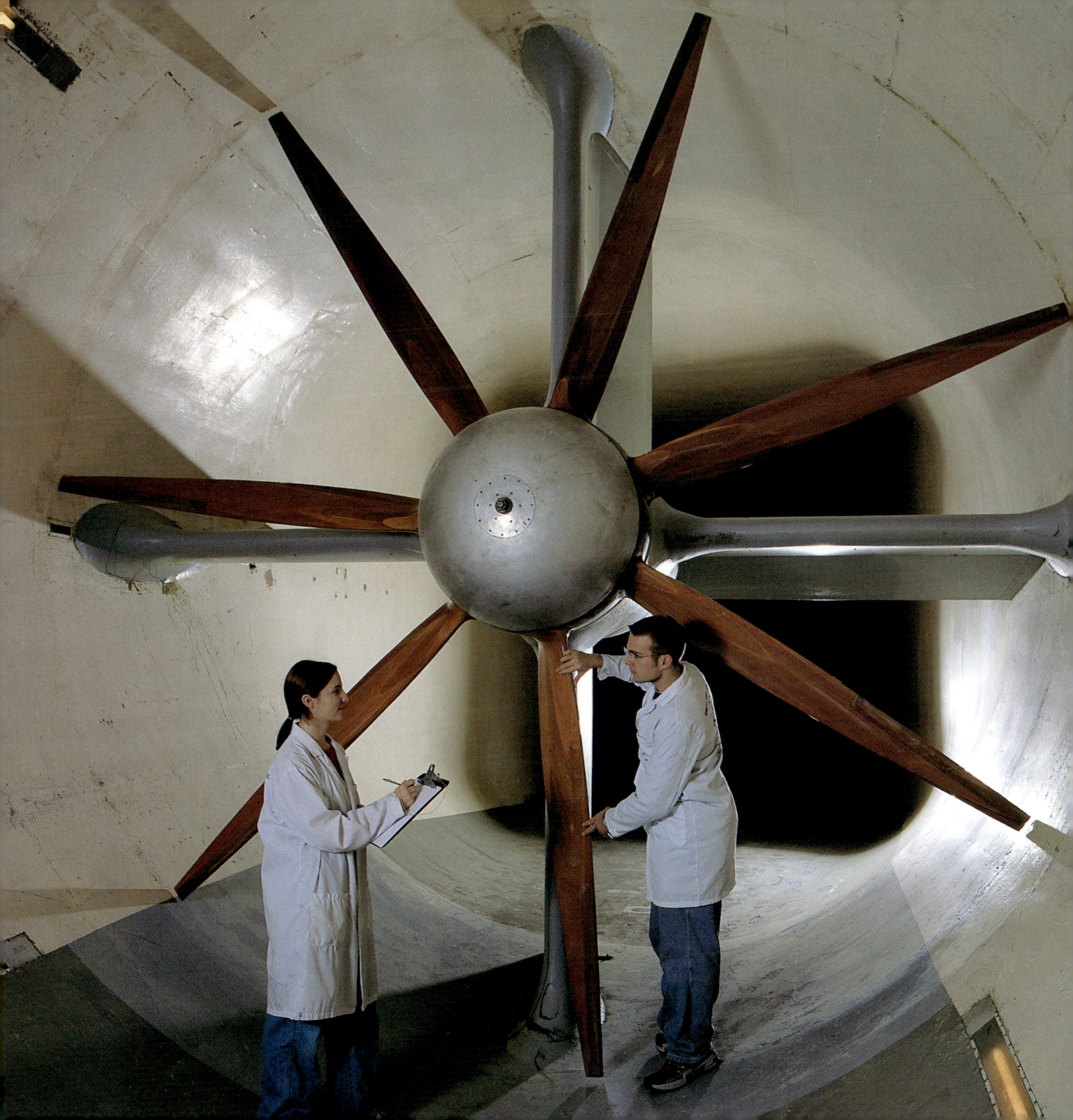

Architecture Hall is the only permanent building left from the Alaska-Yukon-Pacific Exposition, held on campus in 1909. Its beige brick walls and Neoclassical touches came before the UW chose Collegiate Gothic as its architectural style.

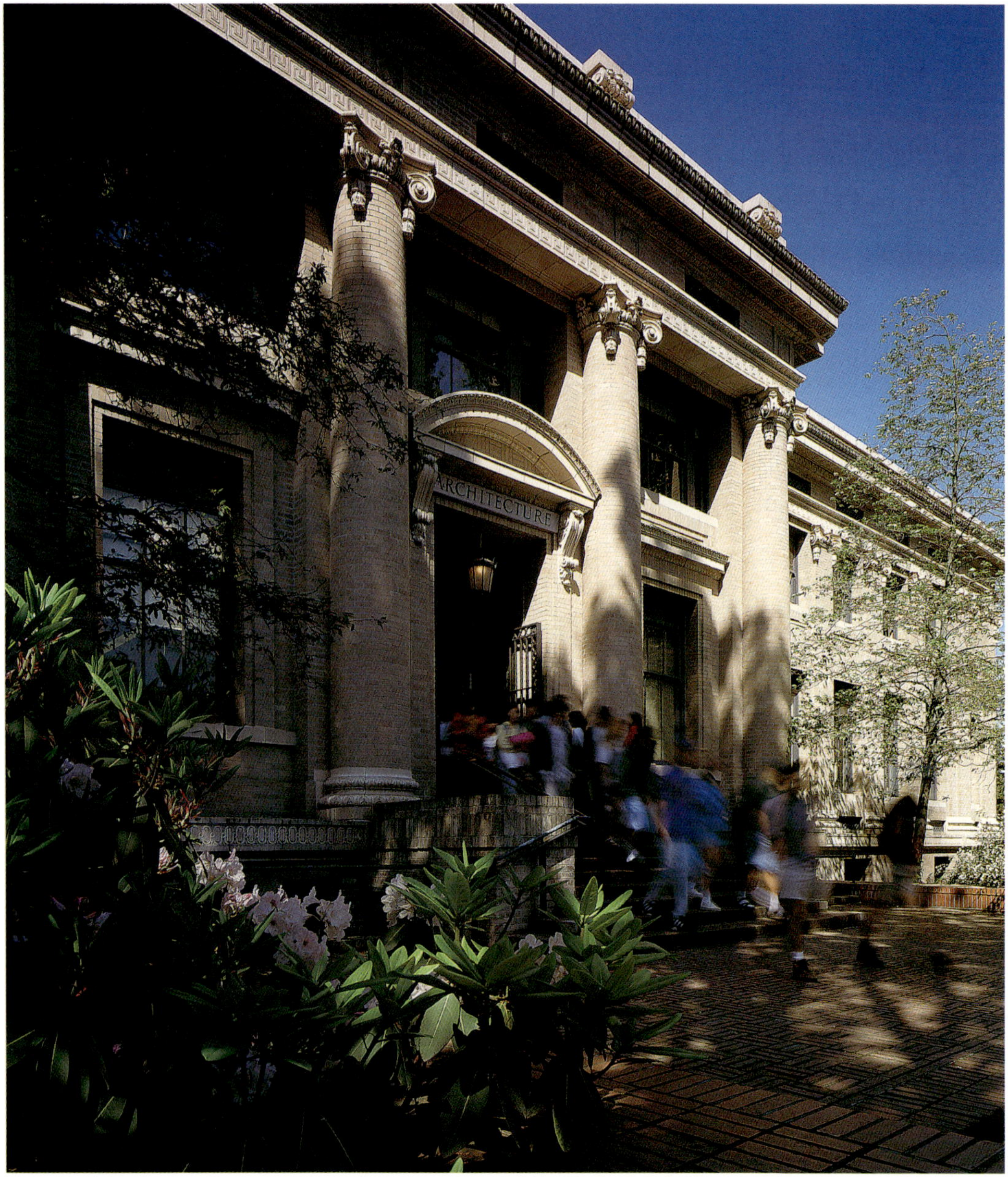

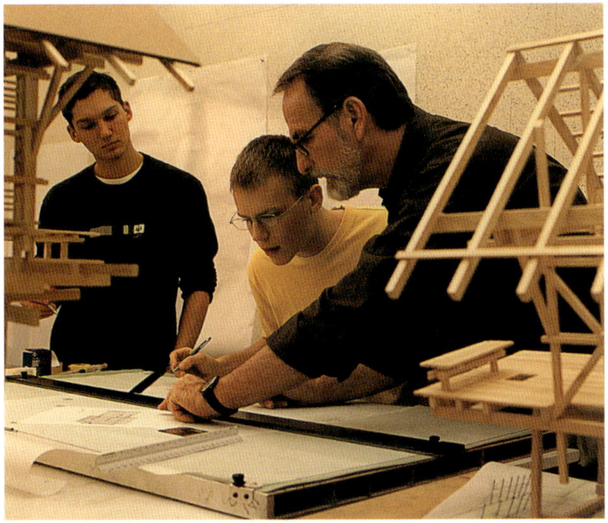

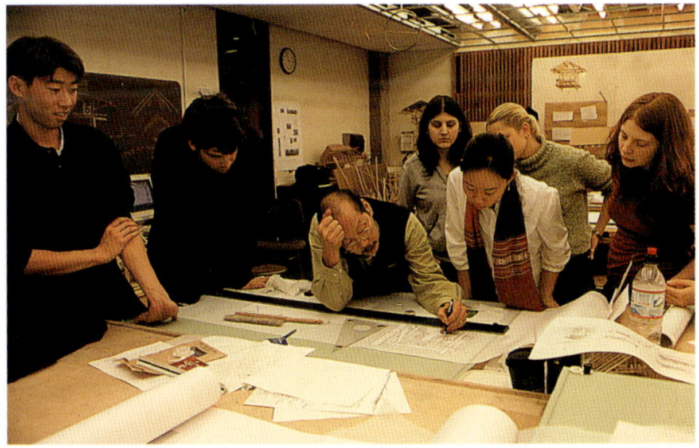

Architecture students plot out their designs with the help of faculty and practicing architects.

Left: The Botany Greenhouse, along Stevens Way, has bright colors, exotic smells and tropical temperatures—a perfect environment for a class in the middle of winter.

Right: A plant technician conducts soil tests on flats of seedlings.

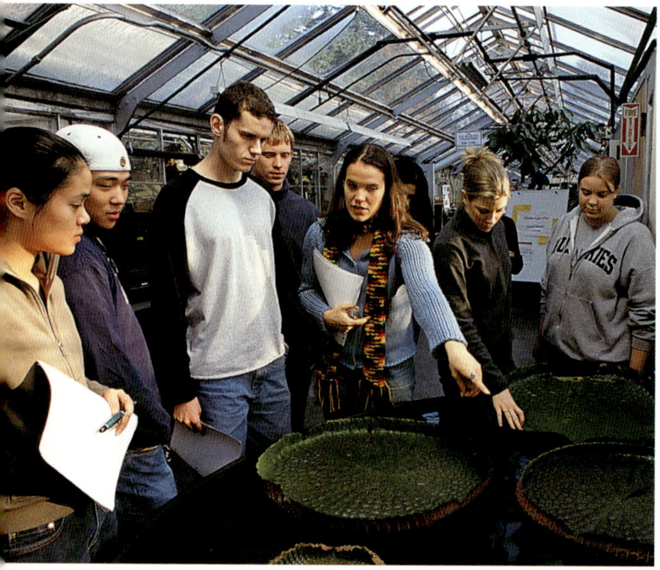

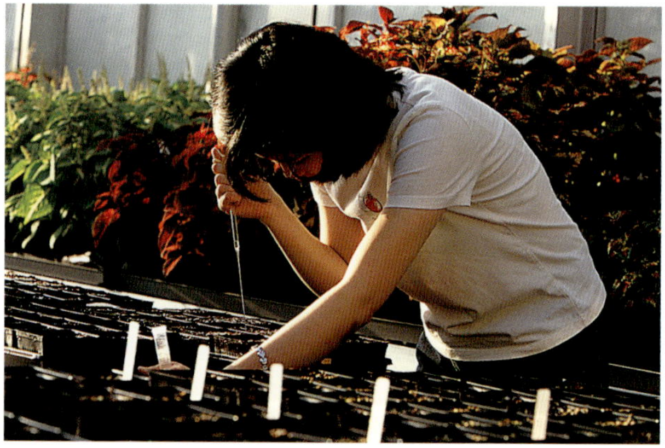

Opposite page: The greenhouse manager inspects a chili plant.

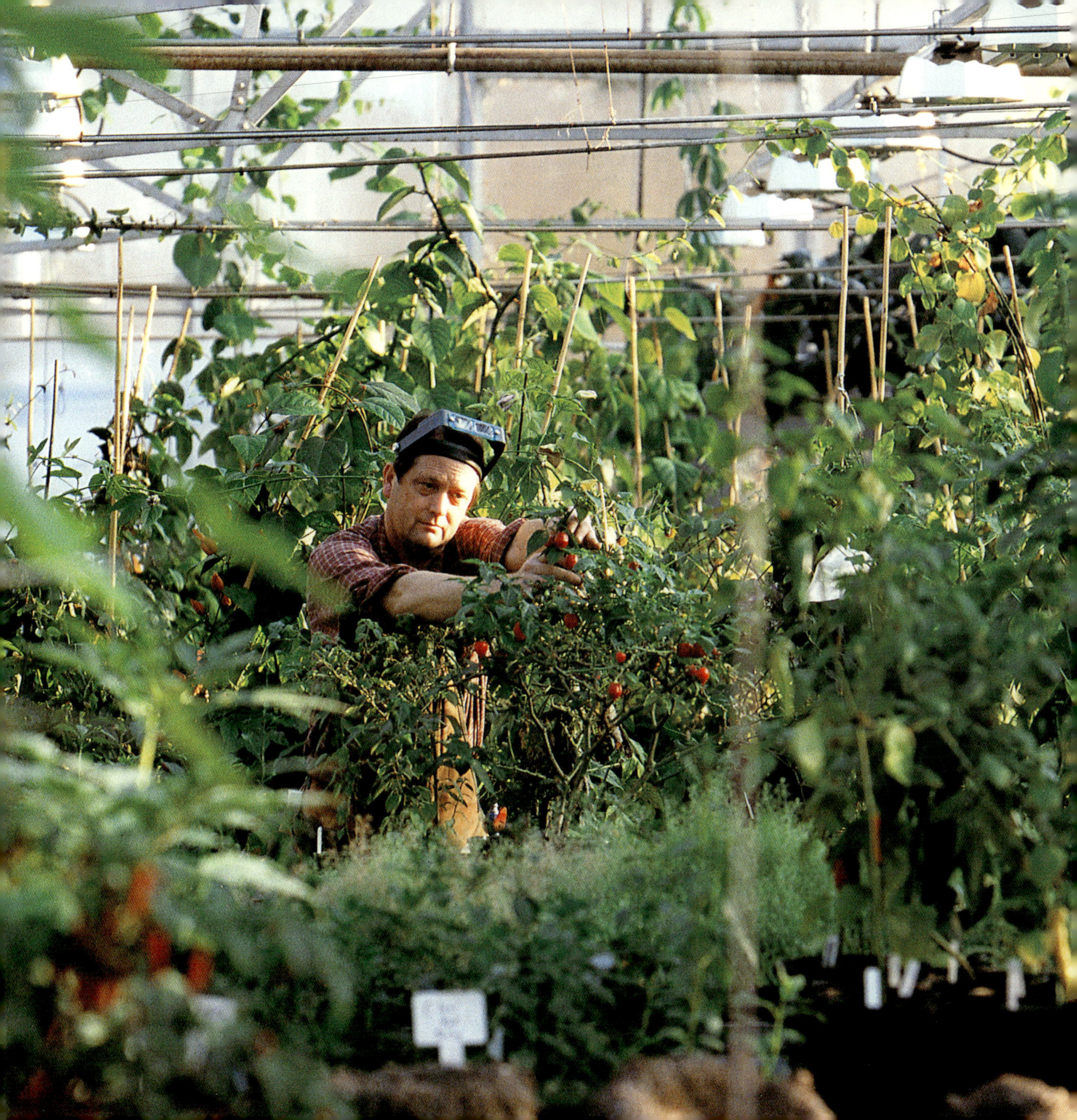

Once the right-of-way for a railroad that followed the shoreline of Lake Washington, the Burke-Gilman Trail is now a popular path for joggers, bicyclists and walkers.

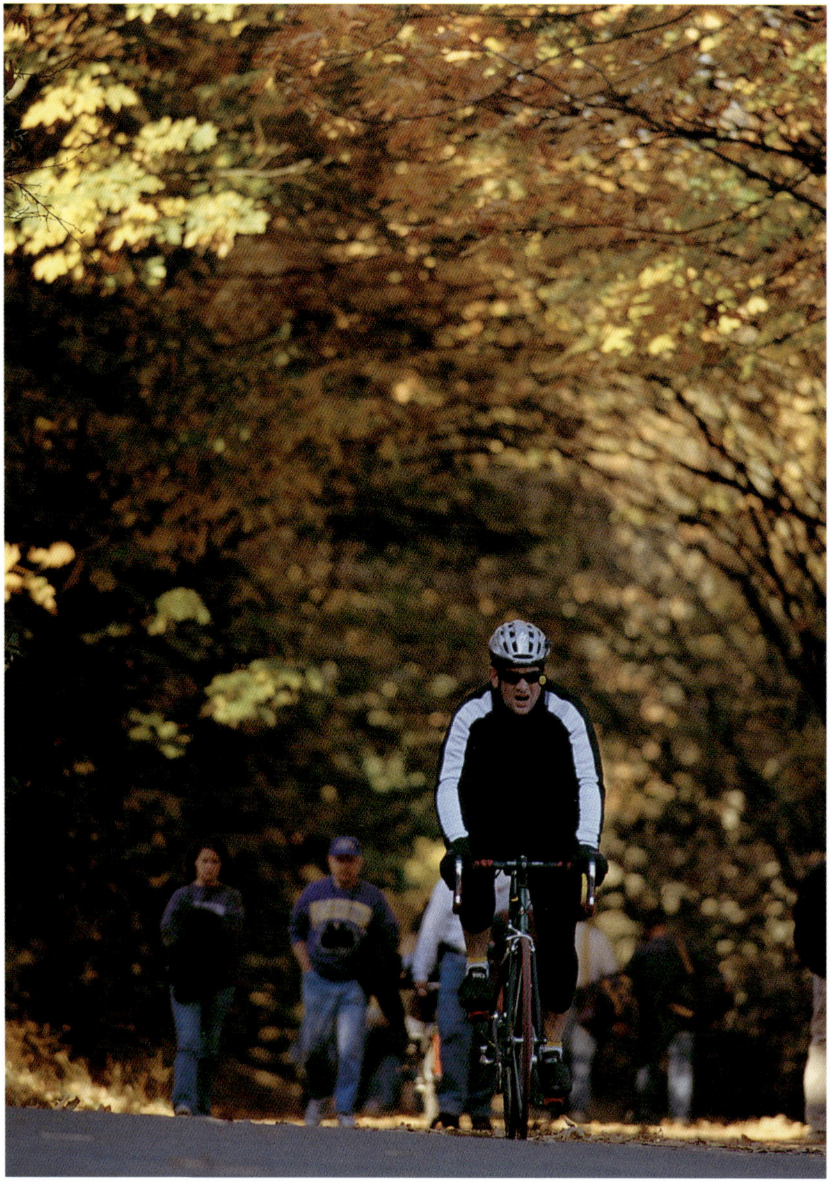

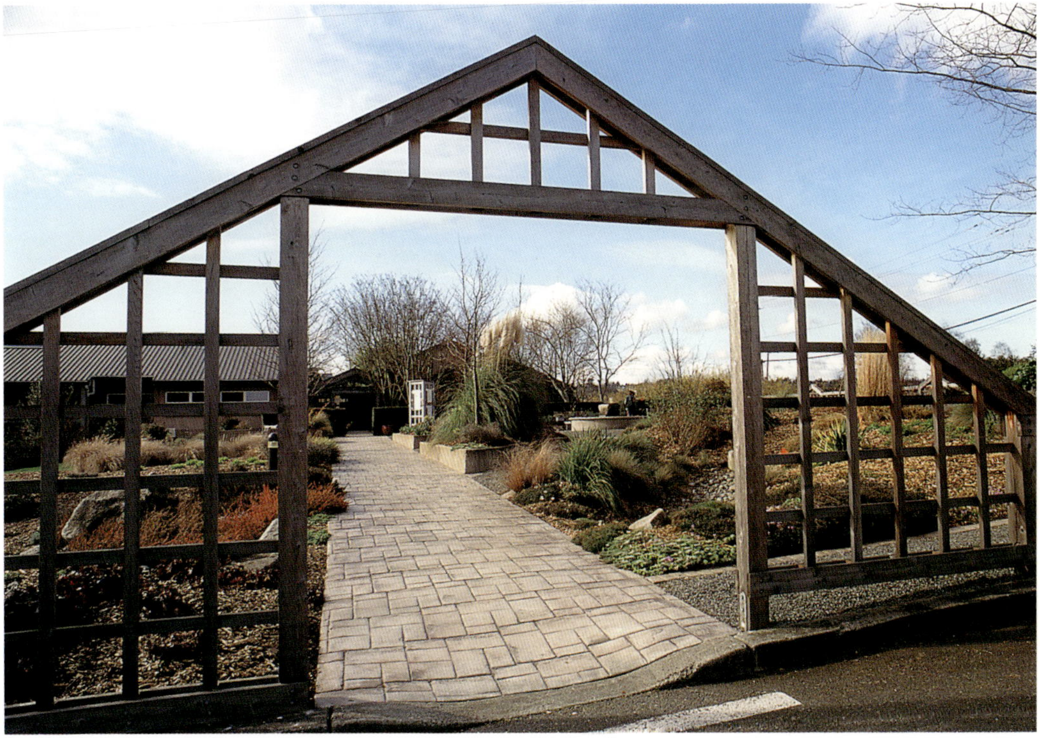

The Center for Urban Horticulture, in the eastern part of campus, features lush demonstration gardens.

Home of the College of Forest Resources, Anderson Hall is a prime example of Collegiate Gothic architecture. It was built in 1925 with funds donated by Agnes H. Anderson.

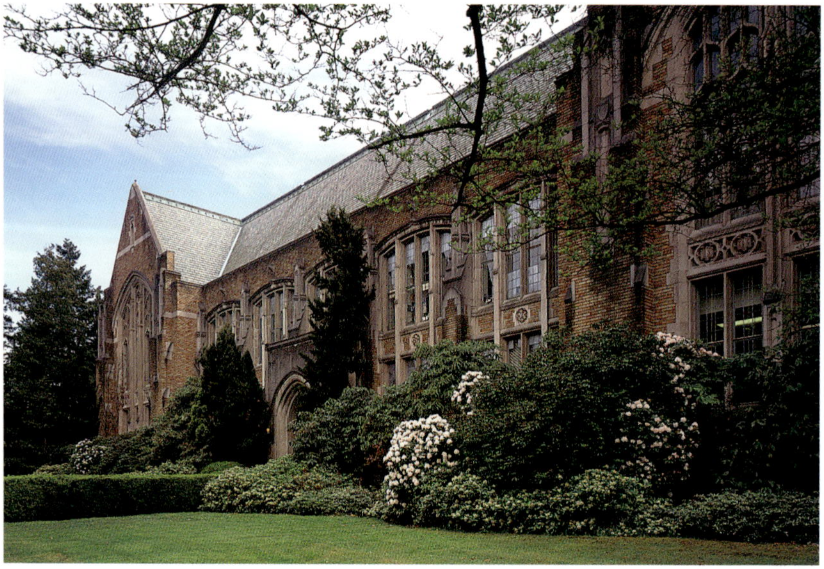

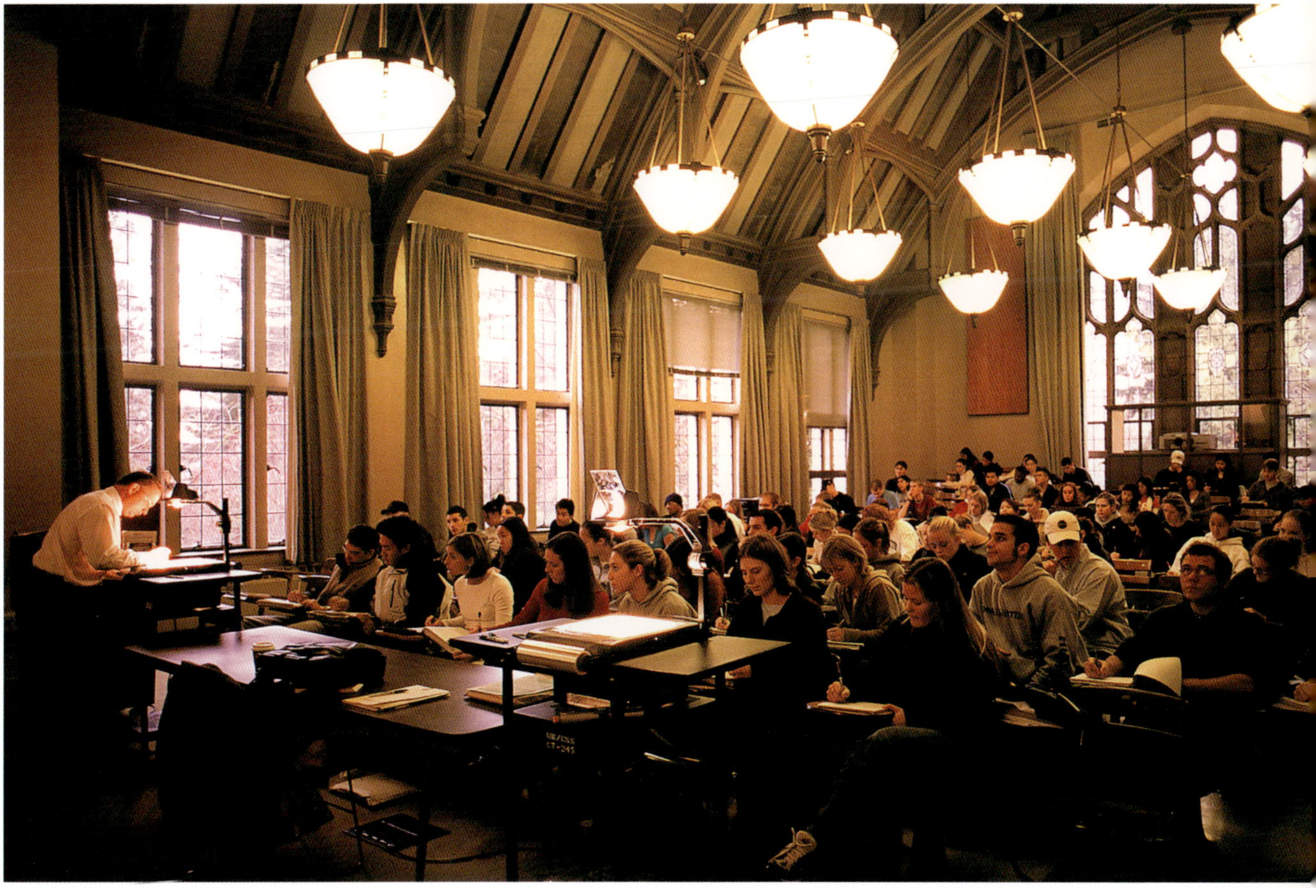

Inside Anderson Hall, there are plenty of Gothic touches as well. Here, accounting students take a class in a grand lecture hall.

Designed for open spaces and grand vistas, the UW is spectacular from the air. This shot looks northwest over the main campus. The green circle in the foreground conceals the roof of the Triangle Parking Garage.

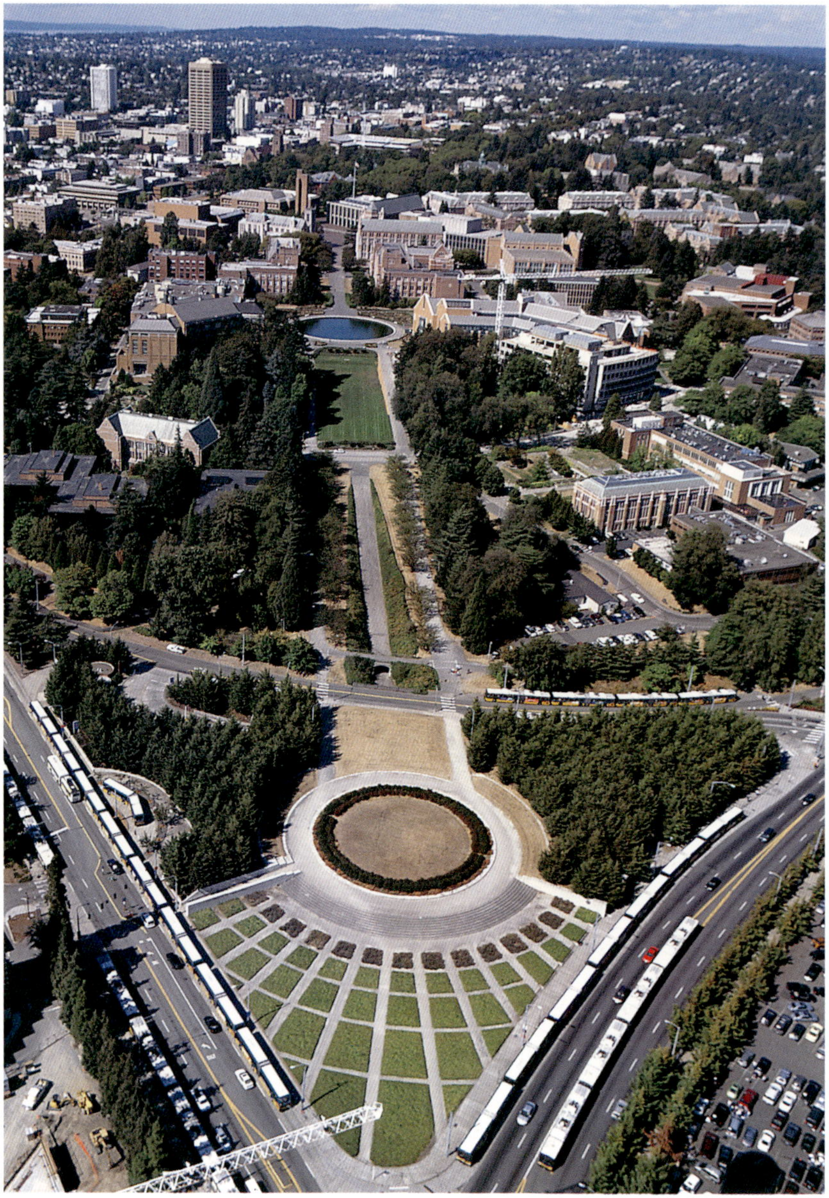

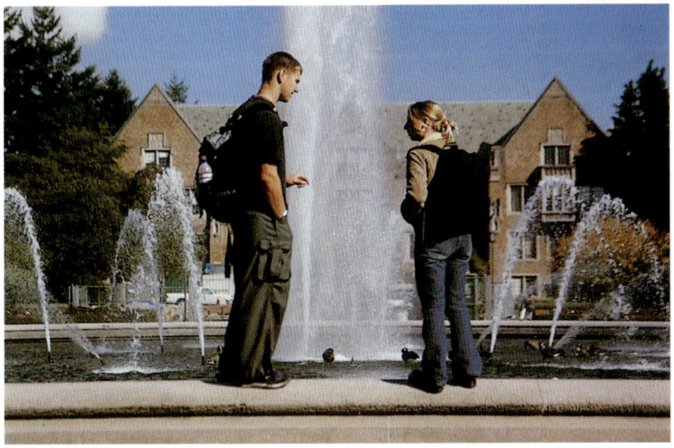

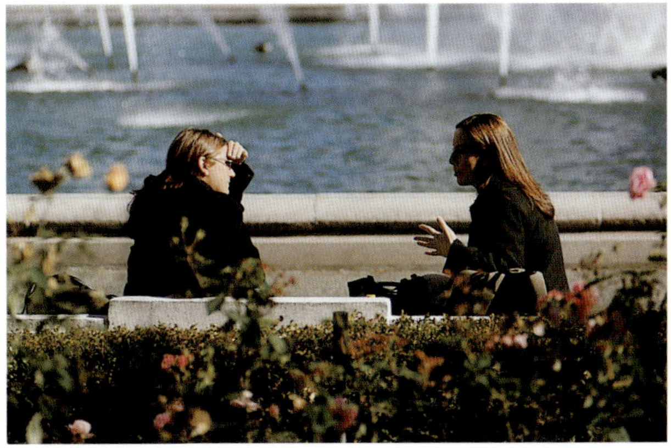

Drumheller Fountain is a great place to take a break from classes or the library, but it wasn't always so restful. A reflecting pool left over from a 1909 fair, it quickly became a spot to haze freshmen by tossing them into the water (hence its nickname, Frosh Pond). The fountain was installed in 1961 to commemorate the UW's 100th anniversary.

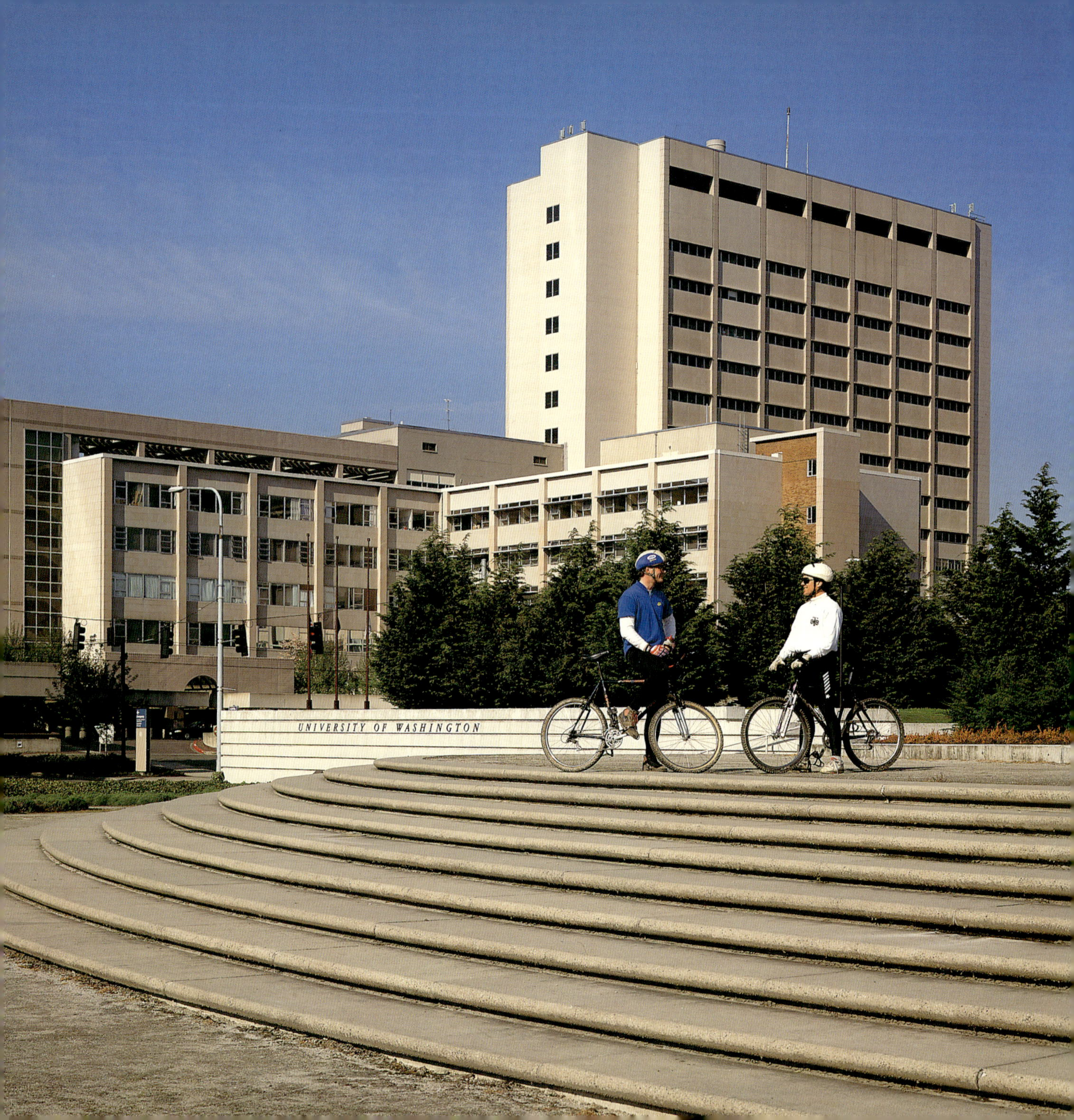
UNIVERSITY OF WASHINGTON

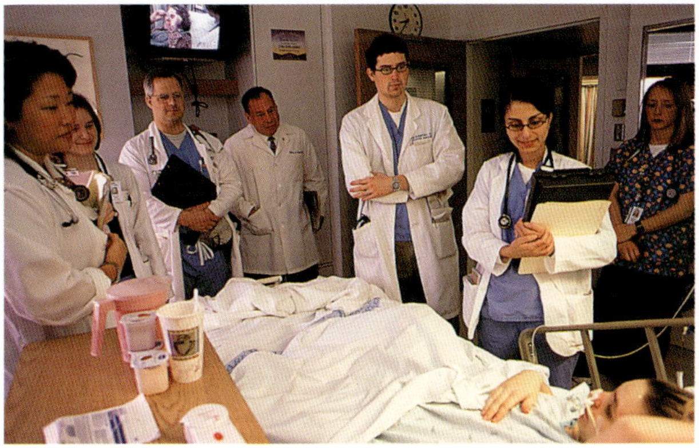

The UW's south campus features one of the top medical schools in the nation. Here interns perform rounds with resident doctors in a post-op ward.

Opposite page:
One section of the huge UW health sciences complex includes the 17-story Aagaard Tower, the tallest building on campus.

Left: A dentistry student gazes into a mechanical mouth as his professor demonstrates a procedure.

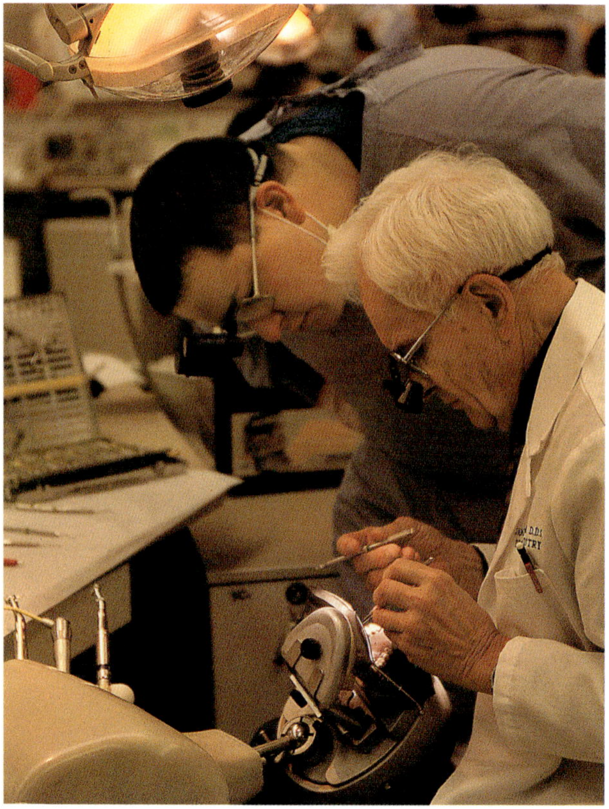

Right: Medical students confer with their professor in the dissecting lab during an anatomy class.

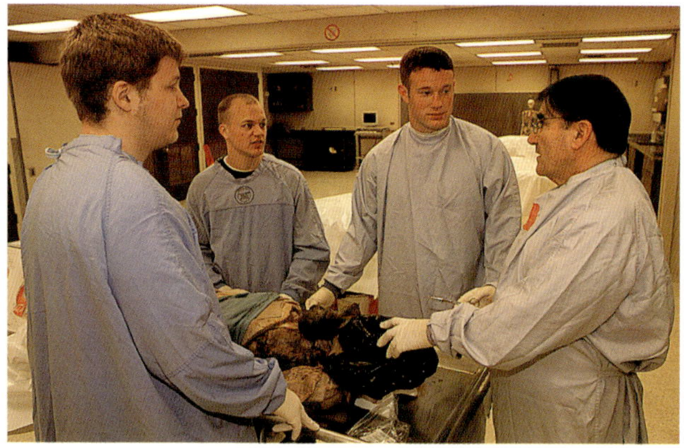

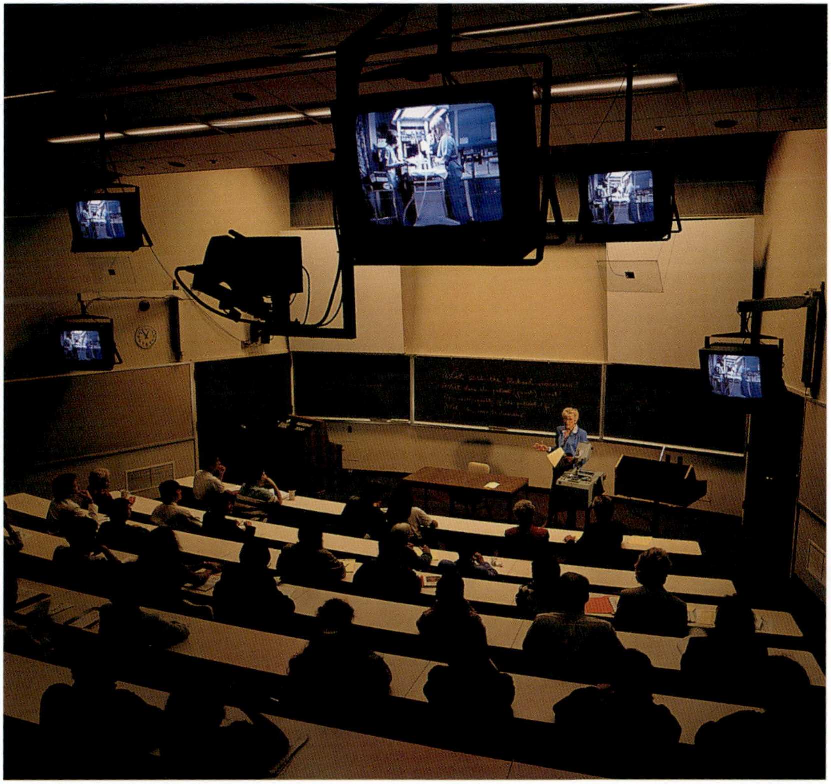

Medical School students hear a lecture in a high-tech classroom.

Next page: Boats glide past one of the top health sciences centers in the nation. The Medical School faculty includes four Nobel Prize winners.

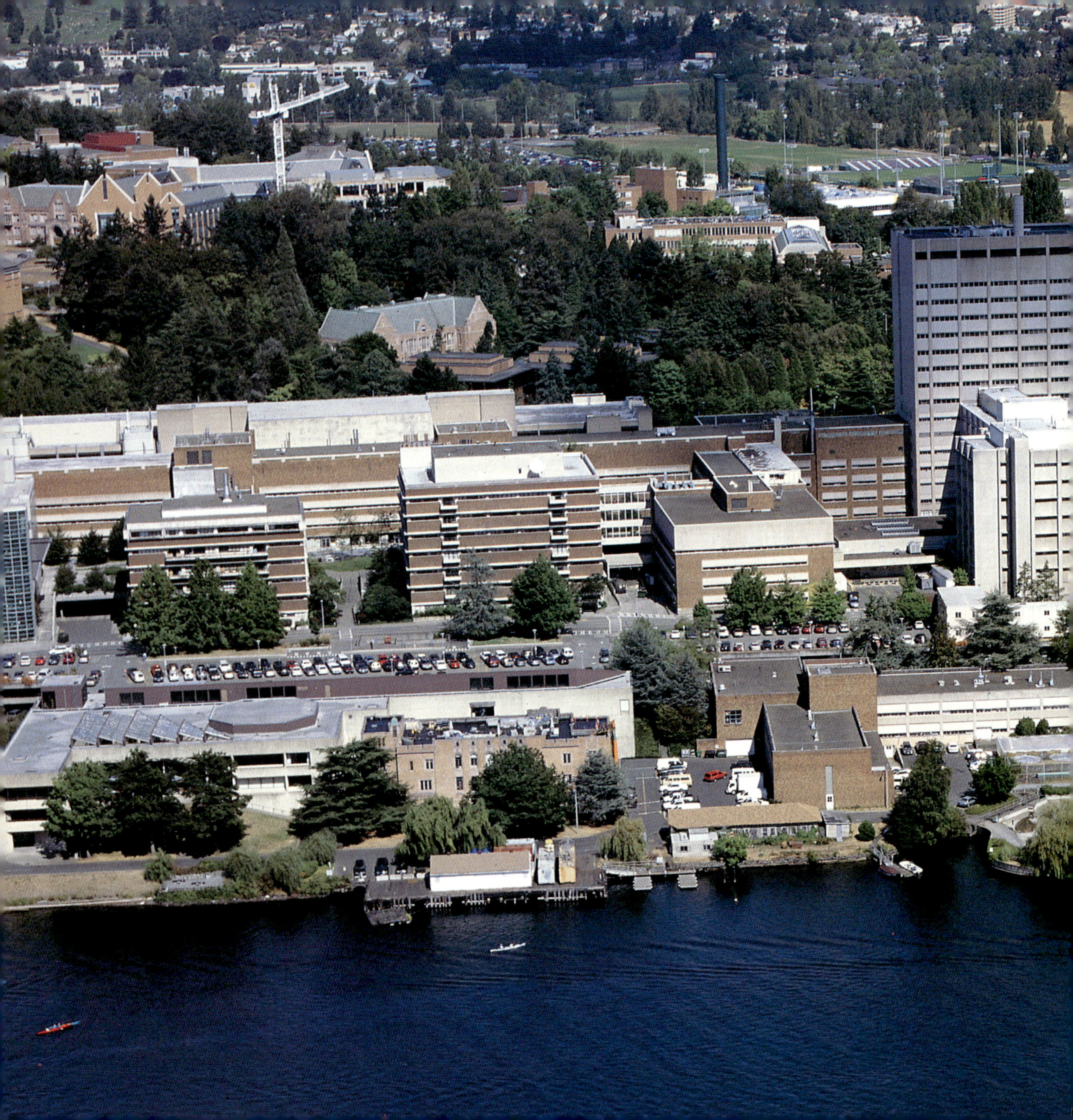

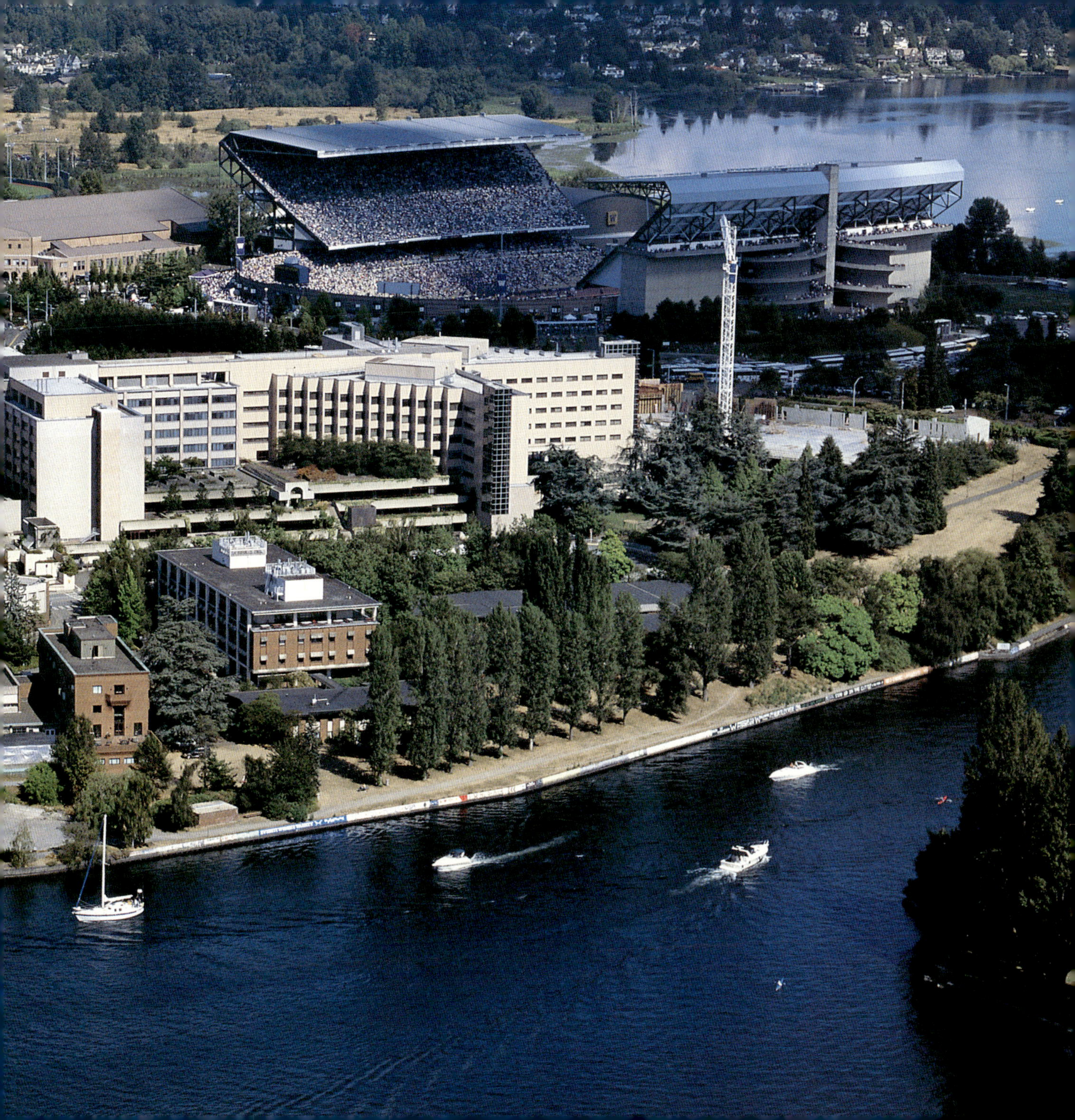

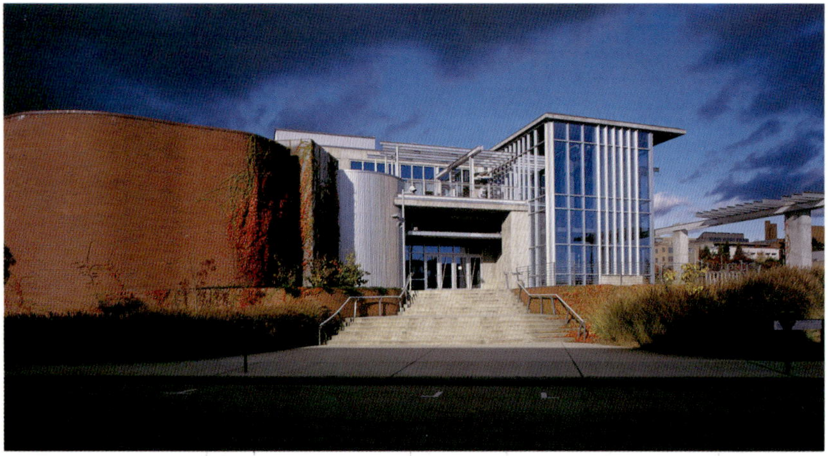

The new Fishery Sciences Building opened in 1999 in the southwest part of campus, consolidating offices, classrooms and labs for the School of Aquatic and Fishery Sciences.

A lab worker checks recently hatched salmon in the school's experimental hatchery.

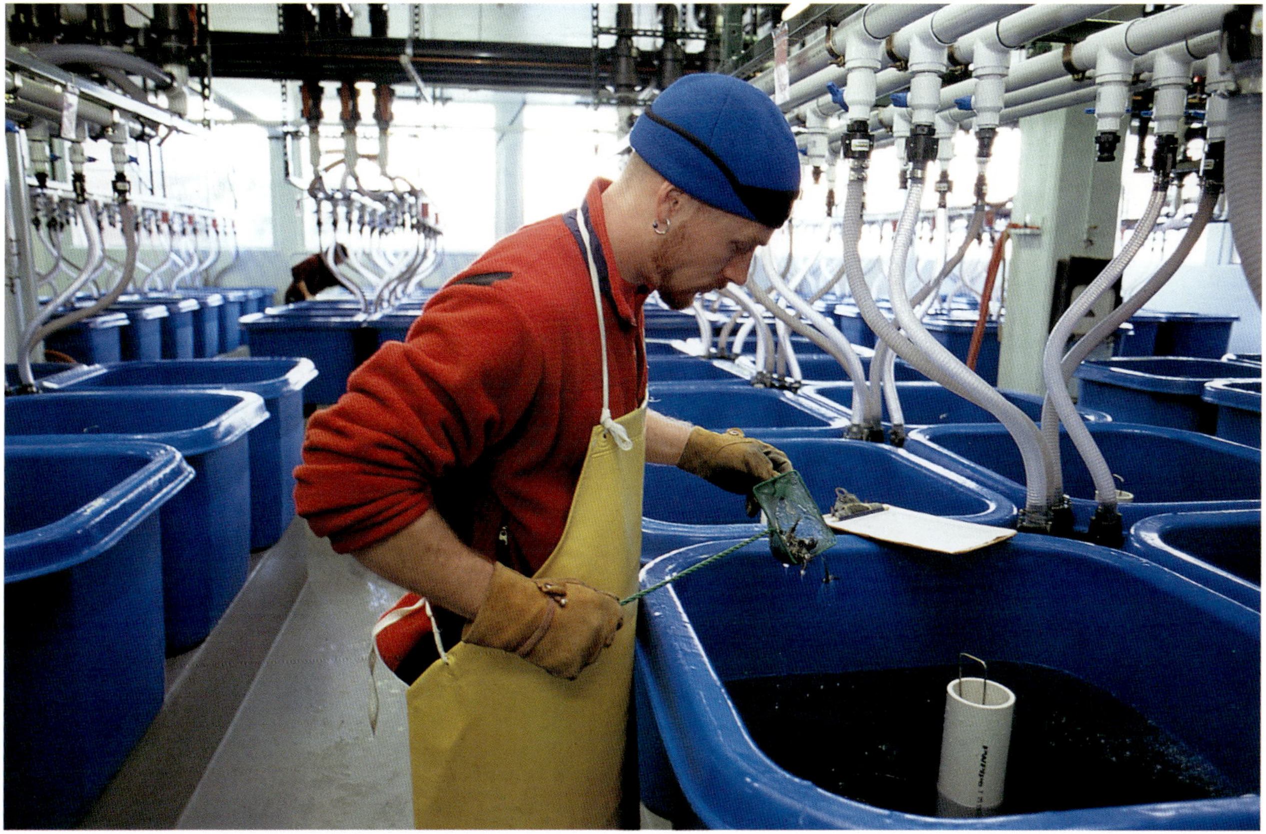

Left: Taking a break from scientific work, these students on the *Thomas G. Thompson* research vessel give each other back rubs.

Right: Built with funds from the Navy, the RV *Thompson* was acquired by the UW School of Oceanography in 1991 and operates primarily in the Pacific.

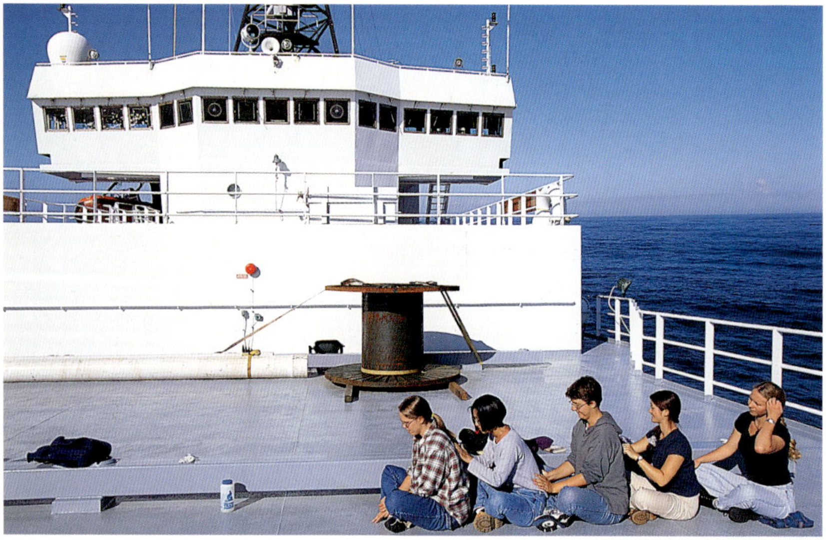

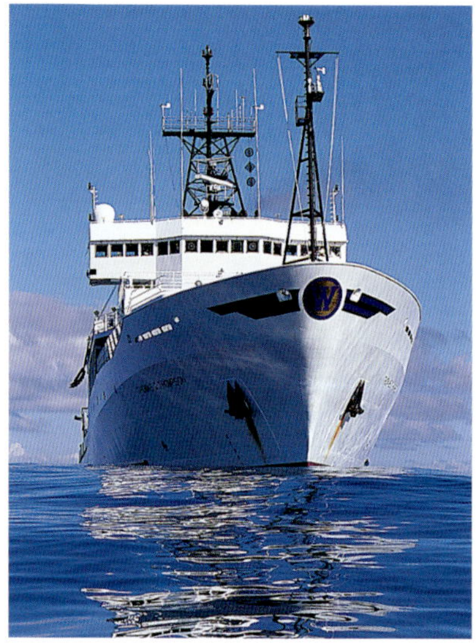

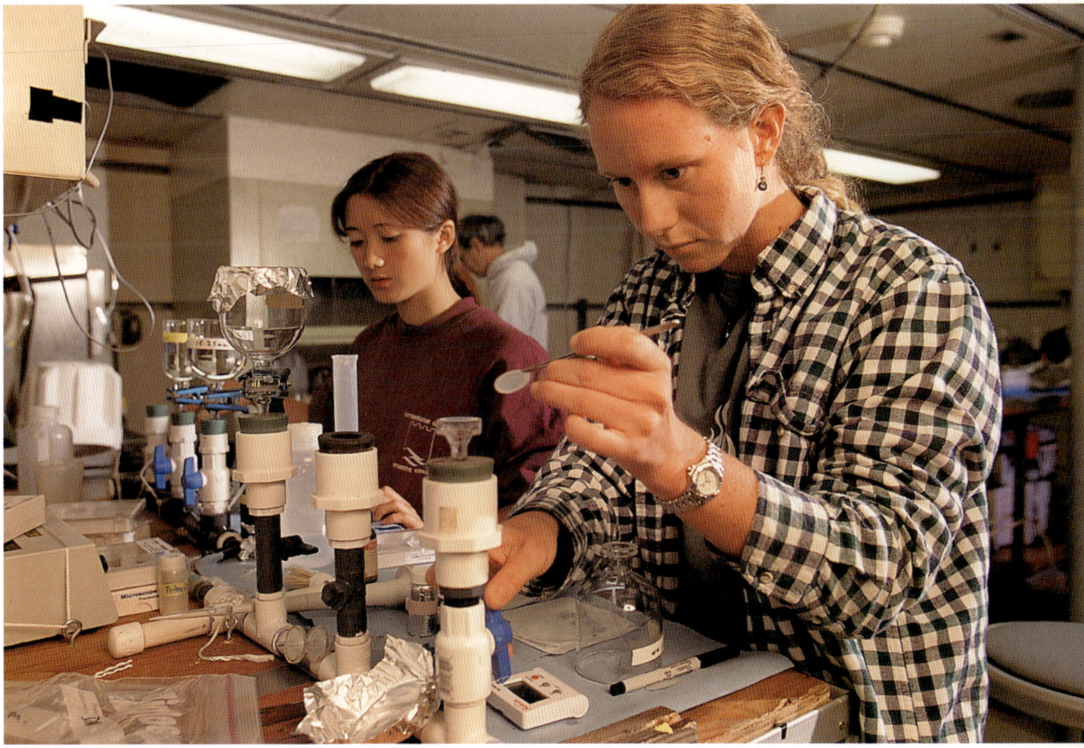

Oceanography graduate students take part in biological experiments aboard the research ship.

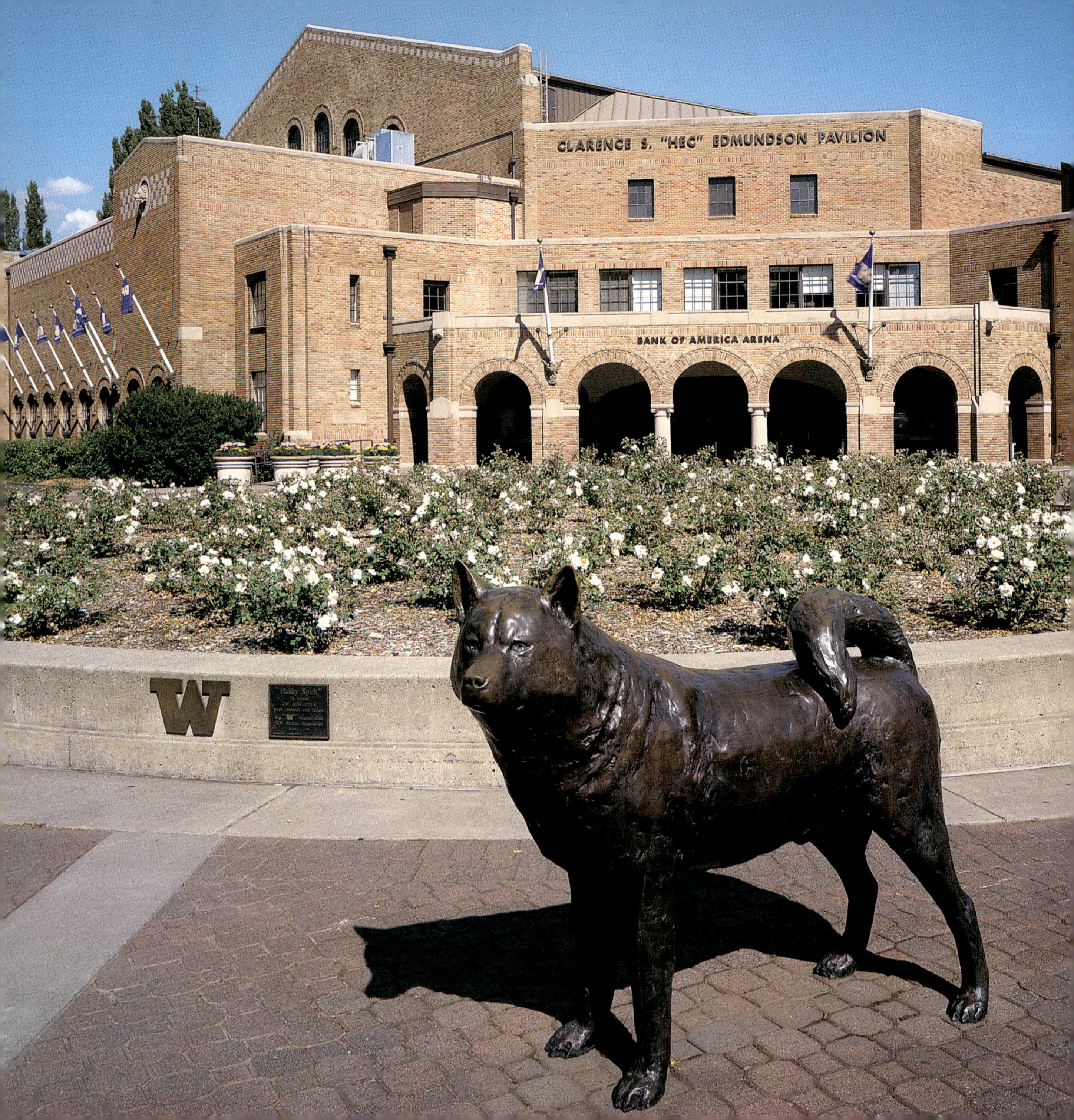
CLARENCE S. "HEC" EDMUNDSON PAVILION
BANK OF AMERICA ARENA

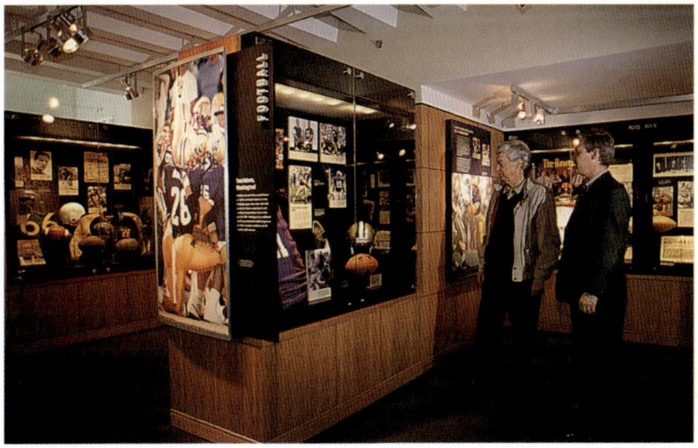

The history of UW varsity sports is preserved in the Husky Hall of Fame Museum, inside Hec Ed.

Opposite page:
A bronze statue of a Husky guards the entrance to Hec Edmundson Pavilion.

The Husky Women's Basketball team battles Oregon in the pavilion. A $40 million renovation improved the sight lines and upgraded the seismic strength of the 1927 field house.

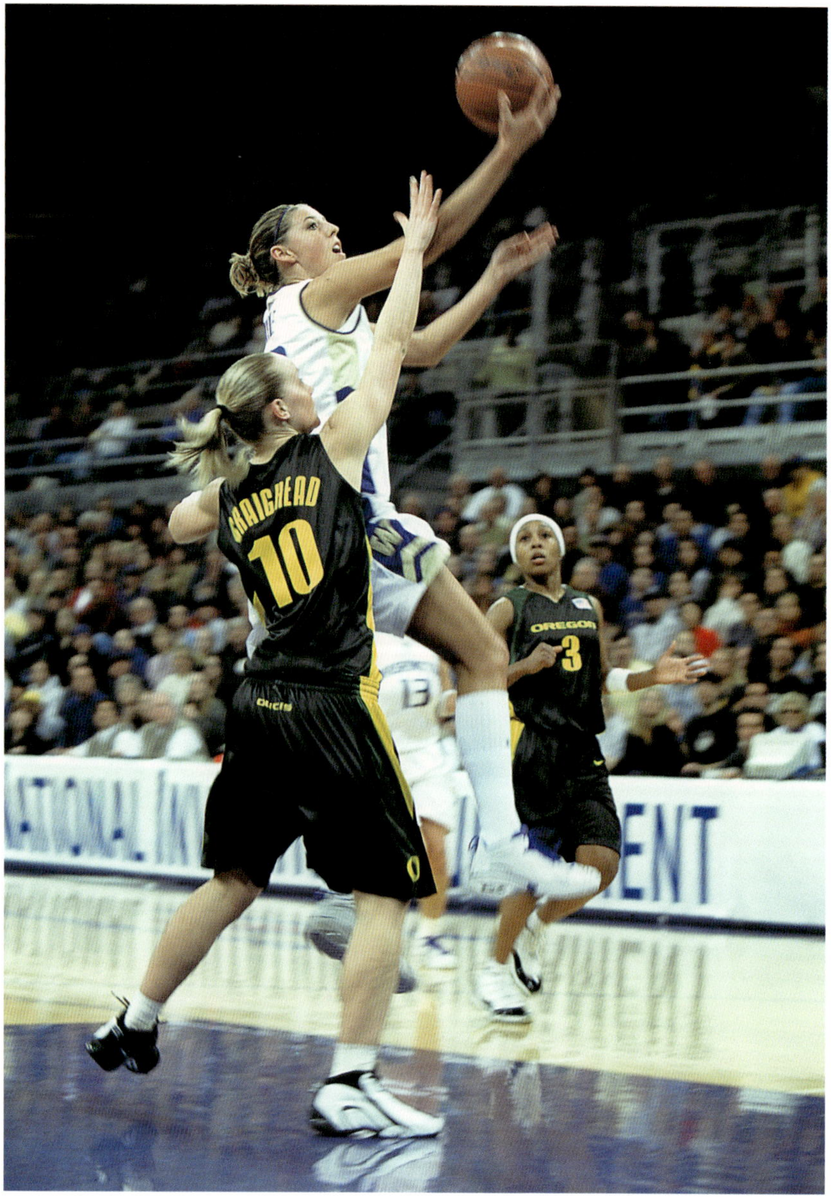

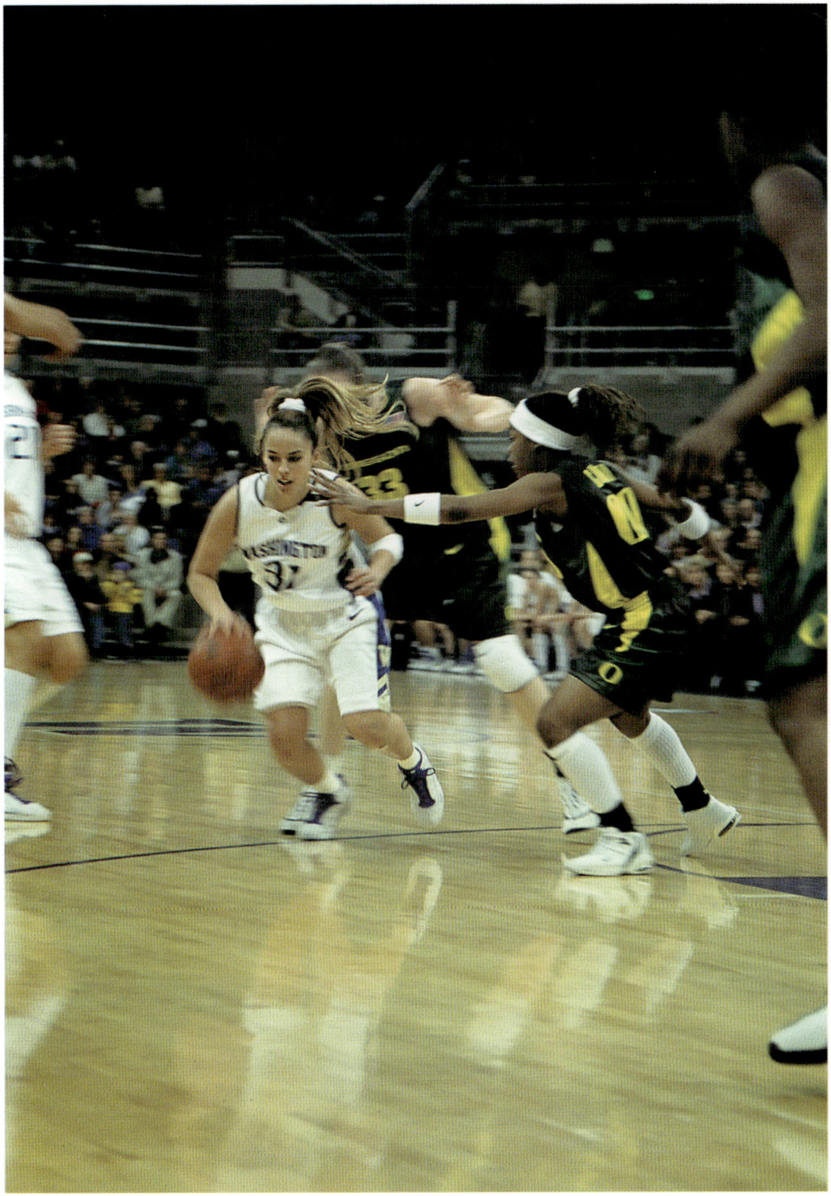

Next page:
The new Dempsey Indoor Practice Facility has 95,000 square feet for varsity sports such as football, baseball, softball, track and soccer. It is large enough to hold a 100-yard football field, and its 1/5-mile indoor track is already helping to set new records.

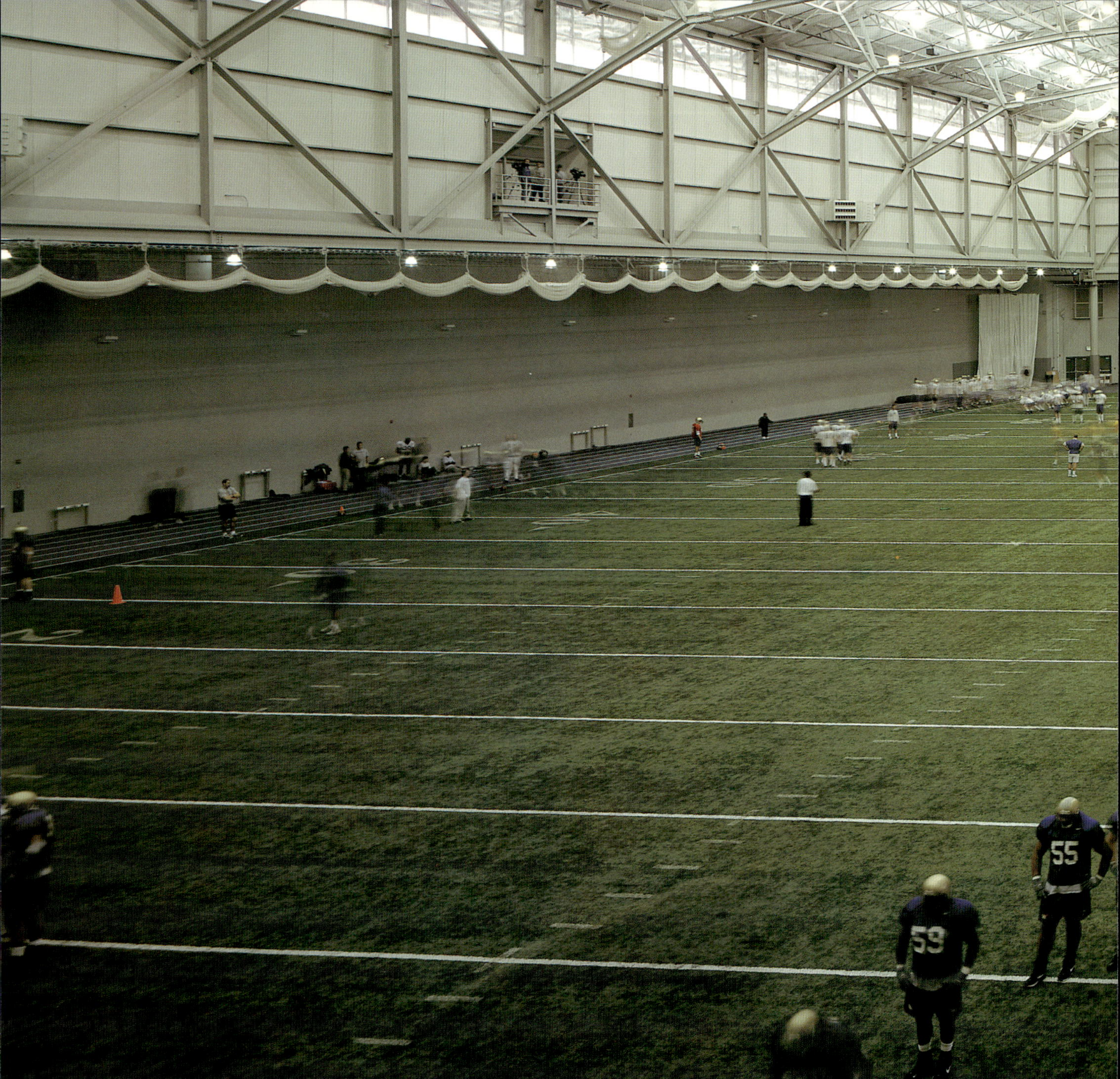
55
59

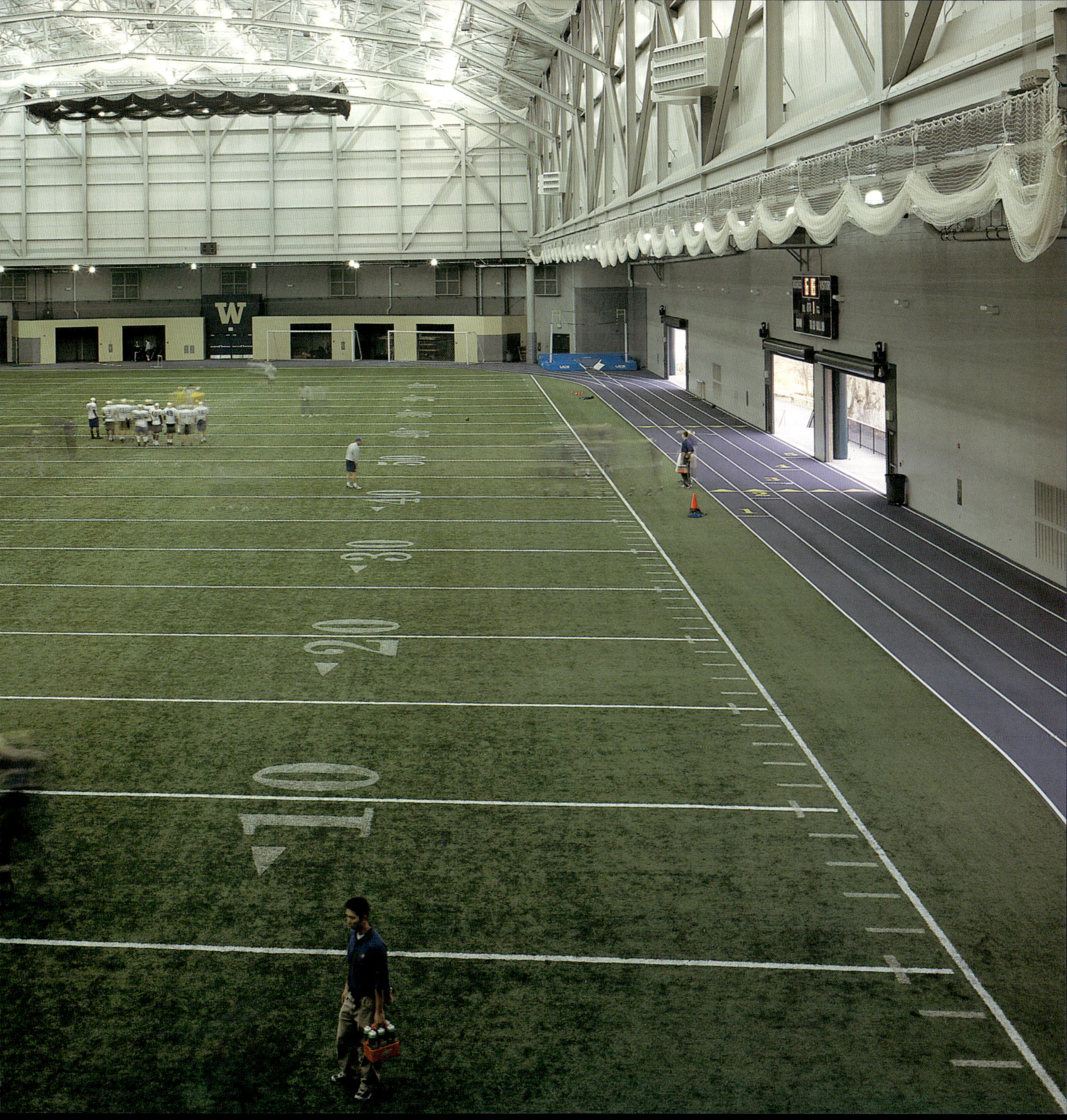

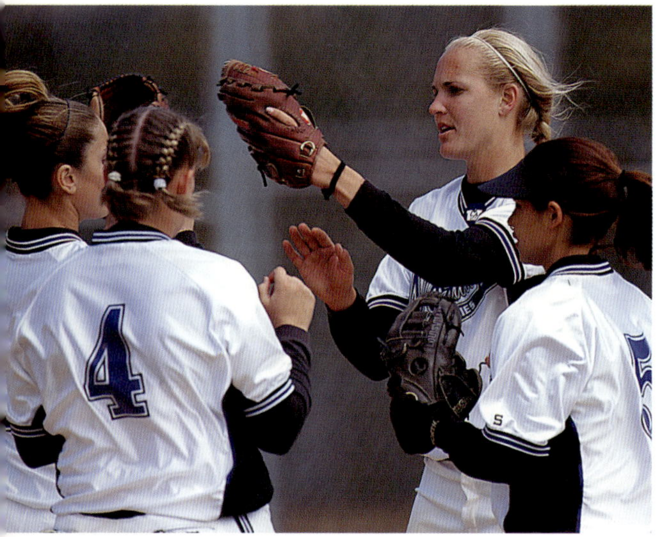

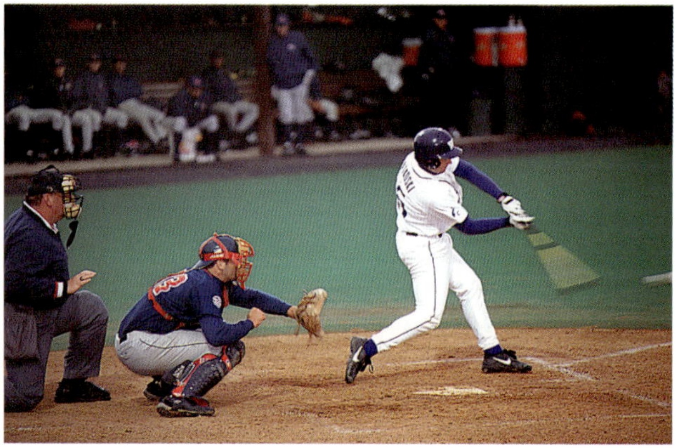

Left: Members of UW's top-ranked softball team congratulate each other after another victory.

Right: A Husky player takes a swing during a game in the new baseball complex. Like Husky Stadium, the base-ball field overlooks Lake Washington and Mount Rainier.

Recreation leagues and club sports—such as rugby—draw thousands of students to playing fields near the Intramural Activities Building (IMA).

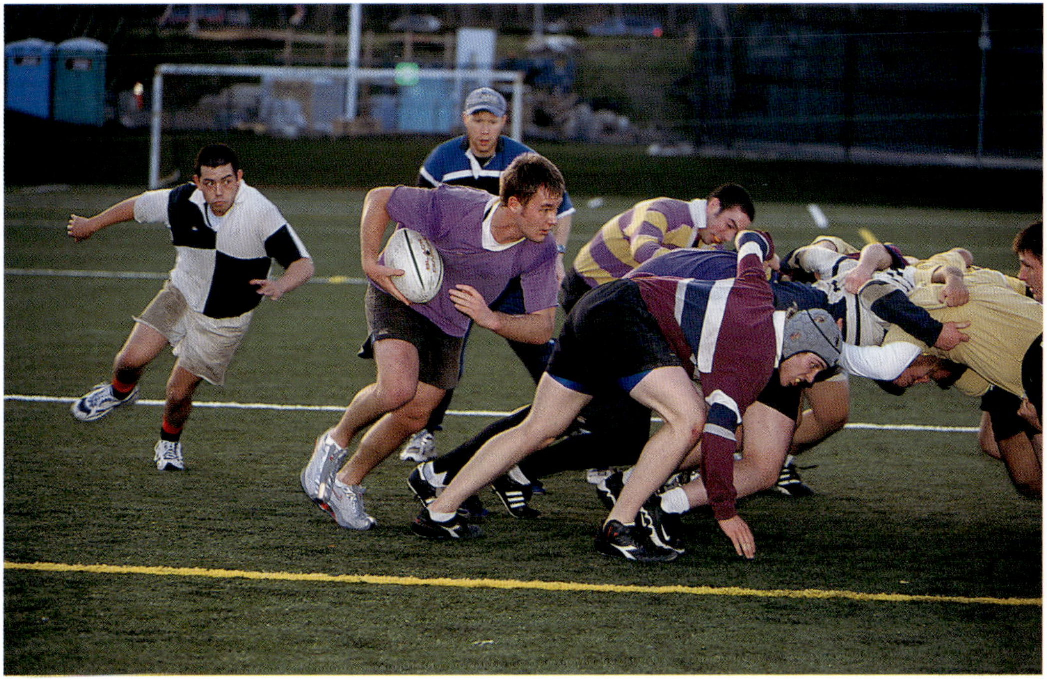

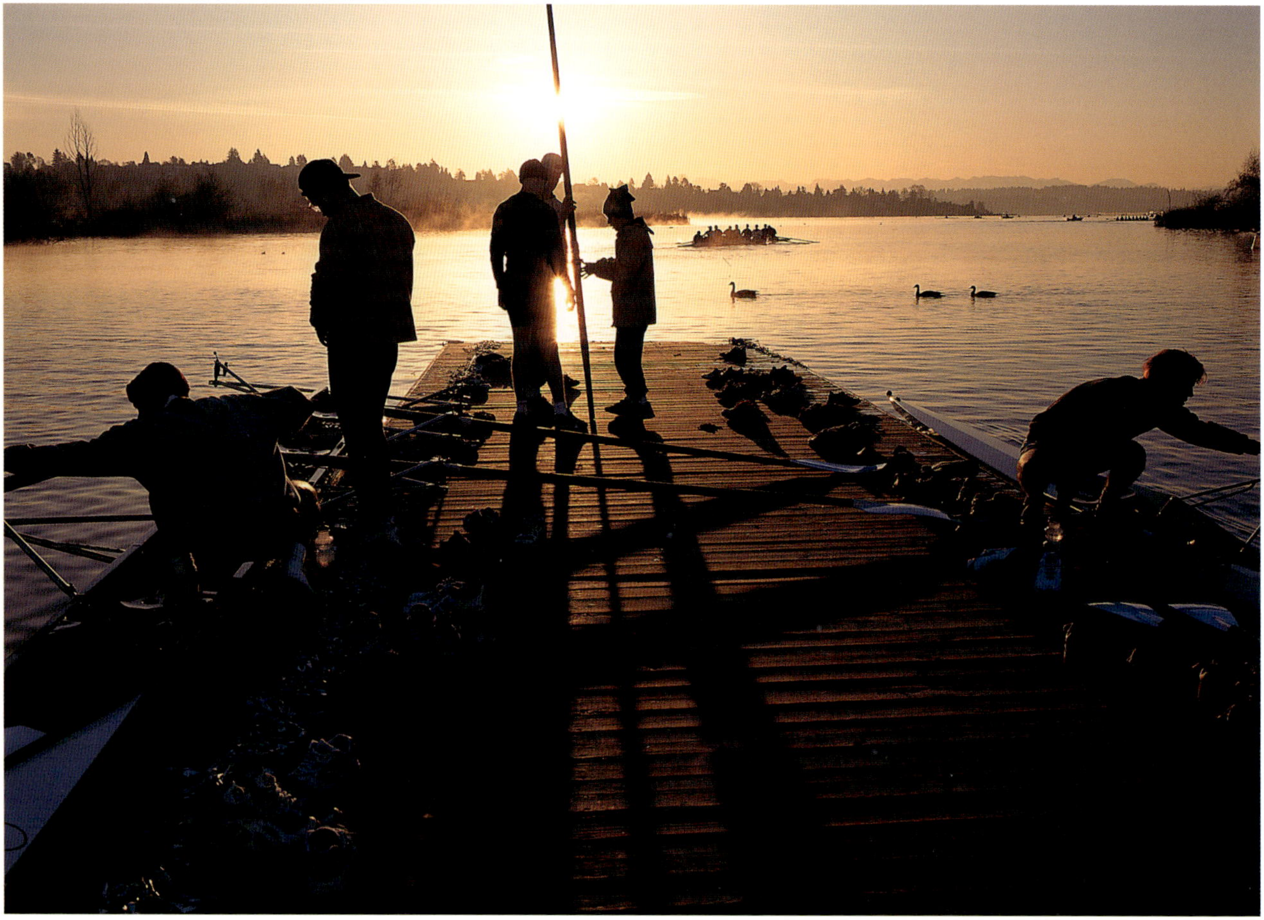

Members of the men's crew team rise at dawn to practice on the smooth waters of Lake Washington.

With easy access to Lake Washington and a tradition that goes back to 1903, the UW has one of the top-ranked crew programs in the nation for both men and women.

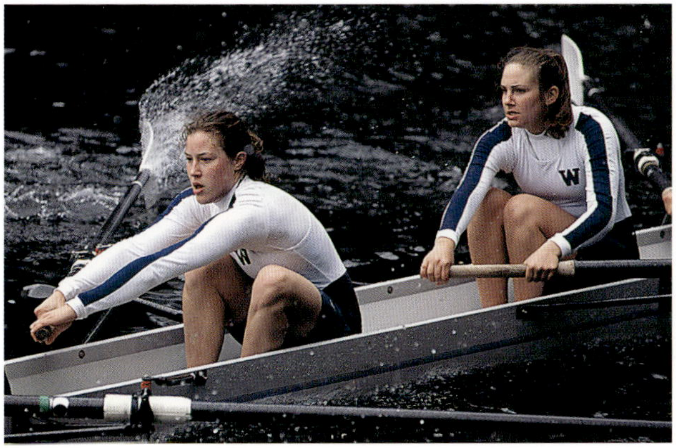

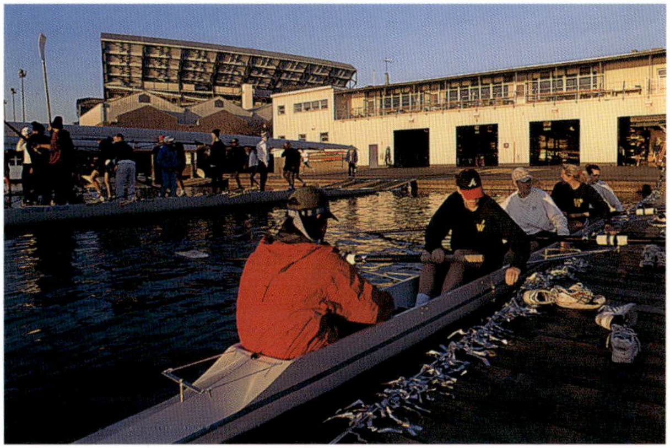

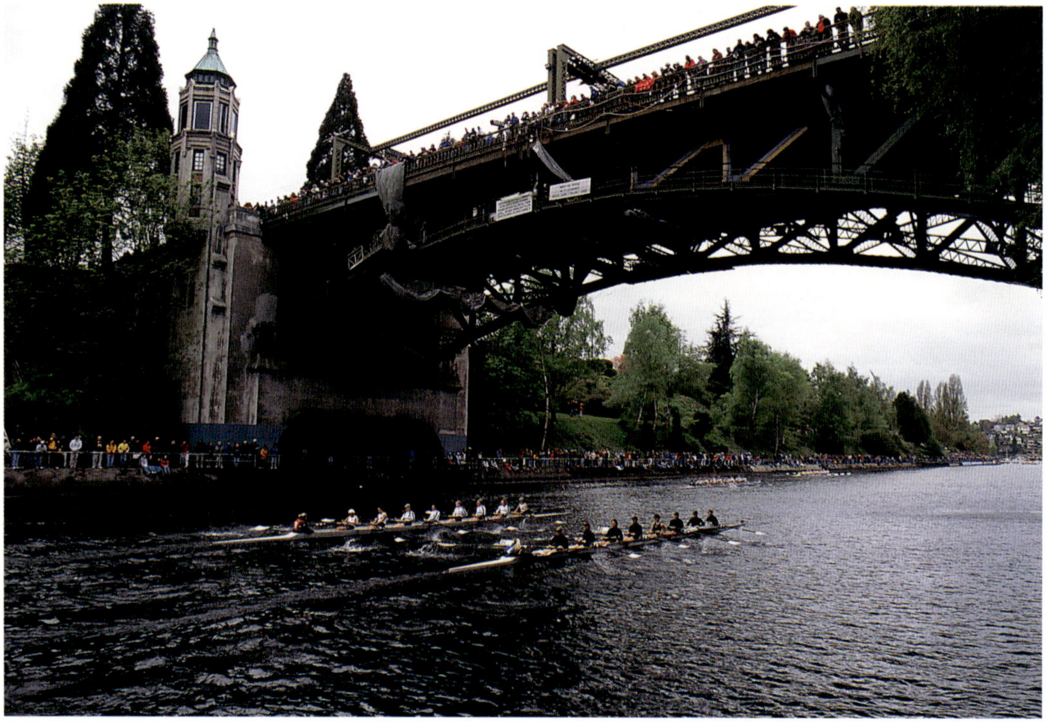

Spectators line the shore and hug the bridge rails as crew teams race down the Montlake Cut during opening day of boating season.

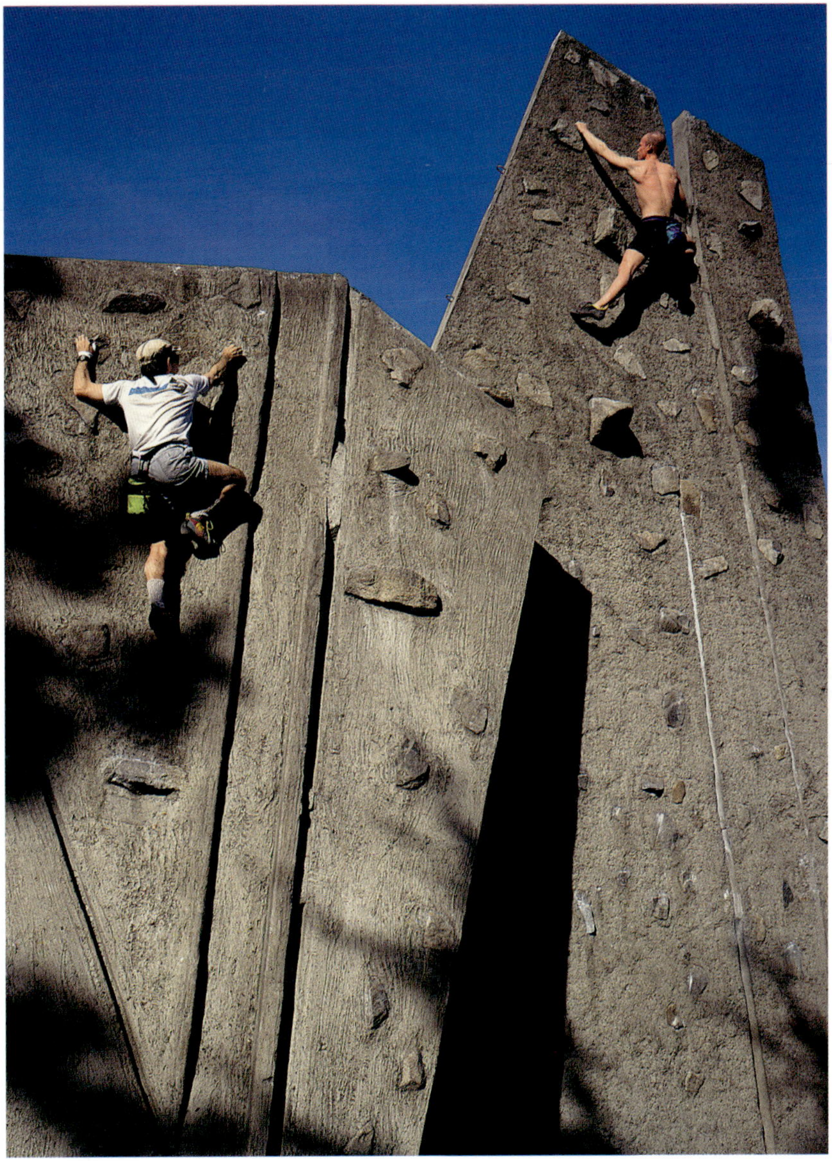

Climbing Rock, south of Husky Stadium, has both easy and challenging approaches. Built in 1974, it was one of the first climbing walls in the United States.

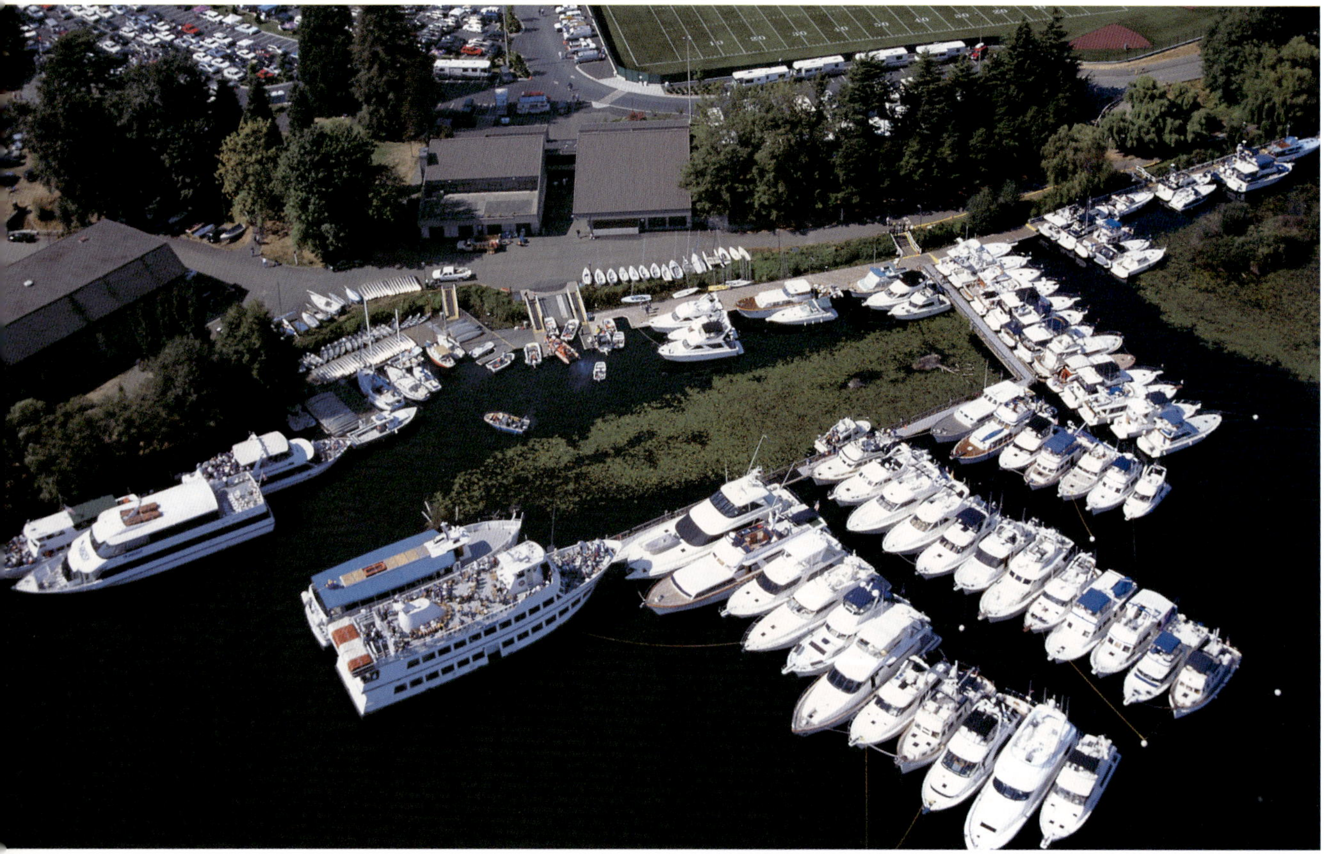

Seattle is a boater's paradise. Here, owners tie up their boats before a football game in Husky Stadium.

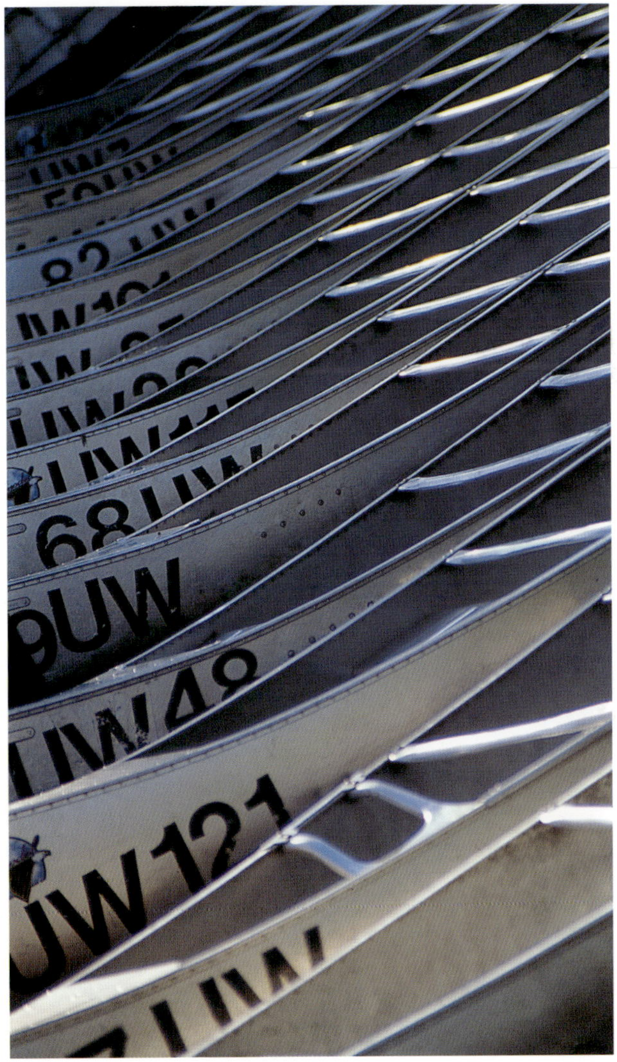

Canoes at the Waterfront Activities Center make a geometric pattern.

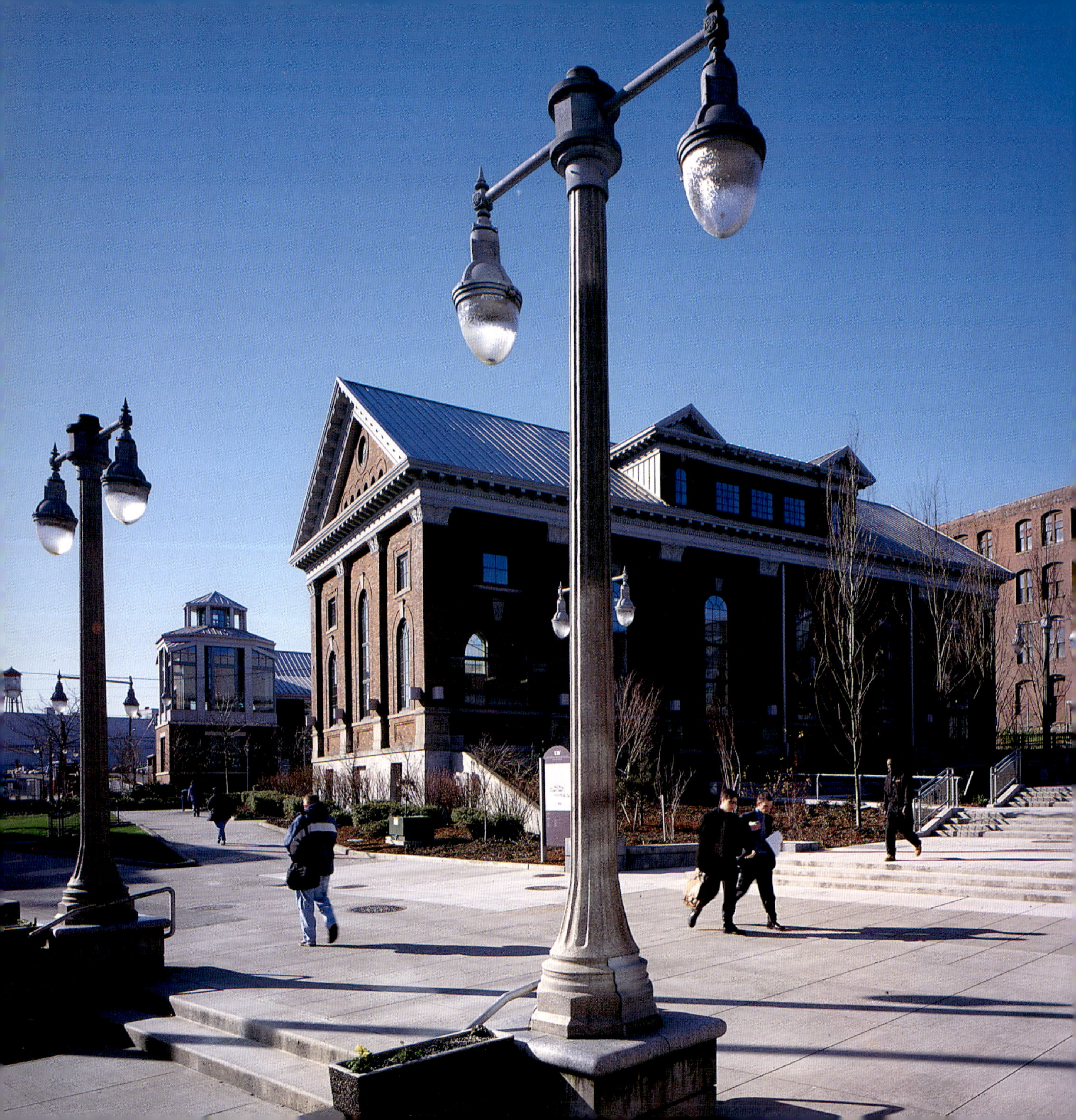

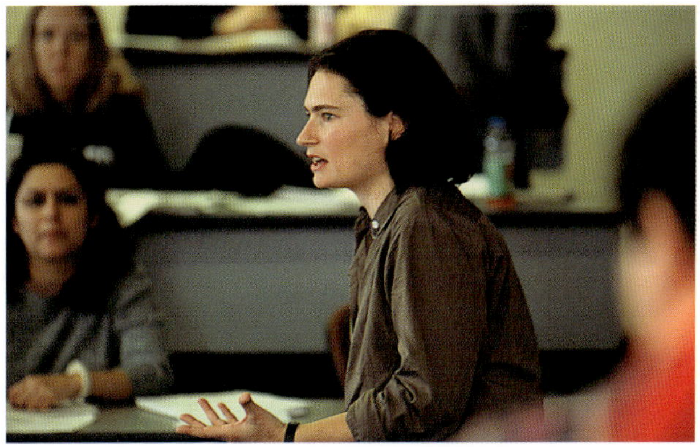

An instructor makes a point in a UW Tacoma classroom.

Opposite page:
It once housed generators for an electric company, but now this ornate Victorian building is the home of the UW Tacoma library.

Only steps from Commencement Bay and Puget Sound, students in these UW Tacoma classrooms are testing water quality and dissecting salmon.

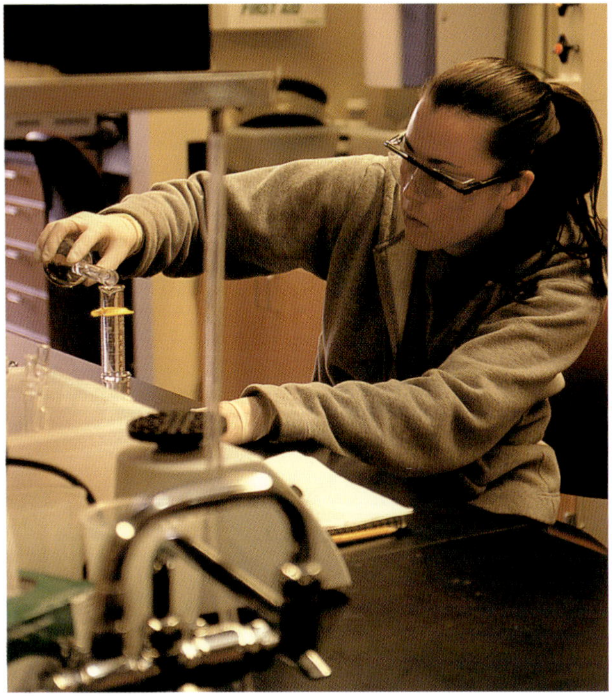

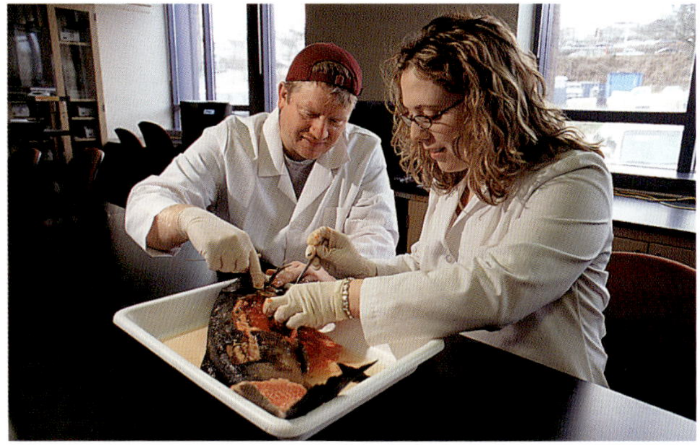

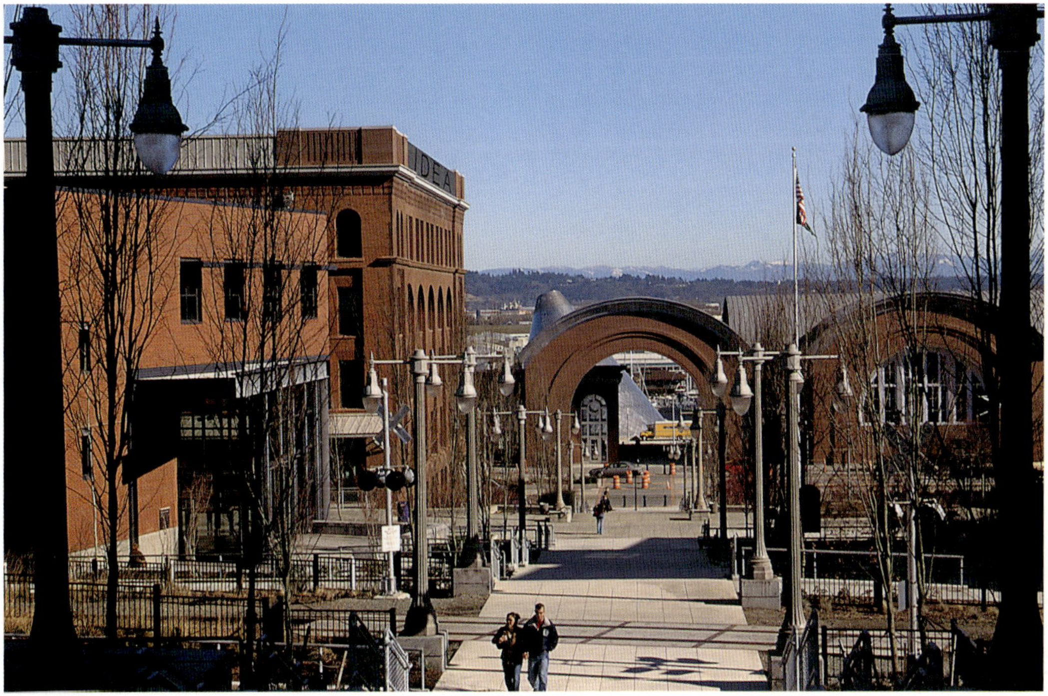

Once an industrial neighborhood, the UW Tacoma campus still has signs of its former uses, such as the railroad tracks in the foreground.

In the distance is an arch linking Tacoma's federal courthouse and its state history museum.

A glass chandelier by Tacoma native and UW alumnus Dale Chihuly hangs in the main reading room of the UW Tacoma library.

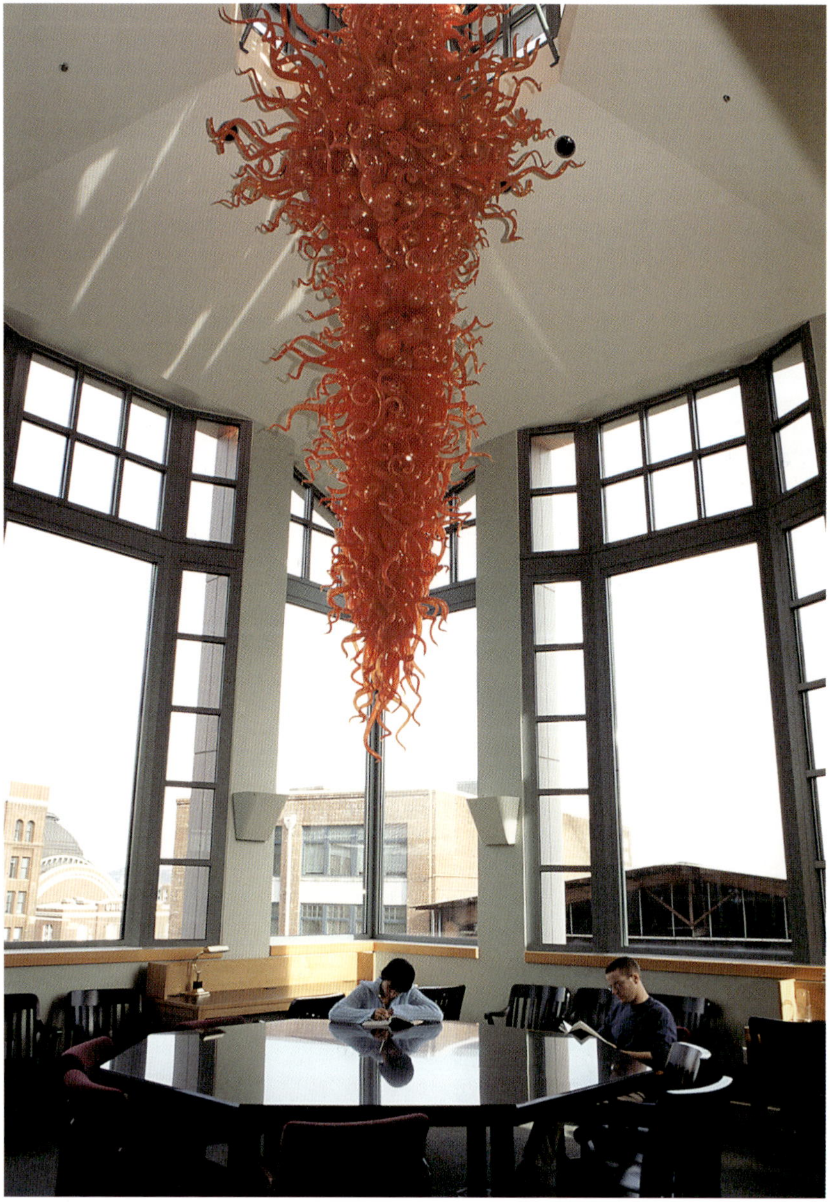

Opposite page: There is plenty of natural light in the reading room of the UW Bothell library.

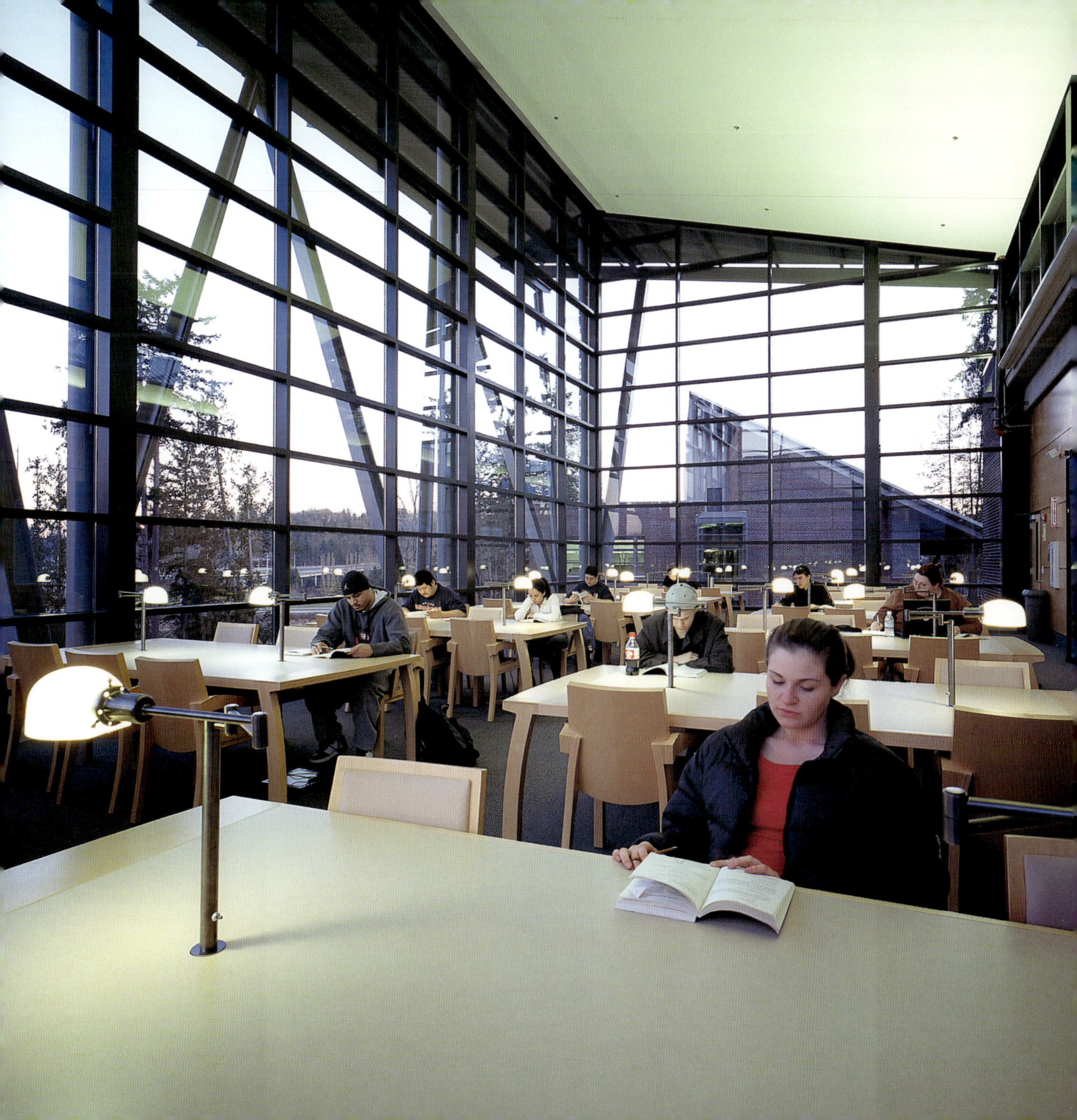

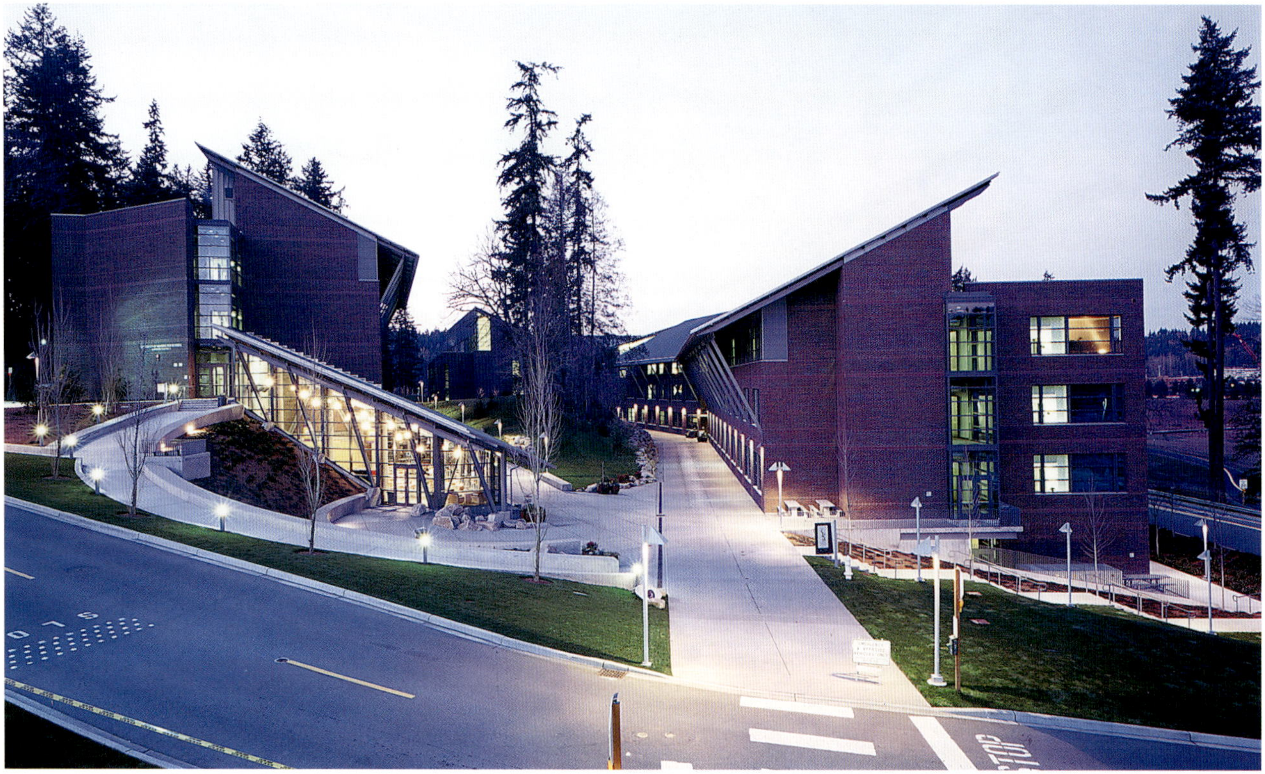

Since its completion in 2000, the UW Bothell campus has been praised for its unique architecture and environmentally sensitive design. Planners preserved 100-year-old Douglas fir trees growing on the property and anchored the offices, laboratories and classrooms into the side of a bluff.

UW Bothell students take advantage of the latest computer technology in the Media Arts Lab.

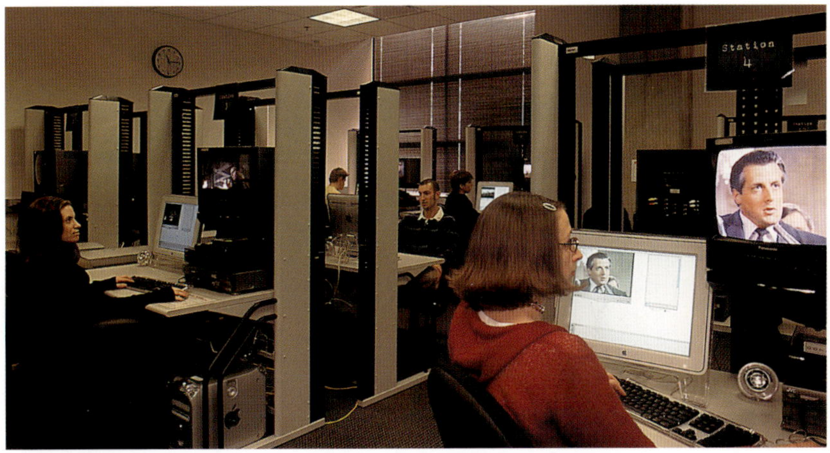

Even the outdoors in Bothell is an experiment. The campus is trying to return overused farmland to its original state—wetlands that might attract migrating salmon. A flock of Canada geese seems at home already.

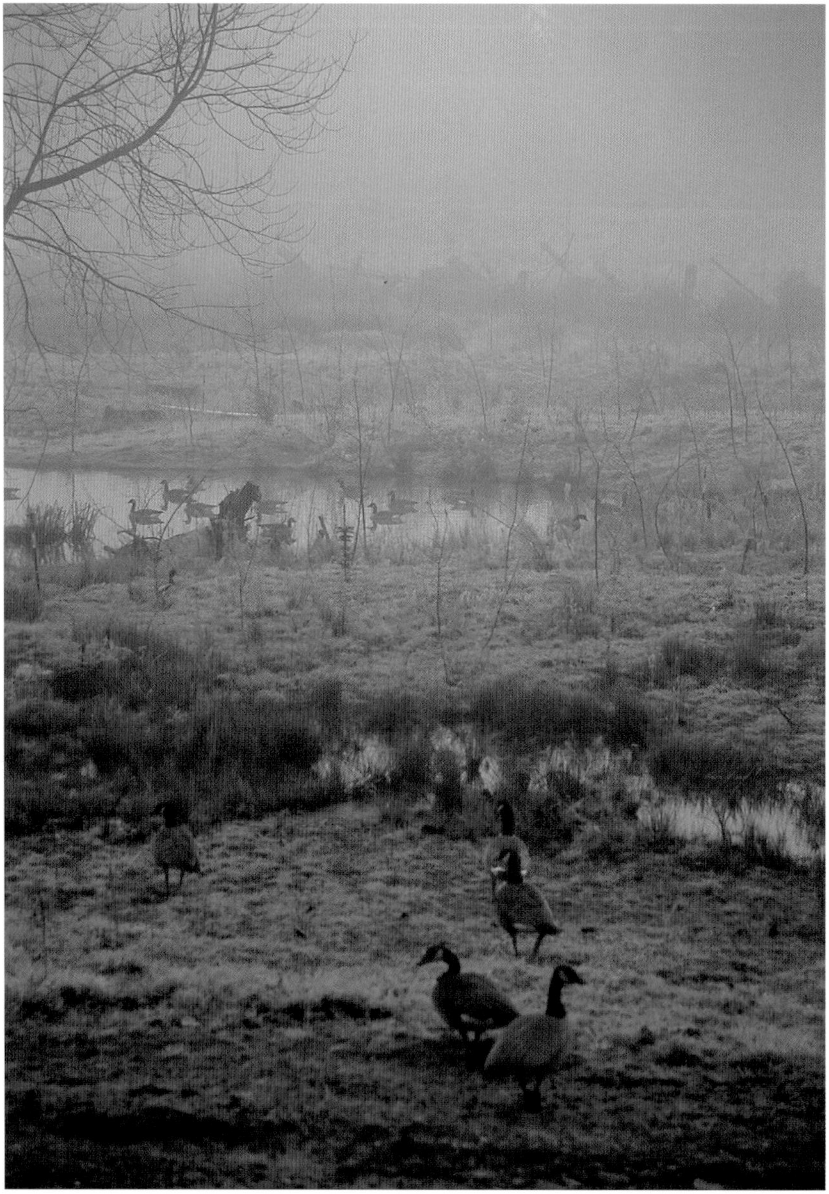

Left: The Bothell library overlooks the wetlands and a stand of fir trees. *Right:* The commons at UW Bothell is a popular meeting place day or night.

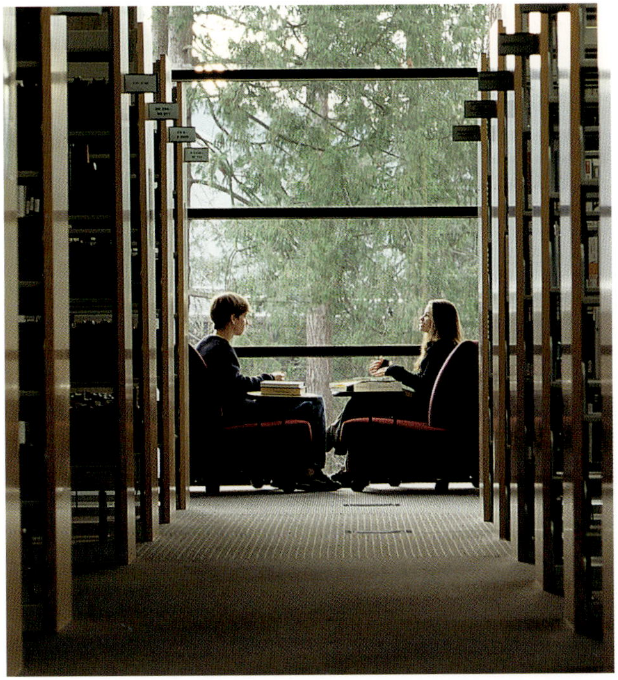

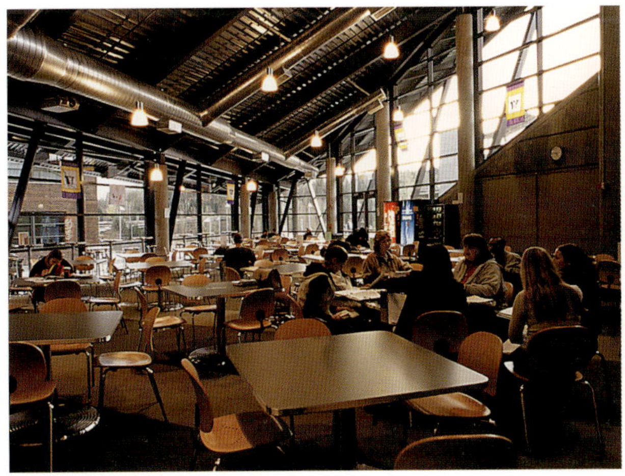

Next page: More than 35,000 people attend the graduation ceremony at Husky Stadium each year.

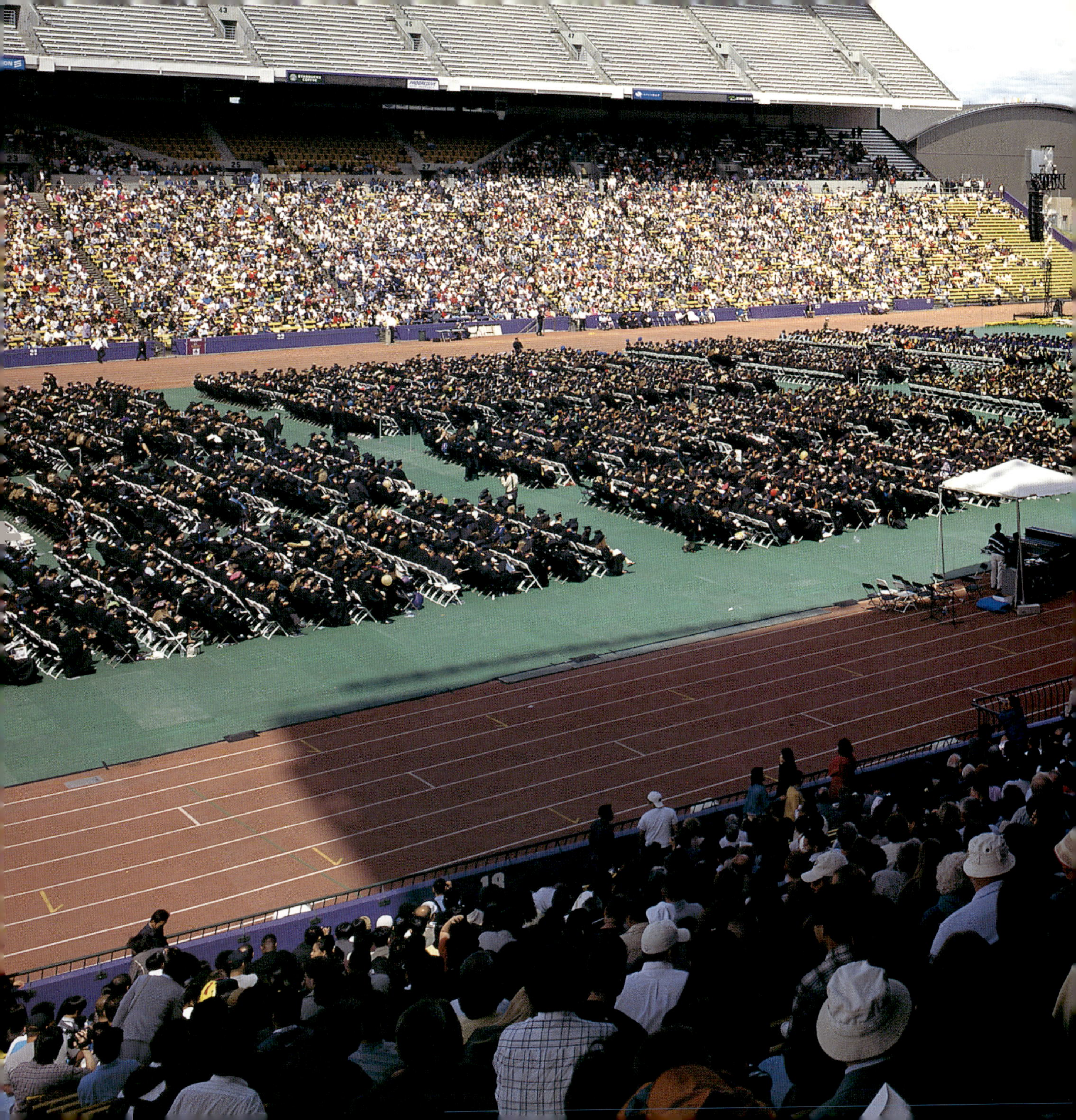

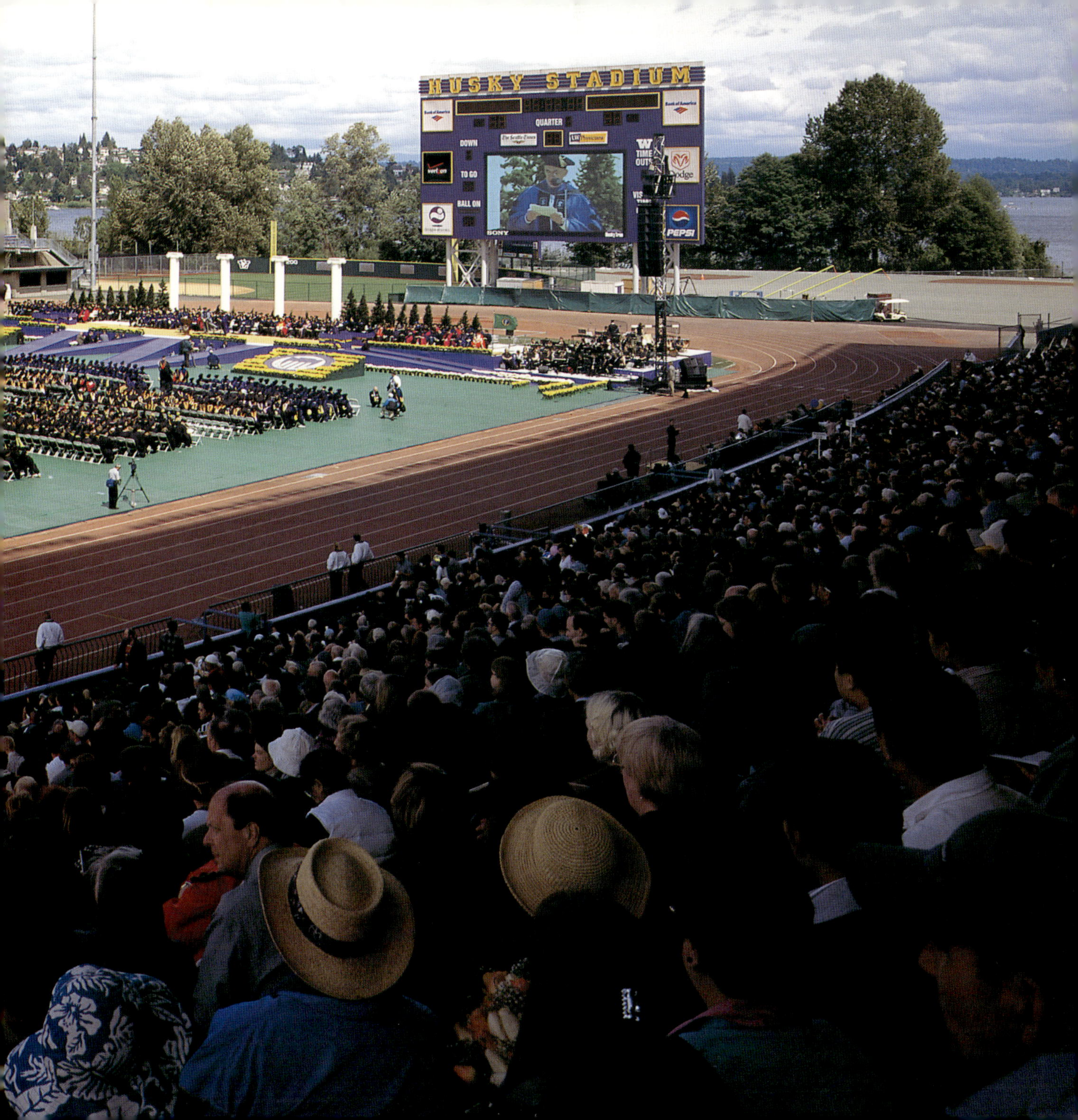
HUSKY STADIUM
QUARTER
DOWN
TO GO
BALL ON
SONY
PEPSI

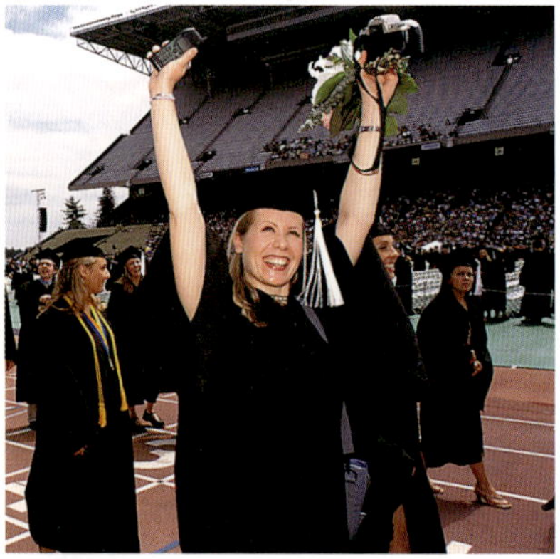

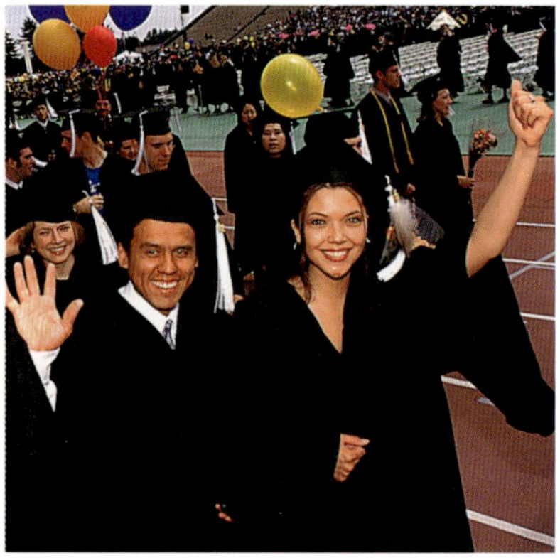

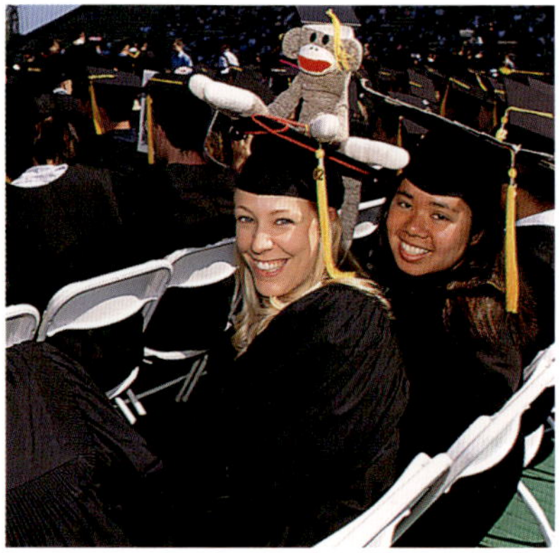

Flowers, balloons and even the occasional stuffed animal are part of the graduation festivities.

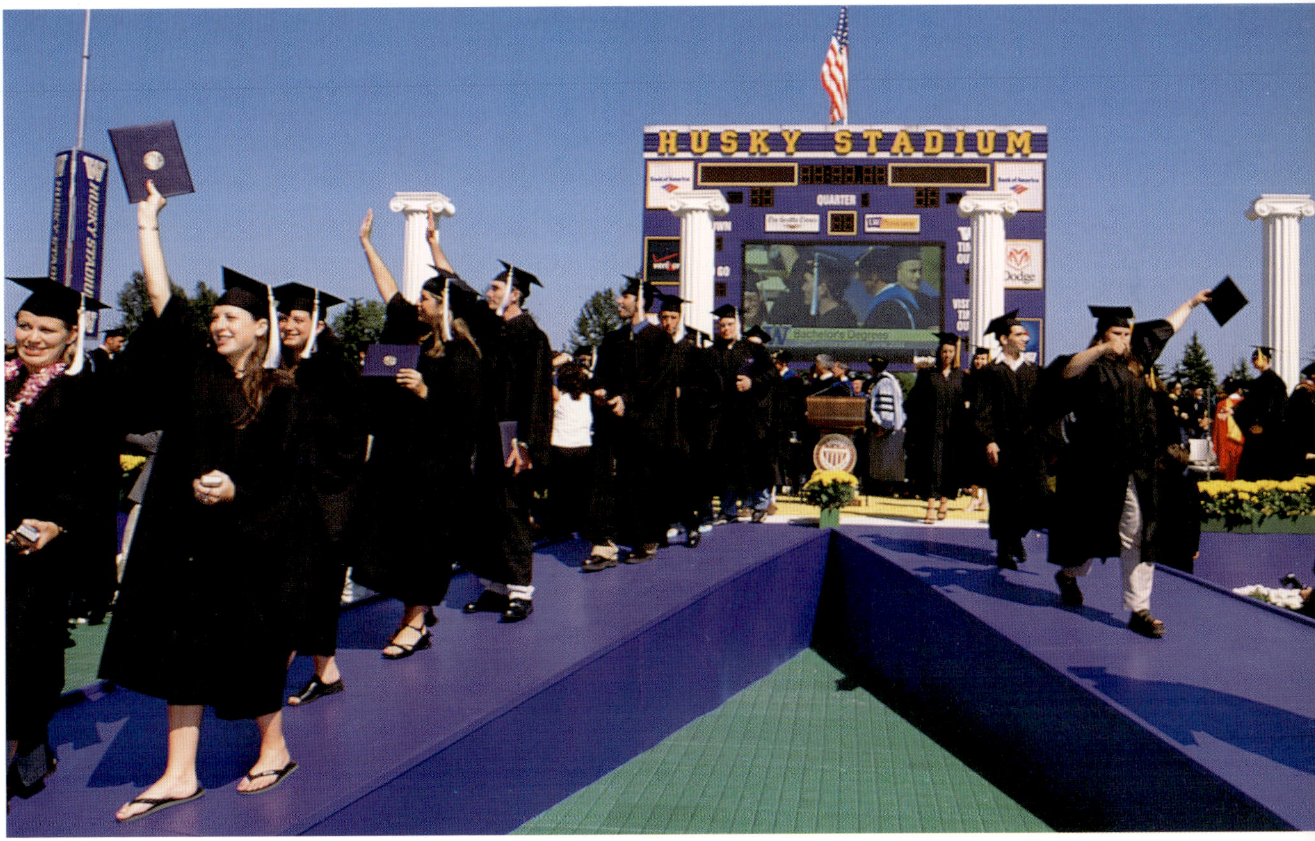

A UW tradition allows each graduate to come on stage to receive his or her diploma and shake the hand of the UW president. Here, happy graduates wave to their families as their images are projected on the video scoreboard.

Photo Credits

1-11	Stewart Hopkins
12	Jaimie Trueblood
13-15	Stewart Hopkins
16a	Jaimie Trueblood
16b-28	Stewart Hopkins
29	Jaimie Trueblood
30-31	Stewart Hopkins
32-33	Jaimie Trueblood
34-35	Stewart Hopkins
36	Jaimie Trueblood
37-41	Stewart Hopkins
42-43	Jaimie Trueblood
44-50	Stewart Hopkins
51-52	Jaimie Trueblood
53	Stewart Hopkins
54	Jaimie Trueblood
55-59	Stewart Hopkins
60-61	Jaimie Trueblood
62	Stewart Hopkins
63	Jaimie Trueblood
64	Stewart Hopkins
65-67	Jaimie Trueblood
68-78	Stewart Hopkins
79	Jeff Zaruba
80-81	Stewart Hopkins
82-83	Jaimie Trueblood
84	Stewart Hopkins
85-86	Jaimie Trueblood
87-91	Stewart Hopkins
92-95	Jaimie Trueblood
96-99	Stewart Hopkins
100	Jaimie Trueblood
101a	Stewart Hopkins
101b	Jaimie Trueblood
102	Stewart Hopkins
103-105	Jaimie Trueblood
106-107	Stewart Hopkins
108-109	Jaimie Trueblood
110-123	Stewart Hopkins
124	Jaimie Trueblood
125-128	Stewart Hopkins
129	Jaimie Trueblood
130-132	Stewart Hopkins
133	Jeff Zaruba
134-137	Stewart Hopkins
138-139	Paul Souders
140-145	Stewart Hopkins
146a	Paul Souders
146b-152	Stewart Hopkins
153	Jaimie Trueblood
154-161	Stewart Hopkins
162	Barry Provorse
163-167	Stewart Hopkins